The Low-Residency
MFA Handbook

The Low-Residency MFA Handbook

A GUIDE FOR PROSPECTIVE CREATIVE WRITING STUDENTS

Lori A. May

continuum

2011

The Continuum International Publishing Group
80 Maiden Lane, New York, NY 10038
The Tower Building, 11 York Road, London SE1 7NX

www.continuumbooks.com

Library of Congress Cataloging-in-Publication Data
May, Lori A.
The low-residency MFA handbook : a guide for prospective
creative writing students by / Lori A. May.
    p. cm.
  ISBN-13: 978-1-4411-9844-0 (pbk. : alk. paper)
  ISBN-10: 1-4411-9844-X (pbk. : alk. paper)
  1. Creative writing (Higher education)—United States—
Handbooks, manuals, etc. 2. Graduate students—United
States—Handbooks, manuals, etc. I. Title.
PE1405.U6M39 2010
808'.042071173—dc22   2010029536

ISBN: PB: 978-1-4411-9844-0

Typeset by Pindar NZ, Auckland, New Zealand
Printed and bound in the United States of America

For the writer who didn't quite think it was possible . . . until now.

Contents

Preface

CONGRATULATIONS. IF YOU ARE reading this handbook, you are most certainly preparing for one of the most exciting times of your life — undertaking a graduate degree in creative writing. There are few experiences in life that will contribute as much, in as little time, as the intense two or three years you will dedicate to creative writing during your graduate studies with a Master of Fine Arts (MFA).

Whether you have been researching the possibilities for years or are just beginning to discover the opportunities, you have undoubtedly noticed the proliferation of programs. Each year, more new programs are introduced and there is currently no sign of such growth coming to a halt. You have also no doubt noticed how overwhelming the research process can be and may have many questions regarding the programs. What makes each program unique? What are the experiences from those who have attended the programs? How do you know which program is right for you? This handbook aims to help you answer these questions and more.

The purpose of this handbook is to complement your own independent research and provide an additional tool to help you in the selection process. It is not, however, meant to substitute individual research: viewing current information on program websites, talking to graduates, calling directors and faculty, and creating your own checklist of "must-haves" in a graduate program.

With so many programs to choose from, it can be an overwhelming task to call or email everyone you want to talk to; with that in mind, this handbook aims to emulate one-on-one conversations with directors, faculty, visiting writers, alumni, and current students. Through reading a variety of comments and Q&As, you will meet some of the many people behind the programs and those who have personally experienced the curriculums.

While this handbook is meant to save you some time and legwork, it may not answer all of your questions. I encourage you to use this handbook as a way to familiarize yourself with the programs and focus in on your research. You will still want to call programs and I hope you will still reach out to alumni and current students to ask questions specific to your own needs. As I have experienced, those involved with low-residency writing programs are very generous with their time when it comes to speaking to prospective students.

In fact, if I had another 300 pages, I still wouldn't have enough room to include all the possible interviewees. Given time and space constraints, I hope this handbook equips you with a solid starting point for determining which programs are right for your own circumstances and creative goals.

I also want to emphasize how important it is for *you* to decide what are the best programs. You will notice there are no rankings in this handbook; the programs represent and speak for themselves. In the end, the number one program that is best for you is the best *for you*, regardless of how it might rank for others. We all have individual needs and goals, and for every writer there are a number of programs that will stand out for one reason or another. It is up to you to research, plan, and embrace the opportunities available to you.

Again, I could have easily included another several hundred interviewees, but what I have provided should be considered a starting point. I encourage you to reach out to others to learn about additional experiences not accounted for within this handbook. You should also note that the proportion of comments per institution is not representative of the program's quality, nor do the comments represent the entire spectrum of available experiences. This is a mere sampling that shares some of the many conversations I had with directors, faculty, alumni, and current students.

When I first began to research material for this handbook, it was clear there would be an overwhelming response to interview requests. As mentioned, those involved with low-residency writing programs are some of the most giving people I have come across, as they are so enthusiastic to share their experiences with prospective students.

Of important note, I must also state how accommodating and open the program directors were in responding to my many questions. While the experiences of current students and alumni might be your focus, I thought it was important to include comments from directors and faculty so that you may learn more about the teaching philosophies within these creative institutions. After all, you will be committing two or three year's worth of your time, energy, and money to learn from them. It's important to hear from a well-rounded assortment of those who will play such an influential role in your creative life.

It is up to you to determine which programs are most appropriate for reaching your personal creative goals. This handbook aims to provide you with one additional tool for your independent research. A creative writing graduate degree can be one of the most exciting and exhilarating experiences of your life and I wish you the best of success in choosing — and succeeding in — the ideal program for you.

CHAPTER 1

An Introduction to
Low-Residency MFAs

MUCH LIKE A "TRADITIONAL," full-residency creative writing MFA, low-residency programs generally take two or three years to complete. However, instead of spending each day on campus, low-residency students are only on campus — or "in residency" — for a small portion of the year. Many programs get together for two residencies each year, while others meet for residency only once per year. Ranging from one to two weeks in duration, each residency brings together students, faculty, guest speakers, and directors in an intense conference-like setting.

During each residency, students participate in a number of workshops, craft and literature seminars, professional development sessions, and one-on-one meetings with faculty. Creative writing MFAs generally culminate in a book-length thesis and low-residency students will set suitable writing goals with thesis supervisors during residencies.

While Chapters 6 and 7 share some personal residency experiences of faculty and students, here is what one director had to say about her MFA program's residency:

> The ten-day residency, which takes place in January and July on the Warren Wilson campus, provides an intensive and stimulating foundation for the semester's study. Each day, discussion classes and lectures in literature, poetics, and the craft of writing are offered by our faculty. Students also participate in workshops and small seminars; readings by faculty and by graduating students are held in the evenings. Another crucial component of the residency is the individual conference time students spend with their faculty supervisors,

planning the semester-long project. In essence, the curriculum is completely individualized. Thorough narrative evaluations at the end of each semester provide continuity, documenting each student's progress and informing the course of study for the next term.

Debra Allbery, director, Warren Wilson College

Outside of each residency, the rest of the graduate program is completed through any combination of distance studies. Some programs pair students with a mentor to work one-on-one for the duration of one term, alternating between faculties for each of the four to six home-based semesters. Other programs use online classrooms to emulate a campus-based workshop experience. There are also a few hybrid study formats, wherein students work through a combination of one-on-one faculty mentorship and distance classes. Chapter 8 provides more detail regarding the various format options and how students work with their instructors.

While each program is unique in its approach, students have opportunities to pursue fiction, non-fiction, poetry, screenwriting, children's writing, and a number of cross-genre options. While most programs encourage literary esthetics, others are open to exploring commercial and popular fiction and films. You can be sure there is at least one program that offers your desired mode and scope of study, no matter your personal interest.

The goal of any low-residency creative writing MFA program is to provide opportunities for students to explore the writing craft. Each student is encouraged to immerse him- or herself in the community, which is comprised of fellow students, instructors, visiting writers, and directors. The programs aim to equip student writers with a support system during the focused time each will spend on developing their craft and working on a substantial body of work.

The main attraction to enrolling in a low-residency program is the ability to obtain a graduate degree while living your usual lifestyle. The low-residency format allows writers to tend to life's responsibilities and joys, including family, work, and friendships, based in the student's current location. There is no need to pack up the family and move, and no need to quit the day job if you so choose. Apart from the residencies, you create your own schedule and complete assignments when it suits you. As such, low-residency programs offer increased flexibility for writers who desire a graduate degree but are unable, or uninterested, in making major life changes.

How are low-residency MFAs different from other programs?

While all creative writing MFAs provide challenging learning experiences, the low-residency format requires a particular amount of self-discipline. Students are accountable for their own success, perhaps more so than full-residency programs, as there are no traditional classes to attend. No one will notice if you stay in your pajamas and watch television all day. No one will reprimand you if you check your social media pages every ten minutes. Deadlines come quick, though, so you can be sure that others will notice if you do not submit your assignments by the agreed deadline.

During those months of study at home, it is up to you to do the work. While you have a built-in support system of peers and instructors, no one will check your progress each day, much like real-world editors often won't check in until deadline. You don't need to show up for class, but if you don't "show up" at your writing desk your graduate school experience — and your writing — will suffer. Thus, it is up to you to commit to self-discipline and produce the work.

While writers are often naturally independent, there is a great sense of community available through online discussions, emails, and phone calls, and regular correspondence with faculty. Students and instructors can connect at any time of day and from all across the country and beyond. Many of the comments throughout Chapter 6 will reveal how a genuine sense of community is one of the greatest benefits of low-residency programs. By relying on distance communication, students are that much more accessible to one another at all hours and, in turn, the residencies often feel like a reunion among close friends.

Most campus-based programs bring together a group of students to workshop one another's material. The writing workshop is indeed a valuable experience as it allows students to reflect on others' comments, reactions, and suggestions. For low-residency programs, the workshop experience is delivered in various ways: through one-on-one mentorship with published mentors, through online discussions among peers and instructors, and through activities offered during each residency.

One major difference between campus-based and low-residency programs is the proportion of time spent on *your* work. Predominately, low-residency programs have a low faculty-to-student ratio; your mentor will likely be working with four or five students each term. This translates to dedicated, individualized attention to your writing.

Also, while many low-residency programs include craft and literary lectures and workshops during residencies, the approach to incorporating literary criticism during the non-residency terms varies from program to program. Some programs have a "book in common," wherein all students and faculty read the same assigned book, regardless of the genre track; this instills a greater sense of community across the various genres. Most programs also require students to create a reading list of up to twenty or thirty books, which they will comment on and discuss with the faculty mentor.

As Chapter 9 demonstrates, there are also a number of peda-gogical training opportunities offered through low-residency programs. A creative writing MFA is regarded as the terminal degree — the final degree qualifying creative writers to teach other writers at the college level. However, pedagogical training is generally not required, nor is it offered in every program. While some students want such training, others do not. Thus, the variety of low-residency formats allows students to select programming options based on individual preferences.

By no means is any of this meant to imply that low-residency programs are better than campus-based programs. For many students, the traditional, full-residency format is best. For others, low-residency is best. These differences are pointed out only to provide one more tool to help you decide what is best for your own specific needs and interests.

Do writers need an MFA?

No. That's the easy answer. All you need to write is a pen and paper, or computer, and you're good to go wherever your imagination takes you. You're the only one who can make yourself write. If you are looking to improve your craft, there are countless opportunities to do so: community workshops, festivals, conferences, and con-tinuing education courses are just a few of the ways you can work on your craft. Then there is the old-fashioned way: just write.

One graduate of University of Southern Maine worked to develop her craft for a number of years before considering a writing program. During our interview, she shared her decision-making process.

> I had been struggling with whether or not to get my MFA, having listened carefully to the arguments against it — that one can just read books and practice writing and that I could learn that way. I had taken several classes at Grub Street, a local writing class, and had loved each class and had even gotten into the Bread Loaf Writers' Conference. I looked longingly at those initials — MFA — after some of my friends' names. I was sending out poems for publication with no success. But really, it wasn't the publications that I was after; I wanted to seriously study poetry. I wanted to be challenged. In the summer of 2007, I had had a child and I had a mortgage. Somewhere deep inside me a voice insisted that this was the moment; I had to get my MFA right now. And I listened.
>
> *Carol Berg, alumnus, University of Southern Maine*

A writing program is merely one vehicle for moving a writer's career forward, but it is certainly not the only path to success. A dedicated, ambitious writer will find personal success one way or another; it is up to you to decide whether a graduate degree in creative writing is ideal for you and your goals.

The creative writing MFA will also not guarantee you a "job" as a writer, whatever that definition is to you. It will not guarantee you an academic position, either. There are few guarantees in life, after all. There are even less guarantees for creative writers.

The creative writing MFA is an artistic, or studio, degree in that it only qualifies you to become the writer you want to be and might become even if you don't pursue such a venture.

What the MFA will do for you, however, is offer a support system that you might find inspiring, motivating, and exhilarating. Throughout your studies, you will learn to discipline yourself, set and attain goals, and work on your craft for an intense period of time, while aiming to equip yourself with the tools to succeed as a writer *after* the MFA.

So, why might you consider a low-residency program specifically? Many believe the low-residency model is ideal for writers as it most emulates a real writing life, complete with deadlines, hours of solitude, and the need to self-motivate. One director summarizes the benefits and challenges of the low-res model in this way:

> Beyond the opportunities our students have to learn about craft issues and to discuss literature, the low-residency model helps writing students learn discipline . . . In a low-residency MFA, it is imperative students recognize the need to create a routine that includes both reading and writing so that these "habits" become second nature to them. The nature of our curriculum and the mentoring methods that our faculty use in working with students help provide them [with] both models to develop the habit of writing and to develop the habit of reading. In looking for MFA candidates for our program, we do what we can to determine if the applicant is someone who might thrive, who can be disciplined enough to work independently without a daily reminder to go to class or make time to write.
>
> In addition, the low-residency model also provides writing students with a network of writing colleagues and friends. Though writing is solitary work, a community of writers not only helps to lessen the isolation of being a writer, but it can be a source of inspiration. I think some student writers imagine that it might be harder to develop a community of writing colleagues in a low-residency program compared to a residential studio/academic MFA, but students and faculty in low-residency programs develop very strong bonds and a very supportive community.
>
> *Rick Mulkey, director, Converse College*

As Mulkey says, the low-residency MFA is meant to pair you with writing mentors who will push you to become your best, surround you with a community of like-minded peers, and support you with feedback on your book-length thesis or other substantial body of work. The residencies will provide you with an intense learning experience and the creative high you need to complete the non-residency semesters. The one-on-one mentorships provide one of life's few opportunities to work intimately with published writers, as they give careful attention to your writing. For many authors, such opportunities are only available through a graduate writing program.

If you're reading this book, you probably *want* the MFA, but, no, you don't *need* it to write. Many published writers don't have an MFA and many don't want one. It's okay if you don't want to pursue the degree and it's certainly okay if the only reason you do want a creative writing MFA is to fulfill a personal desire or lifelong dream. In fact, perhaps the best reason to undertake an MFA is exactly that: the desire to dedicate two or three years to improving your craft under the guidance of critical — but supportive — voices. Ultimately, it is up to you to decide which path is best for you and your artistic development.

If you have determined that a creative writing MFA is right for you, how do you know if the low-residency format is ideal for your lifestyle and for your creative goals? Chapter 2 aims to help you decide.

CHAPTER 2

Is the Low-Residency Model Right for Me?

IF YOU ARE ASKING yourself this question and are unfamiliar with low-residency programs, this handbook will certainly help you gain a better understanding of what to expect during the brief residencies and at-home semesters. Even if you have researched a few programs, this handbook will hopefully expose you to a wide variety of experiences. All of this is meant to help you determine (a) if a low-residency program is right for you, and (b) which programs speak to your personal goals and ambitions.

At the heart of every low-residency program is the flexibility that comes with completing a degree from a distance. If you long for the graduate student experience, but cannot imagine moving your family to another city or quitting a job you enjoy, then you should give serious consideration to the many low-residency options available to you.

The one thing a low-residency MFA is not, by any means, is a quick and easy way to earn a degree. The fact that you are expected to be highly independent during your studies does not imply you have no responsibilities. On the contrary, you will be expected to turn in an agreed amount of creative writing at regular intervals. Your writing schedule is ultimately your decision, but the workload is non-negotiable.

As you review the following considerations, you'll be that much closer to determining if the low-residency model is appropriate for you and your needs.

Considerations for prospective students
Self-discipline

Most writers enjoy their independence and are appreciative for the quiet times in life that allow us to put words down on paper. Some of us, however, lack motivation and drive when we are left to our own devices. The low-residency MFA requires that each student maintain a certain level of discipline in order to complete numerous assignments.

Based on her experience with the demands of low-residency studies, one graduate has this to share with prospective students:

> These programs aren't for everybody. They are for serious, independent-minded individuals who are ready to work. There's no hiding in the back of the class. Low-residency programs provide the most intense kind of instruction imaginable, and they are ideal for developing the intuition for writing and the structure for a continued writing life.
> *Jenn Scheck-Kahn, alumnus, Bennington College*

Each term, you will have a specific amount of pages and/or chapters due and you need to ask yourself if you are able to manage your own schedule and push yourself to meet regular deadlines. Of course, this is a good learning exercise for the real world; writers aiming for publication need to get comfortable with setting daily word count or page goals in order to meet editorial deadlines.

One faculty member who has seen new students struggle with time management, has this to offer:

> I think students sometimes get the impression that because you can do this from your home, it's a sort of "MFA Light." Nothing could be farther from the truth. It's a real, full-fledged MFA program, and so sometimes those with full-time jobs get a bit of a shock. We try very hard to inform them about this, but it doesn't always work. So time management can be an issue for students.
> *Richard Goodman, faculty, Spalding University*

Dedicated time

The benefit of a low-residency program is the flexibility to create a writing schedule that fits the needs of your lifestyle. Still, family commitments and work obligations can play havoc on some of our best intentions. Do you have the ability to set aside a reasonable amount of time to dedicate to your studies? Are you able to designate a writing space in your home that will provide a study space that is free of interruption? Can you envision reading a number of assigned books each year in addition to writing your own masterpiece?

Also, while you have flexibility to dictate when you write each day, you will be required to attend one or two residencies each year, depending on which program you select. These residencies are scheduled in advance and are necessary to attend for successful program completion. Are you able to take one or two weeks off from work or responsibilities at home to attend residencies twice a year?

One thing to note is that some low-residency programs allow students to take more than two or three years to complete the module requirements. The allowance varies from program to program, so you should inquire about this flexibility prior to making an application.

One director has this to say about the option to extend studies beyond two years:

> Students may take from two years to six years or anywhere in between to complete the program. We have two current students who refer to themselves as being "on the six-year plan" but I think they'll probably both finish in five.
>
> *Wayne Ude, director, Northwest Institute of Literary Arts*

Funding

You will be responsible for most, if not all, of your tuition and related expenses. Many programs offer modest scholarships, editorships, awards, and other funding opportunities, but these will only reduce your financial responsibility by a small amount. Thus, you will need to consider if you are able and willing to take out student loans and/or finance your graduate education from your personal savings.

One benefit of a low-residency program is the ability to maintain your usual work schedule and continue to make an income while completing your studies. Chapter 5 provides a more detailed overview of the various funding opportunities offered within low-residency programs.

Pedagogical training

If you have no interest in teaching, this will only concern you in so much that you will perhaps prefer to look for a program that has no specific training component. However, since the MFA is a terminal degree, and thereby qualifies you to teach at the college level, you might want to keep the door of possibilities open.

More and more low-residency programs are offering some form of pedagogical training or, at the very least, an experience in leading a craft seminar or workshop during the brief residencies. Some programs have teaching seminars, while others help you find a teaching practicum within your community. There are also additional add-on terms exclusively devoted to pedagogical training. You will want to consider which of these options, if any, appeal to you and what level of training you desire.

If you want extensive hands-on training within a traditional classroom, you may find that you are more likely to find suitable experience with a full-residency program. Campus-based programs often incorporate teaching assistantships or graderships into their programs, sometimes as a requirement of funding packages. Depending on the level of experience you are hoping to obtain, an on-campus program may be more appropriate for your goals.

That being said, many low-residency students find ample teacher-training opportunities within their programs. Laraine Herring graduated from her MFA in 2001 and now directs the creative writing program at Yavapai College; she has this to say about her decision to enroll with a low-residency program:

> When I was thirty, I had that terrible feeling I was going to be trapped in a moderately well paying job for the rest of my life. The horror! I knew I needed to be writing more, and I felt I needed to teach.
>
> I was working in marketing, getting up before dawn to write, and then trying to figure out how to find a writing community. I'd had a few small things published, and I was afraid I would never expand my career beyond that. I began teaching workshops in the community and discovered I really loved to teach, too. I could not afford to quit my job and go to grad school, so I needed a low-residency program.
>
> My MFA program gave me the discipline to write and . . . complete a novel while working. I learned to manage my time and

to create a permanent place of prominence for my writing. Without the MFA, I wouldn't have been able to teach full-time at the college level. I honestly think that teaching writing has helped make me a better writer.

Laraine Herring, alumnus, Antioch University LA

Workshop approach

Do you prefer to workshop your writing among a dozen other peers? Or does one-on-one mentorship appeal to you? Perhaps a combination is your goal. The workshop experience for low-res students is presented as a one-on-one between you and an instructor and/or via online communication among your peers. As each program approach is different, it is important to consider how you best work with others in order to help during the selection process.

Variety of ages and experiences

On-campus programs tend to draw more recent BA graduates and thus a good portion of your fellow students will be in their mid- to late twenties. However, in a low-residency MFA you are more likely to encounter a wider variety of demographics.

Consider what the following director has to say:

The average age of our students is forty-two. The youngest graduate we had was twenty-two and the oldest was eighty-two. There are various ages and experiences in our workshops.

Sena Jeter Naslund, director, Spalding University

In addition, some incoming students have already published books prior to attending the program while others are currently teachers at community colleges or high schools. Others are coming into writing after working in an unrelated profession for years. Most low-residency students have been away from an academic setting for years, if not decades. If you're a younger writer, you may be drawn to study alongside peers closer to your age. If, however, a wide demographic appeals to you, you will certainly find it within a low-residency program.

If you have been writing for years and not seen the progress you'd like, consider what the following graduate has to say about her decision to pursue a low-residency MFA:

I realized I had come to a place in my writing where I was no longer able to reliably diagnose what was wrong with my stories. I saw clearly that my work was not as good as what I was seeing in literary magazines. I felt I could be that good and I wanted to realize that potential.

I considered traditional MFAs but rejected them because there was no program within reasonable commuting distance and I wasn't prepared to live away from my husband. In any case, I was attracted to the model of intensive mentorship. I have learned how to be a good student in the traditional classroom, but that setting is not natural for me.

I had no writing career before I got the MFA. Now I know what kinds of writing careers I might want and how to explore those possibilities. I would not hesitate to e-mail any of my former mentors with questions about how to move forward in any aspect of my writing.

Claire Guyton, alumnus, Vermont College of Fine Arts

Artistic preparedness

Low-residency writing programs require you to work on substantial pieces of work. Often, a student will work on a book-length thesis. You may want to publish books or write screenplays, but only you can tell if you are ready to commit to two or three years of serious writing. By enrolling in a low-residency MFA, you are telling the world you are serious about your craft.

Have you already determined what genres appeal to you? Have you been working on your craft through dedicated independent writing and participating in community workshops? You should already be in the practice of writing regularly, without deadline and without assignment.

A creative writing degree will push you to be at your best and will encourage you to develop an editorial eye. To take advantage of such an intense mode of study, you will want to ask yourself if you are artistically ready to dedicate your time and effort to complete large projects.

One experienced graduate has the following perspective to offer prospective students:

A low-residency program like Seton Hill's isn't a place to decide whether or not you want to write. This type of program is for people fully committed to making the leap into writing as a lifestyle.

Unfortunately, some people don't realize they don't want to write until they struggle through that first novel. They look at a program as some sort of promise of publication, never understanding that the amount of work required may be greater than everything they had to do during undergrad.

Jason Jack Miller, alumnus, Seton Hill University

All things considered

There are an increasing number of low-residency options to choose from and each program aims to offer something unique. It's up to you to decide if the low-residency model is right for you and what *your* selection criteria may be in choosing programs most appropriate for your goals. Thus, in Chapter 3 we'll touch on some of the features you will want to keep in mind as you continue your low-residency MFA research.

The Selection Process

WITH AN EVER-INCREASING SELECTION to choose from, the process of deciding which programs to apply for can be overwhelming. Ultimately, the program you choose to attend is your decision and yours alone.

So, how do you decide where to submit an application? You'll want to keep a notebook or computer file to document your research and you should first start with a checklist of desirable qualities. As you continue your research, the checklist may grow or change and that's okay. You're learning about what appeals to you in a program. You may discover options you previously didn't know existed. Be open-minded, but try to narrow your focus to some key program components. This will help you stay on track as you approach decision time.

Think about what you most desire in a program; this will go hand in hand with thinking about the writer you currently are and the writer you *want* to be. The MFA won't teach you how to write, but it will teach you ways to improve yourself as a writer and it will push you to challenge your artistic capabilities. It's always a good practice to think about how to move your writing forward and, if you haven't already, it's a good idea to start thinking about setting goals for your creative development.

Program features to consider

As you read this handbook and continue your individual research, you will discover an incredible variety of programs. Each program is unique in its own way, but most programs share some common components. Depending on your interests, you will want to understand how your selected programs approach the following elements.

Residency

The nice thing about low-residency study is that you can choose any program that interests you, regardless of geography. Some programs are based in a lively urban center, while others are more remote, maybe in a retreat-like setting. Since you will only travel to residencies once or twice a year — or never, if you select a strictly online program — you can be a student just about anywhere. However, you will need to consider the cost of travel and whether that will require ground or air transportation. Also, some programs offer international residencies, which may or may not interest you. As you review each program, be sure to keep in mind your personal travel and/or budgetary preferences.

Program curriculum

As Chapter 6 will demonstrate, there are a wide variety of pedagogical philosophies and curricula to review. Thus you will want to consider what genre(s) you want to focus on, and whether or not you prefer to include a program of study that is light or heavy on critical theory. If it interests you, there are program options including translation as well.

Time/flexibility

Most programs offer a two-year duration of study, with four or five residencies. Others take three years to complete and thus might have additional residencies to attend. Many programs also allow students to take a leave of absence for a term in order to complete the degree over a longer period of time. This can be beneficial for students needing to take into account work or family obligations or for those who want to spread out the cost of tuition over a longer duration.

Faculty

It is important to look for faculty who you relate to, but keep in mind that faculty will change over time and sometimes from year to year. Look for faculty that interest you and relate well to your writing goals, but be open-minded to whom might be appropriate mentors for your work.

Most, if not all, low-residency faculty members are active in the literary community; writers who continue to write and publish in their chosen genres. To learn more about faculty, ask alumni and current students about their personal experiences. This handbook offers some faculty interviews, but it cannot possibly represent everyone. What is provided herein should be only a starting point for your research.

It is highly recommended that you read some sample work from faculty that interest you; this will help you familiarize yourself with their work and gain a better understanding of how their writing approach may mesh with yours.

Thesis

The point of the low-residency MFA is to generate a substantial body of work within a supportive, intimate educational environment. Most programs encourage students to work on a book-length thesis project, such as a novel or collection of poems or short stories. Other programs may not focus on a book-length collection, per se, but encourage a collection of smaller pieces. Know what you are getting into prior to committing to a program; you will gain that much more from the first year of study if you have some personal writing goals in mind.

Student/alumni success

When reviewing a program, it will be of great interest to you to see how well program graduates are doing with their writing careers. It can take years to establish a publishing record, but you will want to ensure alumni have some substantial published works and are actively involved in the literary community. Many programs share alumni successes on their website and many also boast the publications of current students.

If publication is your goal, be sure to review the recent success stories of your potential program. When you review the alumni stories on program websites, you might also take the opportunity to email a few graduates to ask questions and gather more information.

Alumni community

Many low-residency programs have a lively alumni association or online group to encourage continued community and networking beyond graduation. Some programs also offer brief residencies or retreats to reunite alumni and provide additional professional development opportunities. Such components can provide an excellent bridge to maintaining the element of community that is created during the program. Carrying forward that sense of community may or may not be important to you now, but you may realize you need and want the connections after graduation.

Visiting writers/special guests

During the residencies, it is common for low-residency programs to bring in guest speakers. Most programs use this as an opportunity to introduce students to publishing professionals such as editors, agents, and established writers. These guests may offer workshop sessions or seminars on publishing, the writing life, time management, inspiration, and any number of other relevant topics. If the program you are interested in does not post the residency schedule on their website, email or call the administration to request a sample residency schedule or a sample list of who has presented sessions in the past. This will provide you with a good idea of what to expect during your own time with the program.

Readings/events

Public readings are an important part of low-residency programs. For many students, this will be the first time they have shared their work with a live audience. For some, it will be the first time they hear professional authors read to an audience. Most often scheduled during the residency, some programs also open their doors to the general public for readings to actively share successes with the community. Also, some programs schedule special events throughout the year. While these events are not mandatory for attendance, given the nature of low-residency, these can offer additional opportunities for students to connect and network with others.

Editing/publishing experience

More and more programs are providing opportunities for students to gain hands-on editorial experience. Some programs have a print or online literary journal, while others manage a small press. Students then have the opportunity to read submissions, edit manuscripts, and produce the final product. While many programs manage the day-to-day business of these publishing options, it is not uncommon for a group of students to create such an opportunity.

If editorial experience interests you, seek out those that offer experience working with a literary journal or small press. Alternatively, you might want to consider joining forces with other students to start a print or online journal if one is not already offered within your program of choice.

Teaching

Chapter 9 details just a few of the pedagogical training opportunities offered within low-residency programs. As an overview, however, it is important to note that it *is* possible to gain some teaching experience in many of the programs. While the learning experience may differ from on-campus programs, in that you will not necessarily be teaching campus-based classes several times a week, there are various ways to approach a teaching practicum.

Some programs offer to assist you with a practicum in your hometown. Others provide the opportunity to lead workshops or seminars during residencies. A few programs offer postgraduate semesters or residencies, wherein students may spend a focused amount of time developing teaching skills under the supervision of the faculty. As these options vary from program to program, and not every institution offers the opportunity, you will want to verify with your chosen program what options, if any, exist.

Community outreach

While not directly integral to your success with a graduate degree, many programs offer community outreach activities that you may wish to get involved with. In addition to providing writing conferences and seminars, or miniature literary festivals, some programs use these events not only to provide more opportunities for students but also as a way to connect with the local community. Not every program offers community programming as such and, again, this is not in direct relation to your graduate degree. However, there are a few opportunities out there so if this is something you find interesting, be sure to check with your selected programs to see what is currently offered.

Additional terms/residencies

If you don't want to commit to a three-year program, but find two years is not quite enough, you will be pleased to learn of the many opportunities for pursuing an additional term or residency. Many programs invite students to enroll in extra residencies to take advantage of workshops and professional development sessions. Some programs also offer an elective term in which students may continue to work on a thesis project, gain pedagogical experience, or simply work with yet another mentor. There are also a handful of programs that open up residencies to non-degree applicants or students from other programs. These opportunities can also provide a way to test out a program that interests you, without making a long-term commitment to enrolling.

Tuition/funding

Chapter 5 provides an overview of some — but not all — funding opportunities, in addition to a brief outline of expenses for which you'll want to plan. Do keep in mind that fees will vary from program to program; fees also change year to year, as with any educational program, so you will need to check the program website or call for up-to-date information. It is up to you to decide what you can afford to pay for graduate education and to seek out programs within your comfort zone.

Also, while more and more programs are offering some form of program-specific funding, such as scholarships or editorial assistantships, you will be responsible for funding the majority of your education. Most programs provide information on their websites about applying for federal student loans that may be used to offset your tuition. In addition, graduate education has certain tax benefits you should take advantage of, if applicable. Visit the IRS website for more information detailed in IRS Publication 970: Tax Benefits for Education.

Formats of study

As briefly touched on, there are essentially three formats of study offered through low-residency MFA programs: (1) one-on-one mentorship, (2) a hybridized version of both individual mentorship and online learning, or (3) online courses and workshops. As you research each program, you will want to take into consideration the program format and what appeals to you and your learning style.

To help clarify the distinction between each of these formats of study, I asked a director for an overview.

The heart of a mentor-based program is the one-on-one relationship between a master writer — an accomplished, actively publishing literary artist who should also be an experienced, exceptional teacher — and an apprentice writer, the MFA student, who sometimes is also a published writer herself.

In addition to the intense on-campus residencies — which usually include workshops, seminars, lectures, panels, and readings — some mentor-based programs also offer online group discussion and analysis of assigned literary and critical works to supplement the monthly packets of writing exchanged by student and mentor. In this way, the community of the residency is continued into semester, complementing the student's semester or quarter-long apprenticeship with his/her mentor.

Electronic classroom-based programs offer actual classes online, with syllabi that sometimes would be otherwise indistinguishable from those in a traditional residential writing or literature course. Electronic classroom-based low-residency programs also offer short, intense on-campus residencies.

Steve Heller, chair, Antioch University LA

AWP Hallmarks

In early 2010, the Association of Writers and Writing Programs published a document you may want to review. The "AWP Hallmarks of an Effective Low-Residency MFA Program in Creative Writing" exemplifies some of the best-practices desirable in low-residency programs. While this document is useful to institutions, directors, and faculty, it is also a tool for prospective students.

Kathleen Driskell, associate director of Spalding University's MFA program, was the Low-Residency Hallmarks Workgroup Leader — the group responsible for contributing directorial feedback in creating the Hallmarks. Regarding this document, Driskell has the following to offer:

> Our aim for the hallmarks is to show prospective MFA students that a low-residency program is not simply about convenience. Our programs do allow writers to study and earn the MFA degree without picking up and moving their lives to a campus, but that's a benefit in addition to the rigorous curriculum and meaningful one-on-one study in creative writing that we provide.
>
> *Kathleen Driskell, Low-Residency Hallmarks Workgroup Leader*

To add to that, Steve Heller, director of Antioch LA's program and current AWP Board Secretary and the Pacific West Representative, has this perspective to share:

> One of the key hallmarks for both mentor-based and electronic classroom-based programs is the need for a low faculty-to-student ratio. Students can use these ratios as one way of comparing programs. I should caution, though, that student–faculty ratio is only one means of valuing what a low-residency program has to offer. A program with a slightly higher mentor–mentee or faculty–student ratio might have more to offer particular students in other ways. Prospective students should pay attention to special features that distinguish one low-residency program from another, including the program's philosophy or mission.
>
> *Steve Heller, AWP Board Member*

The "AWP Hallmarks of an Effective Low-Residency MFA Program in Creative Writing" document is available from the AWP website (www.awpwriter.org/membership/documents. htm) at no cost.

The AWP has other benefits and services for prospective, current, and graduated writing students. More information about AWP is outlined in Chapter 12, which also includes an interview with Matt Burriesci, Acting Executive Director of AWP.

Making *your* decision

As you review the various program offerings, you will develop your own personalized checklist of "wants" in a program. Be firm in the "must-haves" you want in a program, although it's a good idea to keep an open mind. You might be surprised to learn about a new program feature, or an educational component that sounds good that you hadn't previously considered. Once you narrow down your selection, though, it's time to prepare for the application package.

CHAPTER 4

The Application Process

THIS IS PROBABLY THE one area that causes the most anxiety for prospective students. Between the personal essay and the oh-so-critical writing sample, students have a few short pages of opportunity to prove themselves to a selection committee. Rest assured, every applicant feels the same way. This is a big moment, after all. Yet, it needn't be stressful.

I asked a handful of directors some of the questions you no doubt have in the hope of dispelling some of the mystery behind what they want to see in the applications they receive.

What are some general tips for success?

Stan Rubin, director, Pacific Lutheran University: Be honest. Let us hear your real voice and real motivations. There are no strategies or tricks for [a] successful application. Your work, your motivation, and your promise of growth speak for you. We do want avid readers as well as talented writers. They go together.

Meg Kearney, director, Pine Manor College: Following our guidelines might sound simple, but it's worth saying here. We accept students on a rolling basis, so the earlier you apply, the better. Applicants hoping for a specific fellowship or need-based scholarship should pay close attention to our deadlines.

Why do we need to submit reference letters?

Louise Crowley, director, Vermont College of Fine Arts: Such letters can sort of "fill in the blanks" that the application itself might not. They can help tell us how this student receives and uses feedback and criticism; they can tell us how the student might interact in workshop; they can tell us more about a student's attitude, how serious and motivated the individual may be.

Debra Allbery, director, Warren Wilson College: Reference letters rarely provide information that isn't evident in the creative and critical work submitted by the student, but they can be useful in confirming what the manuscript and essays suggest.

What do you look for in the writing sample?
James Harms, director, New England College: Naturally the most important element of the application packet is the writing sample; if the poems aren't ready, then nothing else really matters.

Louise Crowley, director, Vermont College of Fine Arts: It's important for them to choose carefully the piece(s) of creative work that they submit; in a competitive program they need to select what is really the strongest example of their creative ability.

Michael Kobre, director, Queens University of Charlotte: Those pages should represent the very best of their abilities . . . In many significant ways the process of applying to an MFA program is like the process of submitting work for publication. Just as you should know the publication you're submitting to, have read some work published in it, you should take a look at the work of the faculty who are teaching in the program that you'll apply to. And just as you should wait to submit work for publication until you're confident about the work, you should study and revise and polish your work until you're ready for the sort of total immersion that an MFA program requires.

Richard Duggin, director, University of Nebraska: They need to submit the strongest example of their writing to date in the genre they wish to pursue to show the committee they possess the fundamental skills, originality, and artistic vision necessary to take them to the next level of study of their craft.

What do you look for in the personal essay?

Patsy Sims, director, Goucher College: It should talk about their experience and interest in writing, as well as why they want to study in Goucher's program. The essay that deals with their reading backgrounds should also explore their interest in writing and the genre.

Louise Crowley, director, Vermont College of Fine Arts: We look for someone who seems very motivated and eager for critique, someone we believe can work well with the independent nature of a low-residency program, and, of course, someone who clearly has been reflecting on what they may be looking for or recognizing that they need to learn as a writer.

David Stevenson, director, University of Alaska Anchorage: Voice. And the ability to articulate their desire to write. I think it's a hard essay to write. It should appear that it came naturally, as opposed to as a response to a prompt or an academic chore.

Peter Oresick, director, Chatham University: We look for an articulation of how their own work and career goals are a good fit with Chatham's mission. If prospects have an undergraduate background in creative writing, we want to hear about that experience. If prospects lack undergraduate training in writing, we want to hear about how they have learned their craft and how they participate in the literary community where they live. Finally, we look for a statement of commitment to a single genre. Students . . . who are focused and who can articulate a thesis goal [interest us the most], even in their letter of application.

Can you walk us through the process of what happens after an application is received?

Sena Jeter Naslund, director, Spalding University: Our intake varies but, as an example, our biggest incoming class was forty-two and last year's class was twenty-five. Sometimes an applicant will have no workshop experience and that's reflected in the quality of the writing sample. We will encourage them to work on their craft a little more, grow as a writer, and invite them to reapply in the future. We're pleased to see applicants who have been previously rejected come back and try a second time.

Once an applicant has submitted an application, two faculty members review the submitted material, including the writing sample and essays. A third faculty member will review the applicant's entire package. Then, Kathleen Driskell, associate director, and I review faculty-recommended applications and make the final approvals. The news of acceptance is delivered by phone, whereas rejected applicants receive a letter.

Karen Mann, administrative director, sends each accepted student the necessary information about registering for the first residency. The program associate, Katy Yocom, is available to respond to all incoming student questions, but we also assign one or two current students to talk to the newcomers.

The application checklist

In addition to the personal essay, writing sample, and letters of reference, you will want to check with each program about specific institutional application requirements. In addition to a four-year undergraduate degree, in a field not necessarily related to writing, the application package will generally also include an application fee, transcripts, and some institutions — but not all — require the GRE (Graduate Record Examinations). Each program will have a specific application form to submit, sometimes in multiple copies.

Now that you have narrowed down and polished your writing samples, it's time to think about ways to pay for your education.

CHAPTER 5

Funding

WHILE TUITION AND RESIDENCY fees vary from program to program, this chapter provides a brief overview of some of the common expenses students can expect and a few examples of ways to offset the cost of your education. However, it is very important to conduct independent research and inquire about the specific fees and potential funding opportunities associated with your program(s) of choice.

Planning for expenses

In addition to tuition expenses, you will also need to pay for travel to and from each residency. This will vary depending on how close you live to your MFA program and whether the travel requires ground or air transportation. This amount will also vary if you have been accepted into a program that includes international residencies.

Also, be sure to inquire about the residency costs payable to your program. This figure may or may not include meals or lodging during the residency. Be sure to consider these add-on amounts when you plan for the big picture.

There will inevitably be some additional expenses related to books, supplies, and internet access. You will also need to consider postage costs if you have a mentorship requiring packet exchanges through the mail.

Student loans

As suggested in Chapter 3, you may want to approach your program about applying for federal student loans. Many program websites provide the necessary information, but it's perfectly fine to make a phone call if you need to verify any details. I also encourage you to visit the website for the Free Application for Federal Student Aid (FAFSA) at www.fafsa.ed.gov, and the IRS website, www.irs.gov, to review any potential tax benefits as outlined in Publication 970: Tax Benefits for Education.

It is important to consider your comfort level in how much student loan debt you are willing to take on. Based on their experiences, here is what a few MFA alumni have to say about the prospect of student loans.

Carol Berg, alumnus, University of Southern Maine: I heard one poet say that if you plan on getting student loans, you should think about it as buying one less car in your lifetime. I may not have that exactly correct, but what I think the poet is trying to say is that you will probably spend the money anyways — why not spend it on your writing?

Melanie Faith, alumnus, Queens University of Charlotte: I had just paid off my undergraduate debt six months before, when I made the decision to go back into even more debt to pursue the degree. It was not a decision I took lightly, but in retrospect, it was worth every penny of the money borrowed, both in literary knowledge gleaned as well as entrance into a continuing community of writers. One cannot put a price on such experiences, although I certainly understand the frustration and disappointment for writers when learning there is no financial aid. I will be paying my Queens loans back for another seven years, which is a depressing thought, and yet I will have my memories and knowledge for a lifetime. In the end, I consider it a worthwhile trade-off.

In-program funding
Some, but not all, low-residency MFA programs offer financial assistance in the form of scholarships, merit or need-based awards, teaching or administrative assistantships, editorships, and other related work opportunities. Verify with each program what funding opportunities, if any, they have and what monetary value these carry. To provide an idea of what some programs are able to offer, I asked a few directors to share a sample of opportunities.

Wayne Ude, director, Northwest Institute of Literary Arts: We usually have four or five students on partial scholarships each semester. Those are granted based on the quality of student writing. Incoming students are eligible for scholarships.

Michael C. White, director, Fairfield University: We offer our MFA students and alumni the chance to apply for the Fairfield MFA Book Prize, a $1000 First Prize for the best collection of fiction, creative non-fiction, or poetry, as chosen by a judge of national reputation. This contest is only open to Fairfield MFA students, and thus it provides our students with a unique opportunity of getting published. The winning prize is published by the noted literary press New Rivers Press and the book is marketed and distributed nationally with a standard royalty contract.

Meg Kearney, director, Pine Manor College: While our admissions process is competitive, we keep our tuition as low as possible in order to keep the Solstice program accessible to talented writers with financial need. We also feature genre-specific fellowships as well as partial, need-based scholarships.

Stan Rubin, director, Pacific Lutheran University: At present, we have some half-dozen fellowships in addition to the endowed Jack Cady Promise Scholarship.

Bonnie Culver, director, Wilkes University: We have two small scholarships that are awarded to students nearing the end of the program. We also offer five graduate assistantships per year that pay full tuition, but require in-house work with our office. Incoming MA students likely work with me in the office on a variety of clerical, support positions. Upper-level MFA assistants work more closely with curriculum development, support Etruscan Press, and other more in-depth projects.

Kathleen Driskell, associate director, Spalding University: We offer new student scholarships ranging from $500 to $1,000. These are based on merit, but we welcome incoming students to send us a letter expressing need. We generally offer fifteen to twenty scholarships to new students.

Students in their second to fourth semester may receive

graduate assistantships by conducting online research or providing marketing assistance. The value of these range from $600 to $2,400.

Students also have the unique opportunity to gain editorial experience with *The Louisville Review*. For this, we offer graduate assistantships. All students in their first, second, and fourth semester must read a minimum of ten submissions. They each spend about ten hours a week working on the journal, which was established in 1976. Through their editorial work, students learn about the different uses of language, gain valuable experience for setting standards, and learn about submission etiquette. Students do not need to live near Louisville to take advantage of the assistantships. The value of these assistantships varies with the time and demands of each student, but they range [from] $600 to $1,800 per semester.

Again, every program is different in what financial assistance it is able to offer students. These amounts also may vary from year to year, so you should inquire with your chosen program(s) prior to admission.

Now that you've set a budget and considered financial aid, it's time to take a closer look at each of the programs.

CHAPTER 6

The Programs

THIS CHAPTER IS THE heart of the handbook. Through these "conversations" with low-residency directors, faculty, alumni, and current students, you will read about the various philosophies and personalities behind each program. The comments expressed herein should provide enough of an introductory taste to help you decide whether to seek out additional information. I encourage you to email faculty and students from your final "wish list" of programs. You will most certainly have questions specific to your own situation and will want to seek out additional people who can respond to your queries.

As touched on earlier, the quantity of the comments is not reflective of the *quality* of the program. Why might some programs have fewer comments? Some are purposefully smaller than others, more than a handful have only been in existence for a few years, and a few will accept their first applicants after the publication date of this book. By the time you read this book, there may be even more new programs in development.

There is a small selection of international programs included and if these appeal to you, I suggest doing a web search for additional options. Those included herein aim to provide a sampler of what options are available to you.

The programs are listed alphabetically by institution; "University of" programs are placed in alphabetical order as a result of the keyword identifier. Also, where appropriate, I have indicated those programs that are Master of Arts (MA) programs, rather than MFAs.

As you have already experienced, there are additional comments spread throughout this handbook from various interviewees who speak on various topics. Appendix A also shares a selection of extended interviews, while Chapters 7 through 12 offer an assortment of comments on specific topics.

Finally, application deadlines and tuition fees are not included, as these may vary from year to year and it is best to verify the current information by visiting the program website. Similarly, while program genres are included, it is important to note that programs frequently update and enhance their offerings. The years required to complete the degree and the number of residencies are provided as an approximation. Many programs allow students to take more than the minimum time to complete a degree, but I have included the generally accepted minimum for each program, for matters of consistency. I recommend you verify all of the above points with programs you are interested in, prior to making an application.

Now, let's meet the programs . . .

UNIVERSITY OF ALASKA ANCHORAGE
Poetry, Fiction, Literary Non-Fiction
Anchorage, AK
3 years, 4 residencies
www.uaa.alaska.edu/cwla

The interviewees
David Stevenson is the director of the Creative Writing and Literary Arts program. He often writes about the mountaineering experience, both in fiction and non-fiction prose, and has published widely in journals such as *Ascent*, *Alpinist*, *Isotope*, and *Weber Studies*, as well as in *The American Alpine Journal*, where he has been book review editor since 1996.

Judith Barrington is a non-fiction instructor with UAA. She is the author of *Lifesaving: A Memoir*, which won the 2001 Lambda Book Award and was a finalist for the PEN/Martha Albrand Award for the Art of the Memoir. She is also the author of *Writing the Memoir: From Truth to Art* and three collections of poetry, most recently *Horses and the Human Soul*.

Anne Caston is a poetry instructor with UAA. Her work has recently been anthologized in collections such as *The New American*

Poets: A Bread Loaf Anthology, Where Books Fall Open, Sustenance &
Desire, and *Long Journey: Contemporary Northwest Poets.*

Jeffery Oliver is a poet and digital media artist who graduated
from the UAA poetry program in December 2008.

Sandra Kleven is a student who has work in *Cirque, Alaska*
Quarterly Review, and *Oklahoma Review.*

The program

Jeffery Oliver, alumnus: Professionally, I'm a web designer,
developer, and consultant and I enjoy my career and work. I
chose to pursue an MFA in poetry because pragmatic/personal
creativity and artistic/personal creativity feed different needs in
my life. With the program at UAA, I was able to continue to
work professionally while meeting a personal need to refine my
abilities as a poet. Basically, I realized I was getting older and not
engaged with art — this MFA was part of getting my priorities
in the right place.

David Stevenson, director: Alaska makes our program unique.
Our faculty are wonderful — talented and generous. And our
students bring a lot of energy to the program. We value interdisciplinary, cultural diversity, and writing that is particularly
place-based and environmentally aware, but these cast a wide net
and are shared with other programs. Our really unique aspects are
our people and our place.

Anne Caston, faculty: In general, I find that students who are
drawn to this program — one which is pretty far-removed from
the literary center of America — come to us with a sense of
wanting to experience something remarkably different from their
peers at more-established university programs of study. Yes, there
is sometimes a bit of the "romance of the far arctic" in place, but
there is also a desire to be a writer in a geographical landscape
that's somehow bigger than they are, one that puts things into
perspective, one that allows them to explore the significance of
place (both external and internal) to them and to their stories.

Judith Barrington, faculty: I think the program is truly unique.

First of all, the faculty is wonderfully supportive of each other and the students, and committed to giving a three-year, in-depth writing experience. Because of the unavoidable interaction between the university campus-life and the natural world (moose on bike paths, snow-covered mountains all around), there is a focus, though not an exclusive one, on environmental writing. Even if it were not emphasized in any descriptions of the program, it seems to me that it would happen organically, so close are many of the students to the world of fish and bear and mountain. The three-year format, with three summer residencies, allows the students to develop a project at a reasonable pace and with time to re-think, to dig deep, and to edit. It also offers plenty of time to read widely and report on the books which help each student develop his or her critical faculties.

Faculty/teaching philosophy

Anne Caston, faculty: My students are in the last formal stages of their studies and training in the art and craft of poetry. After graduation, they'll have to educate themselves the way all artists must: by developing a dynamic and ongoing relationship to their art. By that, I mean that they'll continue to grow, to learn, but it will be life and the art itself which will be their teachers rather than the writing mentors they currently have nurturing them along. I hope that I am the kind of mentor who can encourage them along towards that independence, by introducing them to the enduring works of literature, by reminding them that the arts are inextricably linked to human experience and feeling, and by asking the tough questions of them they'll need to wrestle with — those questions they'll hear in their minds over and over again when they're working in solitude again, outside of a formal program of study.

Judith Barrington, faculty: I hope to offer my students a one-on-one experience that will give them new insights into the possible ways they can shape and craft their writing, as well as building their confidence and their ability to read the work of others with a writerly eye and ear.

David Stevenson, director: We like to keep our faculty diverse, in all the ways that word may resonate. I'm thinking mostly of a mix of writers who live in Alaska and those from "outside" — as the lower forty-eight is referred to here. One thing student-writers need is a variety of readers — to be exposed to as many different esthetic sensibilities as possible during their time here.

Residency/community

Judith Barrington, faculty: The summer residencies at UAA take place on the campus in Anchorage. The atmosphere is informal, very friendly, and non-competitive. The evening readings by faculty are a highlight, staged with a good sound system, an appreciative audience including members of the public, and a well-run bookstore selling an array of works by faculty and others. The field trip in the middle of the residency has, both times I've taken it, been terrific: a trip by bus to a beautiful area, a hike with a knowledgeable botanist, a visit to an old mine, a walk on a glacier, and more.

David Stevenson, director: The Northern Renaissance Arts and Sciences Series is where our residency intersects with the "public square." All of our faculty and our guests give a public reading in the evenings during the residency. An important function of the Series is to keep our writers engaged in the larger world, to expose them to ideas and processes within other disciplines, to allow writers to hear from historians, scientists, visual artists, etc., all in keeping with this notion of nurturing and cultivating the students' whole being, to broaden their intellects and ways of seeing. It's a great atmosphere — when the readings are over there are still a couple hours of daylight.

Jeffery Oliver, alumnus: Art is created by individuals, so the low-res model works really well if you've got a good residency that challenges — and the UAA residency does this. The residency-model allowed me to interact with fantastic faculty and not only poets — but fiction and non-fiction writers too. I think this is most appealing to me about the UAA residencies — the multi-disciplinary approach. I've learned as much about writing a good line in poetry from advertising as from workshops — everything is useful to the artist. The overall tone of the UAA residency is friendly and faculty are very approachable. I was able to talk with everyone I wanted throughout the residency. The evening reading series is amazing and allows us as students to understand better where faculty come from with their art, which enriches the instruction and workshop comments tremendously. Because of the intensity of the residency, I felt a quick bond with other students.

Sandra Kleven, student: The residency periods are certainly the heart of the program. During the traditional academic year, I have the benefit of close proximity to the staff and the office. This is a personal benefit because the year round staff, director David Stevenson and coordinator Kathy Tarr, are wonderful people, generous in their support and their interest in all things literary. But the summer residency is alive and rollicking . . . Almost every night, faculty members give readings in an event open to the community. The group dinners and lunches give time for students to mix informally.

Format/study

Judith Barrington, faculty: I like the low-residency format . . . I enjoy the freedom to think about my students' work as long as necessary, and to communicate with them on a schedule, which gives me flexibility too. Students considering a low-residency program should be sure that they have enough motivation to keep writing and reading without the structure of a classroom. At UAA, there is a well-developed internet community through which the students can keep in touch with each other, but they should be sure that will work for them. It is ideal for self-directing students who can use the deadlines to keep writing.

Jeffery Oliver, alumnus: Because I pursued poetry as art and spent a lot of time pushing my own perceptions of form, I didn't think so much about creating a collection of poems for publication. This allowed me to practice different modes and forms including digital poems, video poems, and poems set to music. Anne Caston (poetry) and Sherry Simpson (creative non-fiction) both encouraged me to the level of overseeing independent study in these areas. However, when it came time to get my creative thesis together, my poems were all over the map. Anne Caston mentored me through finding ways to assemble a narrative to create a cohesive collection. I feel that Anne supported me completely and was able to mentor me when I really was unsure how to proceed.

David Stevenson, director: The low-residency model appeals to people who are working in careers or jobs that they want or need to continue working in — it's flexible in that way. I think students can make the most of their MFA experience, whatever the delivery model, by keeping in mind that it's about their writing, not about "the degree."

ALBERTUS MAGNUS COLLEGE
Poetry, Fiction, Non-Fiction
Launched in fall 2010
New Haven, CT
2 years, 3 Saturday residencies each semester
www.albertus.edu/masters-degrees/mfa/index.html

The interviewee
Sarah Harris Wallman is an assistant professor of English and Creative Writing at Albertus Magnus College. Her work has been published in Brooklyn's *L Magazine* and produced off-Broadway. She was a founding staff member of *Meridian*, the literary magazine of the graduate program at the University of Virginia.

The program
Sarah Wallman, faculty: Albertus Magnus believes that students should not be shut out from an advanced degree in writing just because they lead full lives. Our blended curriculum allows students to follow their dreams on a schedule they devise. The blended approach means much of the course will be delivered in an online format, though every fifteen-week course also involves three on-campus Saturday meetings. We're reaching out to busy writers who want to take the next step: to formally study the genre they've been privately practicing and to produce a publishable manuscript as their final project.

Faculty/teaching philosophy
Sarah Wallman, faculty: We started the MFA in Writing program at Albertus Magnus because we have a passionate writing community here at the college, as well as in the larger New Haven

community and across the state of Connecticut (and the region of New England). This surplus of talent and passion was being harnessed by two types of writing programs: the traditional residential and the low-residency programs. We believe that there are talented writers out there who cannot fit either of these molds. The Dominican tradition encourages us to search for truth in all its dimensions, and we hope this program will open a portal where none existed.

Residency/community
Sarah Wallman, faculty: Over the course of a fifteen-week semester, students will meet on the New Haven campus of Albertus Magnus on three Saturdays (once every five weeks). For every four-credit course, students will meet for two and a half hours during each Saturday session. Students enrolled in a portfolio or mentoring course will meet with their mentor for one hour of each session. These sessions supplement the virtual community established on the MFA website.

Format/study
Sarah Wallman, faculty: The blended approach means that some assignments will be both distributed and collected using the Moodle course-delivery system. Professors are available for physical as well as virtual office hours throughout the semester.

Our curriculum familiarizes students with every aspect of the writing life from understanding the creative process to assessing market trends in specific areas of professional writing. Through rigorous genre-study, students will locate themselves in the creative tradition. Through workshops and one-on-one mentorship, students will produce a portfolio of work in their chosen genre.

ANTIOCH UNIVERSITY LOS ANGELES
Poetry, Fiction, Creative Non-Fiction; Focus on Social Justice
Culver City, CA
2 years, 5 residencies
www.antiochla.edu/academics/mfa-creative-writing

The interviewees
Steve Heller is the MFA program chair at Antioch LA and the Pacific West Representative for the AWP Board of Directors.

Heller is also a fiction instructor and is best known for his novel *The Automotive History of Lucky Kellerman*. His short stories have appeared in numerous magazines and national anthologies, and have twice received O. Henry Awards.

Laraine Herring graduated from the AULA fiction program in 2001. She is the author of *Lost Fathers: How Women Can Heal From Adolescent Father Loss*, *Writing Begins with the Breath: Embodying Your Authentic Voice*, *The Writing Warrior: Discovering the Courage to Free Your True Voice* and the novel *Ghost Swamp Blues*. She directs the creative writing program at Yavapai College.

Mandy Farrington is a student, writer, and employee of a small liberal arts college in Los Angeles. She has published a few short stories and is now hard at work on a novel about an interracial relationship in the post-civil-rights-era south.

The program
Steve Heller, chair: Many MFA programs are tightly focused on helping an author complete their first book, find an agent, and get it published. At Antioch LA, we take a broader view of educating writers. Our purpose is to educate writers for life. This includes not only helping them sharpen their craft and develop their vision, but educating them in the varied roles writers perform in society and their many communities. We address these goals at each residency in faculty or guest seminars: "Arts, Culture, and Society I & II" and "Writers at Work." Our most significant way of addressing this issue, however, is the MFA Field Study.

Laraine Herring, alumnus: I really appreciated the service component that was a requirement of the Antioch MFA program. I thought it would be wonderful to learn how to use writing as a way to help and enrich the community, and was thrilled that it was part of the degree requirement.

Faculty/teaching philosophy
Steve Heller, chair: We look for actively publishing writers of fiction, poetry, and creative non-fiction who are also excellent teachers. We want faculty whose students' successes are as important to them as their own. We also strive to hire faculty from

underrepresented groups. Most importantly, despite the fact that AULA has earned a reputation as a progressive, liberal institution, there is no Antioch way to think or write. So we make certain that our faculty reflects a broad diversity of viewpoint on the act of writing, in terms of craft and vision.

Laraine Herring, alumnus: I am still in touch with one of my mentors, Alma Luz Villanueva, the former chair of the program, Eloise Klein Healy, and several of the women who were in my cohort. One of them, Gayle Brandeis, is my first reader. My friendship with her was one of the highlights of the program.

Mandy Farrington, student: My first mentor was especially encouraging of my attempt at a novel. I admire her as a writer, especially her ability to be so prolific while teaching and raising her own kids. I chose her after hearing her read her own work. Then I sat down with her at the first residency and told her I wanted to try a novel after attending a workshop by another faculty member who suggested the "page-a-day" routine. His workshop stressed writing a page a day, without looking back until you reach 100 pages. I had always wanted to try a novel, but I'm such a perfectionist; I can spend months on an opening paragraph, and I just didn't think I'd live long enough to spend that much time on a novel.

My mentor really helped me fight the urge to perfect in those early stages. When she read my work, she made lots of comments, but they were all encouraging — leading questions, suggestions of where to draw out scenes in the future. After I finished the first month's pages, I told her I really wanted to go back and make what I had a better draft. She replied, "You could do that, but I think you'll be happier if you stick with your original plan and press on." I fought the urge — and she was right. I ended the project period with 100 pages. They were far from perfect, but it was so much easier going back in the second project period with 100 pages of prose to mold and shape than it would have been with one perfect paragraph and a lot of ideas not yet on the page.

Residency/community
Steve Heller, chair: Our students and faculty reflect almost every imaginable viewpoint — in terms of politics, religion, art, you

name it. The friendships and professional bonds that are formed at the residencies deepen during the online project period — and continue long after students have graduated. Antioch MFA alumni and faculty are lifelong learners as well as writers, and we continue to read and learn from each other for the whole of our individual lives. The sense of community among our students and alumni is the program's biggest selling point.

[During residency] they can expect the time of their lives. They can expect workshops that are constructive in both tone and substance, faculty and guest seminars that challenge them to think in new ways, graduating student lectures that surprise and provoke, panels that show them the business side of writing and how to get published, and readings of creative work that edify and inspire. They can expect to form relationships that last for the rest of their lives. At the end of ten days, they can expect to [go] home exhausted but rejuvenated, ready to face a blank page and put black on white.

Laraine Herring, alumnus: The residencies were well done. We were paired with a buddy when we first arrived so that we could get acclimated. I found the residencies well organized. We received notification of the seminars and reading lists in plenty of time. We had ample opportunity to meet with our cohorts and to work with mentors. There was always at least one networking and socializing event off campus.

Mandy Farrington, student: I have seen a few readings in Los Angeles. Since I'm local, I try to attend some of the many events of which the program keeps us apprised — though I never manage as many as I'd like. The main way I interact with the community is online, however. We post to the message boards and continue writerly discussions even via personal email or on Facebook. We gripe, we collaborate, and the best part of this is — you are always able to stay in touch with these people at this level, regardless of where they live or their continued connection to the program.

Format/study
Steve Heller, chair: The MFA Field Study provides students with the opportunity to put their knowledge and expertise in service of a cause or institution or issue in their home community that they

personally care about. We insist that each Field Study address at least two of the three aspects of the MFA program's special purpose: the education of literary artists, community service, and the pursuit of social justice. An Antioch Core Faculty serves as the student's Field Study mentor, usually communicating with the student by email, while a local expert in the student's home community serves as On-Site Supervisor and Evaluator. MFA Field Studies vary greatly in their subject matter and scope. A current student just created and taught a writing workshop in Paris. A graduate of just a few years back, a salmon fisherman from Kodiak, Alaska, served as an embedded reporter in Iraq. A young poet from Atlanta, Georgia, interviewed elderly jazz musicians and developed publicity packets for each of them to help them find work. The Field Study is a way students connect most deeply to the mission of all Antioch campuses.

Another unique feature is the Art of Translation Residency Seminar and Project Period Online Conference. This feature does not require knowledge of a foreign language. Rather, using glossaries constructed from various languages, our translation expert teaches students how translators first construct literal translations of poems and prose passages, then transform those literal translations into literature. Students often tell us this was the most surprising and uniquely satisfying aspect of our program.

ANTIOCH UNIVERSITY MIDWEST
Master of Arts (MA)
Individualized Liberal and Professional Studies
Fiction, Poetry, Playwriting, Screenwriting
Yellow Springs, OH
2 years, 2 residencies
http://midwest.antioch.edu/ilps/cw/index.html

The interviewee
Rebecca Kuder teaches and advises students in creative writing at the Individualized Liberal and Professional Studies program at Antioch University Midwest. She has published short stories, essays, and poems, and her novel *The Watery Girl* is forthcoming from Red Hen Press.

The program

Rebecca Kuder, faculty: Horace Mann, Antioch's first president, said, "Be ashamed to die until you have won some victory for humanity." It can be a lofty idea and a heavy burden, but this notion has influenced my work and life. The Antioch program carries forth that mission. And being extremely student-centered, the program allows students to find and follow the paths that will lead them to discover their own potential victories. These victories might be large or small, but I would argue that the ability to write engaging and well-crafted novels, stories, plays, or poems, regardless of the content, influences humanity in powerful ways.

Antioch University [Midwest] offers a self-designed degree. This allows writers in the program to design the curriculum of their dreams. Working one-on-one with stellar writers as instructors (writers who are often not available to students at more traditional programs) is one of the most unique aspects of our program. Our students have worked with great writers in their fields. Many students in the program work in realism or literary genres, but some write mystery, science fiction, fantasy, or horror. These genres are often overlooked or marginalized in more traditional writing programs. This idea of locking whole segments of writers out of academe contradicts Antioch's core values. Antioch University is a place for excellent writing, independent of genre.

Faculty/teaching philosophy

Rebecca Kuder, faculty: Whether students want to teach in a community college, pursue a PhD, or simply strengthen their writing and connect with other writers, we offer students a place to work on craft at their own pace. Personally, I aim to help students take themselves seriously as writers, and step into the community of writers, building writers' confidence. Ideally, this allows students to release any negative messages they may have learned or absorbed over the course of a life that is defined by an urge to write. Negative messages or lack of confidence seem to be primary obstacles to those who would write. As a teacher, I give my students generous, balanced portions of thoughtful support and rigorous challenge. My hope is that students in the program will gain discipline and self-assurance, so that they continue to grow as writers well beyond graduation.

Residency/community

Rebecca Kuder, faculty: Residencies are hosted in Yellow Springs, Ohio, which is a small, unique arts community near Dayton, Cincinnati, and Columbus. The atmosphere is at once strenuous and relaxed. Because the program is self-designed, ample time is devoted to [teaching] how to build curriculum. With a balance of group and individual time, the residency provides connection to the writing community in an informal, friendly setting.

Though the program is individualized, and students work at different paces rather than in a traditional classroom or cohort model, we have built web-based and real community into the program as much as time and space allow. The online forums and discussions are a place where writers can post work and give and get feedback, as well as share information about the writing life.

Format/study

Rebecca Kuder, faculty: We use a variety of technologies: email; web-based learning communities via Sakai; traditional dial-in phone conferencing; voice over IP via Skype; live chats; and, of course, paper mail. Local and regional students often meet with Antioch faculty chairs throughout their study, and students who live near their non-Antioch mentors have the opportunity to meet in person as well.

Some students choose to combine creative writing with fine arts, breaking down the barriers of form to create new types of graduate level curriculum. The openness of our program allows almost endless possibilities, within a context of rigorous academic accountability.

[We have] a strong partnership with the Antioch Writers' Workshop, a week-long summer writing workshop where participants have ample access to faculty — not only through the formal workshop setting, but also through organized lunches and informal talks. Because of this partnership, we can offer students the opportunity to earn graduate credit while attending the workshop. This has opened up an even broader community of writers to our students, and it has expanded our adjunct faculty pool.

ASHLAND UNIVERSITY
Poetry, Creative Non-Fiction
Ashland, OH

2 years, 3 residencies
www.ashland.edu/graduate/mfa

The interviewees

Steven Haven is the director of the MFA program at Ashland University. He is the author of two books of poems, *Dust and Bread* and *The Long Silence of the Mohawk Carpet Smokestacks*, and one memoir, *The River Lock: One Boy's Life Along the Mohawk*.

Ruth L. Schwartz is a poetry faculty member at Ashland. She is the author of four prize-winning books of poems, including *Dear Good Naked Morning* and *Edgewater*, and a memoir, *Death in Reverse*.

Grace Curtis, alumnus, studied poetry in Ashland's MFA program. Her work has appeared in the *Chaffin Journal*, *The Clockwise Cat*, among other publications.

Joan Hanna is currently enrolled in Ashland University's low-residency creative writing program. She is completing a cross-genre study of poetry and creative non-fiction.

Joy Gaines-Friedler, student, is a writer-in-residence for InsideOut Literary Arts Project in the Detroit Public Schools. Mayapple Press published her first poetry book, *Like Vapor*, in 2008.

The program

Stephen Haven, director: The Ashland MFA program is distinct from any other MFA program in the country in that it offers degree tracks in two genres only — poetry and creative non-fiction. Though poetry students study in workshops exclusively with other poetry students, and creative non-fiction students with other non-fiction writers, the influence of both genres is always present in the program. During summer residencies, following morning workshops segregated by genre, all students and faculty attend afternoon craft seminars and evening readings. All craft seminars and many readings are designed to celebrate both genres, and often bring the two into dialogue with one another.

The Ashland MFA program also offers a cross-genre option,

for students who are active in both genres. The exclusive two-genre focus — and the emphasis on what poets can learn from CNF writers and what CNF writers can learn from poets — distinguishes the Ashland MFA program from all other low-residency and traditional MFA programs.

The Ashland MFA program is also one of the few low-residency programs to work on the single annual residency model.

Ruth L. Schwartz, faculty: It's really the most collegial and genuine atmosphere I've ever encountered in the writing world.

Joan Hanna, student: Ashland University was the most personable program I found. From the moment I contacted them for information I began receiving a newsletter, monthly updates, and reminders of upcoming deadlines. They were also the only school that personally invited me to an information session. Both the Administrative Director and Program Director contacted me personally.

It was also clear that the focus of this program was on writing instead of a heavy concentration of courses that were not centralized around my writing. I was at a point where I felt that I wanted to concentrate solely on my writing and to build a body of work.

Faculty/teaching philosophy
Stephen Haven, director: The Ashland MFA program is built on the idea of creating a supportive, literary community that maintains only the highest expectation for new writing. The program embraces the idea that accomplished writers often developed their craft through an association with an audience of other writers who are both supportive and insist on high esthetic standards.

The pedagogical philosophy behind the Ashland program supports the creation of a literary community that extends well beyond degree completion. Alumni, current students, faculty, staff, visiting writers and editors, are all members of the extended Ashland community. Without any sort of demographic distinction whatsoever, we welcome all talented writers who love and celebrate literature and believe in the possibility of adding a book to the canon. We look to draw to the program students and faculty who celebrate the successes of others and feed off that energy to work toward successes of their own.

Ruth L. Schwartz, faculty: Our [program] has unbelievably supportive camaraderie among faculty, and between faculty and students. There is a sense of genuine caring for each other and for the larger art in which we're all engaged. It's inspiring and stimulating.

Joy Gaines-Friedler, student: I did enjoy working with my mentor, Kathryn Winograd. She pointed me to specific books and poets I was grateful for: Yusef Komunyakaa, *The Wild Iris* by Louise Glück, Jori Graham, and others. Her sectional responses were wonderful and I would love the chance to work with her again.

Grace Curtis, alumnus: All of the teachers have their special talent and process of encouraging and teaching. Ruth Schwartz taught me to understand poetry better and has provided some of the most detailed feedback on my own work. Peter Campion has been so encouraging . . . Angie Estes is an extraordinary poet with incredible artistic sensibilities. I have read her books over and over.

Residency/community
Stephen Haven, director: There are three fourteen-day intensive residencies during the process of completing the two-year degree — one gateway residency, one mid-program residency after the first year, and one exit, post-thesis residency. Again, this format accommodates students with regular work lives. Our students can devote each year a single two-week leave from work to the single, annual Ashland MFA summer residency. This residency format also creates more of a full-immersion experience, as it is longer than the ten-day residencies typically found in other low-residency MFA programs. In the Ashland program, students sustain for a full two weeks a non-stop focus on their own writing and on the writing of others. We keep a twelve-hour daily schedule on residency weekdays and a half-day schedule on weekends.

The Midwestern location — on the northeastern edge of the Midwest — is yet another distinctive quality of the Ashland MFA program. While our student body has a foundation in Ohio, there are students in the program from most regions of the United States. Our students currently come from nineteen different states. Ashland MFA faculty mentors also come from many different states — Indiana, Alabama, California, Ohio, New York, Colorado, Georgia, and Wisconsin.

Ruth L. Schwartz, faculty: The residencies are hosted on the Ashland campus for two weeks each summer. They are friendly, rigorous, intense, community-building, collegial, and inspiring. They are exhausting, too, but it's the kind of exhaustion most writers thrive on! I wouldn't say there's much "networking" — the Ashland program really doesn't have that kind of "connection-making" vibe — but there is a lot of friendship happening. People genuinely want to learn from each other, and help each other. We get into some fascinating group conversations during the course of each residency, and since all faculty attend all of the readings and craft talks, we're all able to further those conversations with our students.

Joan Hanna, student: The atmosphere and social elements are very supportive and encouraging. We also share meals with the instructors and the visiting writers. There really is a strong sense of community and accessibility to both instructors and visiting writers.

Since the poetry and creative non-fiction students all participate in the craft sessions and readings together, we can develop many relationships within the two genres. The focus is always on how to improve and get at the heart of your writing. All of the craft sessions are geared to both genres and we are able to apply techniques from both genres.

Format/study
Stephen Haven, director: The Ashland MFA program offers a publishing seminar during every intensive summer residency. We generally invite literary agents or senior editors of journals, independent literary presses, or university presses to address the students and faculty in a 90-minute session. As part of the post-thesis residency, graduating students meet in hour-long sessions with prominent editors to receive additional advice and critical feedback on their theses.

Joan Hanna, student: The non-resident semester workload varies by teacher, but consists of four packets of student writing a semester along with studies of contemporary writers. We are required to participate in online discussions of both the readings and workshopped student writing.

The first semester is designed to generate a large amount of material. The second semester is designed to allow students to begin to see trends and common themes in their writing and to begin to explore those themes more thoroughly. The third semester is designed to allow students to begin grouping writing in anticipation of the fourth and final semester's thesis compilation.

Grace Curtis, alumnus: Ashland brings in editors and publishers as a part of their program, which has been extremely helpful . . . Last year, Ashland brought in publishing editors to review each of the thesis manuscripts of all the graduating poetry and creative non-fiction students. The editors provided important information and feedback on the work of each student with one-on-one review sessions.

Additionally, several of the faculty members have provided me with some very helpful insights, even down to how to handle rejections on submissions. Just today, one of the professors sent me a link to a journal with a note that said, "I thought of you when I saw this site. You should check it out."

BENNINGTON COLLEGE
The Bennington Writing Seminars
Fiction, Poetry, Non-Fiction
Bennington, VT
2 years, 5 residencies
www.bennington.edu/go/graduate/mfa-in-writing

The interviewees
Sven Birkerts, director, has been editor of *AGNI* magazine since July 2002. His most recent books are *Reading Life: Books for the Ages* and *The Other Walk*.

Alice Mattison teaches fiction in the Bennington Writing Seminars. She is the author of four collections of stories, a book of poems, and five novels including *Nothing Is Quite Forgotten in Brooklyn*.

Laura Nathan-Garner, non-fiction alumnus, has written for

The Writer's Chronicle, *Redbook*, and *Cooking Light*, and authored *Day Trips From Houston*. Laura also teaches creative writing to elementary and middle school students.

Jenn Scheck-Kahn, fiction alumnus, has been published in *Forklift, Ohio*, the *Dos Passos Review*, and *Tea Party Magazine*. She's currently at work on a memoir.

Winona Winkler Wendth, non-fiction alumnus, received a BA in English in 1968 and has been taking graduate classes in literature, history, and art almost continually since then.

The program

Sven Birkerts, director: Bennington has a superlative faculty, a strong ongoing culture with bonding at residencies and alumni continuity, visitors chosen for their provocations, a palpable sense of mission about writing — and, of course, the quality of admitted applicants, their powerful chemistry.

Alice Mattison, faculty: The Bennington MFA program is the only one I know of that unashamedly and happily focuses on literature of all times and countries, not primarily on contemporary American literature. The degree is in "writing and literature." Most of us on the faculty write in more than one genre, and we expect students to read poetry whether they write it or not, and to write non-fiction responses to literature, whether their primary work is in poetry, fiction, or non-fiction.

Winona Winkler Wendth, alumnus: Bennington is a literature, rather than craft-centered writing program. The truth is that a smart writer can figure out those nuts-and-bolts requirements on his or her own — and practice them through workshops and interactions with mentors in between residencies, but no craft book or writing prompt can replace careful reading of good literature and good conversations with careful thinkers.

Faculty/teaching philosophy

Sven Birkerts, director: With faculty, I look for passion — about serious writing, passion about reading — and a capacity to respond to a range of students. Publications matter — to testify to ongoing engagement — but what really seals the deal is an ability to work honestly and supportively and insightfully with the writing and aspirations of the student.

Alice Mattison, faculty: I would like to help my students become more attentive to language, more attentive to their own choices as they write so they use common sense instead of trying to follow rules — there are no rules.

Jenn Scheck-Kahn, alumnus: The strategies that governed my instructors' teaching style varied as much as their own creative work did. One instructor tended to the architecture of a story, while another offered a more intuitive approach to narrative movement, twice recommending that I read a specific poem before considering a new ending. Some amended my reading list based on my current work; others stressed the annotations, which were the small evaluations we wrote in response to the books we read. Never did I receive a compliment that wasn't hard earned. I developed a disciplined schedule to compensate for their standards, which were challenging, not discouraging. I recall my instructors with affection and admiration.

Winona Winkler Wendth, alumnus: Bennington gives a student a wide variety of mentors, so each semester I had a different take on what I was doing, although all my teachers agreed about my strong and weak suits — that was helpful. Tom Bissell provided a semester of sentence-level editing, which drove me nuts, but his suggestions affected my writing invaluably, even though his voice is very different from mine. Sven Birkerts and Philip Lopate have expansive intellects and challenged me to think hard and carefully while still maintaining my own voice and stance. I think some programs do not emphasize this enough — I know too many new writers who go through programs without developing intellectual sinew or literary sensitivity and write quickly and effectively but have little to add to the life of letters. Bissell taught me a lot about editing for for-profit publications, and Birkerts actually made me believe that I had something to say. Simply having access to Lopate — and we all had open access to any of the professors at almost any time — was helpful in reminding me how interconnected the fine and liberal arts are.

Residency/community

Sven Birkerts, director: The residencies are intimate, intense and ongoing. I am amazed every time I go to AWP and find myself surrounded by the ongoing Bennington community. The residency is the crucible, but the contacts that then continue over the distance are a flourishing thing.

Alice Mattison, faculty: I was wary the first time I arrived at a Bennington residency, worried that I'd find would-be writers competing with one another. Instead I found friends hurling themselves into one another's arms after the unbearable separation between residencies. That was fifteen years ago, before email and social networking sites. Now, as far as I can tell, some Bennington students are in touch every minute, though some find that the residencies provide a half year's worth of social contact, and remain solitary most of the year.

I don't keep in touch between packets with my current students, unless questions that can't wait come up, but I have happy relationships with alumni, and hear from some every week, sometimes with a request for advice or a letter of recommendation, often just with news and greetings and friendliness. Some colleagues and former students have become my close friends. For many of us, however far along our careers may be, the Bennington community is the most reliable source of people who believe in books and writing: we go to that community to be understood.

Jenn Scheck-Kahn, alumnus: The bombardment of lectures and readings alongside so many hours with creative individuals was invigorating. Because the students have families and jobs and competing commitments, being at residency truly felt like a retreat and we all felt grateful to be in each other's company. You hear about the competition among students at other MFA programs, but that didn't exist at Bennington. We cherished the opportunity to be together.

Winona Winkler Wendth, alumnus: The residencies were intense: well over a hundred contact hours in ten days. I attended almost all the lectures, which were terrific — even the mediocre ones — and I took and refer to copious notes. Both graduating student and faculty lectures — visiting and core — were a great benefit. Readings came in the evenings — both graduating student and faculty readings; these were instrumental in building community and giving us a glimpse of what a writer's life is like. In fact, the residencies, generally, were set up to build community and introduce us to a life of letters.

Format/study

Alice Mattison, faculty: When I started teaching at Bennington, I wondered whether students in a low-residency program could possibly learn as much and work as hard as students who attend classes at a university all year long. Now I think they work harder and learn more; the low-residency format means they read not the books an instructor chooses for a class syllabus, but the books they need to educate themselves — supplemented by books their instructors suggest. At Bennington residencies we teach, aside from workshops every other day, mostly by means of lectures — about literature, about writing, about the state of letters today: there are lectures by graduating students, by faculty, by visitors. All of us attend most lectures, and they become starting points for a community's talk at meals, in workshop, and in the dorms. For ten days twice a year, we live as a bunch of mad intellectuals. This has to be good.

Laura Nathan-Garner, alumnus: At Bennington, we corresponded with our instructors in a somewhat old-fashioned method, but it was one that enabled us to focus more on our writing and to get a significant amount of personal attention. Each month, we had to write something — an essay, a chapter, a short story or set of short stories, a set of poems — as well as the requisite book critiques, and send them by snail mail to our respective faculty member. The instructor then spent a week to ten days reading and annotating the materials before sending them back, along with a long letter critiquing and responding to your work. I also often emailed with and, in some cases, called my instructors during the semester to ask about things they had said in their letters or for other guidance.

Since each instructor only has four or five students a semester, my faculty advisors really got to know my writing and helped me work on very specific things over the course of a semester. They couldn't possibly have devoted this much attention to my work had I been in a class with ten or fifteen other people, as I almost certainly would have been at a full-residency residency program. The value of this kind of personal attention was evident in the transformation of my writing each semester. Unless you've got a great mentor or a great editor, the odds of getting that kind of detailed and thoughtful feedback on your writing are slim. Plus, by exchanging packets like this and forcing students to make time to fit writing into their "normal" lives, the low-residency format really mimics the writer–editor relationship.

UNIVERSITY OF BRITISH COLUMBIA
Fiction, Poetry, Non-Fiction, Children's, Translation, Screenwriting, Playwriting
Vancouver, BC
2 years, optional residencies
www.creativewriting.ubc.ca

The interviewees
Andrew Gray, director, authored the short fiction collection *Small Accidents*. His stories and poetry have appeared in numerous literary publications, including *Malahat Review*, *Prairie Fire*, *Event*, *Grain*, and *Fiddlehead*.

Luanne Armstrong, faculty, is the author of *Jeannie and the Gentle Giants*, *Pete's Gold*, and several award-winning essays.

Elaine Beale, alumnus, was the winner of the 2007 Poets & Writers California Writers Exchange Award in fiction. Her novel, *Another Life Together*, was recently published by Speigel & Grau in the US and by Bond Street Books in Canada.

The program
Andrew Gray, director: I'm the creator of the program. I proposed it because I saw the need for a low-residency program with greater flexibility than many of the existing programs out there. In addition, there was no existing low-residency program in Canada.

We are unique in that we allow students to study part-time, taking up to five years to complete the degree, and our residencies are optional. This allows many students who wouldn't otherwise be able to take an MFA to come to UBC.

Faculty/teaching philosophy

Andrew Gray, director: We have a unique "cross-training" approach to the teaching of writing. Students must write in a minimum of three genres during their MFA degree, and we strongly believe that this dedication to stretching yourself creatively makes for better writers.

Elaine Beale, alumnus: Working with teachers who are published writers was extremely helpful; they gave numerous insights and thoughts and guidance. I took a non-credit course that was specifically about building a writing career. Also, at the residency there were several panels on issues related to this. In addition, many of the students were published before they began the program — some with short stories, but quite a number with novels under their belts. They had a lot of wisdom to share and much of it has been very valuable.

Residency/community

Andrew Gray, director: We have a very strong online community, with a great deal of chatter and support going on outside of workshops. Our residencies, of course, are strongly focused on building student community, but many of our students have become great friends without meeting in person. This online community is available for all students and they continue to have access after graduation — as long as they want.

[Residencies are] an intensive ten days of workshops, panels, seminars, social events, and bonding with other students and faculty members. It's usually exhausting, exhilarating, and a powerful mixture of the personal and creative.

Elaine Beale, alumnus: I really loved the residency portion of the program. It was very stimulating in terms of the panels, classes, and hanging out with other students. People were tremendously friendly and I had a terrific time both times I went. There's a lot packed into a short time, but it didn't feel like too much. Also, the location is fantastically beautiful. If you're fortunate to get good weather when you go it's especially nice. Students are asked for their suggestions on panels and most of the time they felt very relevant and were quite stimulating. There are several organized social activities during the residency, and also a lot of informal socializing.

Format/study

Elaine Beale, alumnus: I liked the flexibility and I also found that having to write a lot, with responses and discussions on the forums in addition to comments on manuscripts and my own writing, was really good in some ways. While verbal discussions can have the kind of spontaneity that you might not get in online interaction, writing responses to others' thoughts and opinions meant I had to be much more thoughtful and considerate in my answers.

Andrew Gray, director: The Teaching Creative Writing course and the optional practicum are new, and quite exciting, additions to our offerings. Luanne Armstrong, our instructor, has a great deal of experience in teaching creative writing — both theory and practice. The course consists of an initial theory part, in which students work through the theory and practical concerns surrounding the teaching of creative writing, both in-class and online. The second term, which is optional, each student then is asked to go into the community and teach writing, putting the knowledge from the first term into practical use. Students must set up the practicum themselves and their work has ranged from local community colleges to free outreach programs. Students stay in touch online during the practicum to share experiences, ask for advice and follow-up on the work done in the first term.

Luanne Armstrong, faculty: The Teaching Creative Writing course is a reading and discussion-based course and so the challenge for the instructor is to ask questions designed to really get students to think and to dig into ideas. My experience so far is that students really respond online, so then the challenge for me is to keep up with their questions, comments and ideas. It can be quite time-consuming, but also extremely interesting. Students can take this course at any point; there are no prerequisites for it. However, it is probably most useful for them when they are in their final year, because part of the course is designed to help them look for and succeed in finding a job teaching in a college or university program.

UNIVERSITY OF CALIFORNIA RIVERSIDE
Palm Desert Graduate Center
Fiction, Poetry, Memoir, Screenwriting, Playwriting

Riverside, CA
2 years, 4 residencies
http://palmdesertmfa.ucr.edu

The interviewees

Tod Goldberg, director, is the author of seven books, including the novels *Living Dead Girl*, *Fake Liar Cheat*, and the popular *Burn Notice* series.

Mark Haskell Smith is the author of four novels, *Moist*, *Delicious*, *Salty* and *Baked*, and an award-winning screenwriter. He is part of the core faculty at UC Riverside Palm Desert MFA in Writing and Writing for the Performing Arts Program.

The program

Tod Goldberg, director: That our program actually focuses on all of the major genres — fiction, non-fiction, screenwriting, poetry and playwriting — is somewhat unusual, as is our devotion to letting people write commercial work, which is viewed with horror in some programs. Many programs won't allow you to write crime or horror or chick-lit or whatever subgenre happens to gain a new moniker at any given time, but we embrace it, particularly as we also have a very significant screenwriting program, which must have a strong commercial emphasis, certainly, just by its nature.

In that light, we also tend to be different in that we bring out a great many professionals to meet one-on-one with our students. We had the Disney film division out recently, editors from Simon & Schuster and Viking and Dzanc, agents from major agencies and boutique ones, e-publishers, publicists, and every other imaginable iteration of writing professional. This is in addition to our wonderful guest writers, like Jane Smiley, Dan Chaon, and Bernard Cooper. In essence, what separates us is very simple: we are a low-residency program for the twenty-first century that is invested in getting our students the best instruction and the best opportunities for success beyond the program.

Faculty/teaching philosophy

Tod Goldberg, director: While we place a premium on the teaching of the craft of creative writing, it's also important to me that our students have a real idea about the world they are entering into. So in that light I was attracted by the opportunity to bring top-flight professionals to the students who can help them with the next phase of their life — namely publication and production. Though we've only been in existence since 2008, I can say without a doubt that vision is a clear success.

Mark Haskell Smith, faculty: I can't teach someone to be talented, but I can teach them how to think about writing and give the tools and encouragement they need to find their own voice. I think that is the single most important thing a writing program can do to help aspiring writers.

Residency/community

Tod Goldberg, director: Because the students work online all during the year, they have a far better connection to each other than in other programs, I believe, as they spend a great deal of time on their message boards talking about books and movies and poems and plays and about their lives, of course, and about their writing. The students have bonded so well, in fact, that they even started their very own — and very successful — literary journal, *The Whistling Fire*, which complements well our official journal, *The Coachella Review*.

We also encourage our students and professors to actually talk during the year and so frequently our students chat on the phone with their professors or meet up for lunch or dinner or just to sit and talk if they're nearby. And this isn't just about our regular faculty — many of our guests remain in contact with the students as well, which I think says something about the kind of people we choose to bring out as guest faculty.

Mark Haskell Smith, faculty: We hold our residencies at resort hotels in Palm Springs — we get a great deal from the hotels — so it feels very relaxed and collegial. Students, faculty, and guests tend to hang out together and it's not surprising to see a guest speaker like Jane Smiley lounging by the pool after her lecture.

The students bond fairly quickly and they are surprisingly supportive of each other. It's become something of a tradition that they hold nightly readings of their own work by the "fire pit" under the desert sky.

Format/study

Tod Goldberg, director: We structure our residency program differently than most low-residency programs: you actually begin work immediately online with your professor — and your class-mates as well, though there is no peer workshopping until the actual residency — and thus you spend ten weeks working on your pages, reading your literature and working in your secondary genre before you ever step foot in residency. This is important, I feel, because that way the residency experience is far more beneficial as the students will already have a base of learning, a shared language and aren't walking into a workshop blind. Their professors already know their work, which makes the workshop a far more useful device during the residency.

Mark Haskell Smith, faculty: At UCR Palm Desert we want students to leave the program with more than just a thesis, we want them to have a completed project that will help them launch their career.

CARLOW UNIVERSITY
Fiction, Poetry, Non-Fiction
Pittsburgh, PA
2½ years, 4 residencies
http://gradstudies.carlow.edu/creative/index.html

The interviewees

Ellie Wymard, director, is the author of *Talking Steel Towns: The Women and Men of America's Steel Valley*. Her critical essays have appeared in academic journals such as *Modern Fiction Studies*, *Southern Studies: An Interdisciplinary Journal of the South*, *Studies in Short Fiction*, and *Cross Currents*.

Celeste Gainey graduated from the poetry program in 2010.

Michelle Stoner is a student in the poetry program at Carlow University.

The program

Ellie Wymard, director: Carlow University's MFA program in creative writing provides the convenience of a low-residency program with the boundless opportunities to work with international-renowned writers in the United States and Ireland. Each year, students complete two residencies. In January, students spend eleven days in Pittsburgh, studying with award-winning writers. In June, students experience the magnificent setting and rich literary tradition of Ireland during eleven days in Sligo or Carlow. When the Irish residency coincides with Bloomsday, on June 16, our students follow in the footsteps of Leopold Bloom, with a Joyce scholar as guide.

Students do not parachute into Ireland and leave without footprints. After returning home, they continue to study for five months with their Irish mentors in either creative non-fiction, fiction, or poetry. After the Pittsburgh residency, students also complete a five-month practicum with the mentor who guided them at Carlow University.

Students and mentors communicate regularly by email about individualized assignments in creative and critical writing that they have agreed upon at the end of a residency. At the completion of four residencies and practica, students produce a manuscript of publishable quality, under the guidance of a mentor with whom they studied in the United States or Ireland. Carlow's program can be completed in five semesters. It is known for providing a respectful, collegial, supportive atmosphere for growth and development.

Faculty/teaching philosophy

Michelle Stoner, student: To me as a student, one of the best parts of the entire program is the student–instructor relationships that [come] out of the residencies and deepen as the distance portion of the semesters unfold. The director of this program does an unparalleled job of selecting excellent mentors. She chooses writers who are wise, personable, kind, and generous. These are mentors who are not only among the best of their craft, but who are also very invested in teaching new writers. As a result, I have at times been baffled by the amount of time that I know my mentors have devoted to their critique of my writing and to the subsequent spot-on instruction that they have offered me.

This program has provided me the opportunity to work with writers I admire who are also the best among teachers. Because of the nature of the mentors this program's director handpicks, I would say that one of the unique qualities of the distance portion of it is that the student–mentor relationship doesn't end when the semester does. I am confident that my personal relationships with my mentors will go beyond my completion of the degree. I now see them as lifelong colleagues and friends.

Celeste Gainey, alumnus: The student–mentor relationship is an intense and demanding one. At the close of each residency the student and mentor come up with a study plan for the ensuing work to be done at home. The plan is drawn up in the form of a contract, signed by both student and mentor. The contract requires tremendous reading, as well as critical and creative writing to be done according to deadlines.

Basically, I had about six books — some poetry, some poetics — one or two critical papers, five or six original poems, and a four-to-six page single-spaced letter discussing my experience with the work, due every four weeks. Within ten days I would receive my packet of work back by US or international mail, completely commented upon, poems marked up, with an equally lengthy letter responding to my letter and work. Sometimes even a lengthy phone consult followed. The first time I received this kind of response from my mentor, I was blown away — she was doing as much if not more work than I was doing! It is a very moving and motivating thing to have a teacher invest so much time in you.

Residency/community
Celeste Gainey, alumnus: The student community at Carlow is friendly and supportive while managing to remain competitive and demanding. This atmosphere is something that seems to have been consciously cultivated by Dr. Wymard and the faculty. There is a demand for excellence, but it coexists with a rare generosity. All students attend cross-genre residency lectures together and the University does a good job of organizing many "after-school" activities and dinners during the residencies. Too, there are opportunities during each residency for all students to read their work before the entire student body. As well, the Irish residencies are a time when all students are away and staying together 24/7 in the same locale, outside of our home culture — a great *esprit de corps* results from this.

Michelle Stoner, student: Students can expect to be challenged in their writing to the fullest extent. Each residency includes seven intense, two-and-a-half-hour long, genre-specific workshops. During this time, mentors and peers focus very closely on the individual concerns and successes of each student's writing. They are difficult and invigorating and they will absolutely improve a person's writing.

In addition, they can expect to develop peer relationships which will likely last and offer them writing support for the remainder of their careers.

Format/study

Michelle Stoner, student: Students are hosted on Carlow University's campus in Pittsburgh, PA, for both January residencies. There they stay at the Shadyside Inn, a wonderful hotel. For the June residencies, they are hosted by St. Angela's College at the Innisfree International Conference and Convention Centre, outside of Sligo, Ireland.

Celeste Gainey, alumnus: It is interesting to note that there are students in their early twenties all the way up into their sixties in the program. In my first residency poetry workshop there were four of us — a young fellow fresh from undergrad, an accomplished musician in his early thirties, a woman in her early fifties, who was a past graduate of the Barnum & Bailey Clown College, and myself, in my late fifties, a lighting designer. The diversity of our tiny group was rich and rewarding. I would say the thoughtfully cultivated MFA community is one of the major assets of the Carlow program.

CHATHAM UNIVERSITY
Focus on Nature, Environment, and Travel
Pittsburgh, PA
2 years, 2 residencies
www.chatham.edu/ccps/mfa

The interviewee

Peter Oresick, director, is editor of *The Fourth River*. He is the author of several books including *Warhol-o-rama* and *For a Living: The Poetry of Work*.

The program

Peter Oresick, director: As a publisher with more than twenty years of experience, I was first attracted to Chatham because it is one of the few MFA programs to recognize the importance of educating young writers about the publishing process. Chatham regularly offers three formal courses in literary publishing and holds a publishing conference annually. Additionally, the thesis experience at Chatham is designed to give students the skills needed for completing long manuscripts, crafting book proposals, and finding publishing success after graduation. A major role of mine at Chatham is to teach these publishing courses and to serve as the in-house publishing consultant for our students.

Faculty/teaching philosophy

Peter Oresick, director: Chatham University's MFA focusing on nature, environment, and travel writing is dedicated to nurturing creative writers interested in the environmental imagination and place-based writing. Our program is inspired by the work of Chatham alumna, Rachel Carson, a scientist and creative writer whose work demonstrates both lyricism and social conscience.

The heart of our program — nature, environmental, and travel writing — honors Carson's legacy, but expands the interpretation of environment to include any place-based writing and all genres — poetry, fiction, and creative non-fiction — shaped by human relationship with place.

We look for faculty who are both masters of their craft and who are committed and passionate teachers. Faculty must be adept at online technologies. They must also be attentive to institutional policies and deadlines even while working off campus.

Residency/community

Peter Oresick, director: The Chatham annual residency in Pittsburgh offers morning writing workshops, afternoon craft lectures, and evening public readings by faculty, visiting writers, and MFA students. Students should also expect a block of time each day to write. Each residency also features a field seminar to a nature preserve with time given to explore and to write. Cultural field trips include the Andy Warhol Museum and Frank Lloyd Wright's Fallingwater. Each residency concludes with a half-day publishing seminar.

The Chatham campus in the heart of the city of Pittsburgh is located on a beautiful arboretum that offers rich opportunities for reflection and meditation, and is minutes from a downtown that transformed itself years ago from a smoky haze into a vibrant city center. Filled with beautiful parks, nestled between three rivers, and surrounded by natural and cultural areas as varied as the Appalachian Trail, the Allegheny National Forest, the Amish and Pennsylvania Dutch countryside, and a bit of the coast of Lake Erie, Pittsburgh offers many opportunities for writers during their residency.

Format/study

Peter Oresick, director: Students are given lots of time to write at Chatham. Mentorships focus on style, form, and literary traditions. We offer regular courses on topics such as Wilderness and Literature, Ecofeminism, Nature and Culture, Women and Nature, and The Environmental Imagination. Students also have the opportunity to work on *The Fourth River*, Chatham's literary journal.Students learn writing career management skills three ways at Chatham. Mentorships cover the fundamentals of publishing according to genre. Our courses in literary publishing offer an in-depth look at how the publishing industry works and how writers can best approach literary publishing houses and agents. Finally, each residency concludes with a half-day publishing seminar, including visiting editors, agents, and literary presses.

CONVERSE COLLEGE
Fiction, Creative Non-Fiction, Poetry
Spartanburg, SC
2 years, 5 residencies
http://old.converse.edu/mfa

The interviewees

Rick Mulkey, director, is the author of four collections including *Toward Any Darkness*, *Before the Age of Reason*, and *Bluefield Breakdown*. His work also appears in the anthologies *American Poetry: the Next Generation*, *The Southern Poetry Anthology: Volume I*, and *A Millennial Sampler of South Carolina Poetry*, among others.

R. T. Smith is a fiction and poetry instructor. He is the author of fourteen volumes of poetry and fiction including *Messenger*, *Trespasser*, and *Brightwood*. Smith's fiction has appeared in publications including *The Pushcart Prize* and *Best American Short Stories*; his poems have appeared in *The Pushcart Prize*, *Atlantic Monthly*, *Georgia Review*, and *Gettysburg Review*.

Susan Tekulve is a fiction and non-fiction instructor. She is the author of *My Mother's War Stories* and *Savage Pilgrims*, and her fiction, non-fiction, and poetry have appeared in journals such as *New Letters*, *Denver Quarterly*, and *The Literary Review*.

Jeffrey R. Schrecongost is a student in the fiction program. He is currently at work on *The Uphill Climb*, a collection of linked short stories, and *Free Throw*, a novel.

The program
Rick Mulkey, director: Unlike some MFA programs, we have no desire to become a large program with 120 students. Our students and our faculty want to remain a selective MFA program with approximately thirty-two to thirty-eight students. When hiring faculty, I look for individuals who plan to remain with the program long-term. We aren't looking for a large list of faculty to rotate in and out of the program, but we are looking for a committed group of highly accomplished writing faculty to work with a selective group of students.

When I see student writers in a classroom at Converse, I want to make clear to them that they are in a program as good as any in the country. One way we've done this at Converse has been to show them the caliber of the poets, writers and editors who teach in the program and who want to come to Converse as visiting faculty to the program. So now our students sit down with Claudia Emerson or Albert Goldbarth, with C. Michael Curtis and R. T. Smith, with Robert Olmstead and Denise Duhamel, and with all the other outstanding faculty and guest faculty in the program. I think our current faculty mentors and students recognize that something exceptional is happening in the program. They recognize that this program isn't about churning out degree recipients; rather it is about developing good writers.

Faculty/teaching philosophy

Jeffrey R. Schrecongost, student: Leslie Pietrzyk, my first semester mentor, is at once inspiring, insightful, generous, and supportive. She challenged me to write in a much less inhibited fashion, encouraged me to free my imagination, which led to a real breakthrough in my fiction. Her counsel has been invaluable.

Susan Tekulve, faculty: The most effective way to teach writing is to work one-on-one with a student. Every student writes differently and learns differently, so I think the mentoring I do in the low-residency program is the most important thing I hope to offer. The mentoring enables me to tailor my comments to an individual student's work, and to create a dialogue between instructor and student that is comfortable, productive and at a sophisticated level. I can make much greater strides while mentoring an individual student than I can working with that student in a traditional classroom setting. Also, it helps to be able to work with students who are genuinely engaged in their own writing and learning. In the low-residency program, I help each student to create her own plan of study that includes the type of creative writing project she wishes to complete during a term and a book list that informs her creative project.

The student must produce a certain amount of work that is in her semester plan; however, because we are working one-on-one, we have the flexibility to tweak that plan if, for instance, she starts off intending to write about one subject, but then finds herself delving into material that she uncovers while writing her initial pieces. This process really just formalizes what writers who aren't in official writing programs do. That is, writers often uncover more interesting subject matter while working on one project. Sometimes, a writer will put down a project to work on the new idea. Other times, a writer will finish working on the original project as the newly discovered idea begins to percolate on the back burner. The mentoring system accommodates this natural process of discovering andmanaging one's material so that by the time the student has graduated, this way of working and thinking will be second nature to her.

R. T. Smith, faculty: I hope to teach students how to translate the realm of sense experience and physical motion into language that conveys the sharpness and dimensionality of things done, observed, imagined, and how to do it with a density of implication that is neither cumbersome nor breezy. I also try to draw their attention to the thresholds where different kinds of narrative, different genres, meet. And I want to infuse them with an unabashed fervor for reading, without which there will be little joy in writing. Wild discipline is one of my mottoes; serious mischief is another.

Rick Mulkey, director: I look for three things in faculty.

1. Strong writers with multiple book and journal publications. A faculty member must be a writer who remains actively engaged in the writing craft, continuing to write and develop. These individuals are also writers whose work should be critically respected, too. Our writing faculty members have been National Book Critics Circle Award winners, finalists for National Book Awards, recipients of national and international fellowships, and contributors to some of our best literary journals and anthologies, including *Best American Poetry*, *Best American Fiction*, *New Stories from the South*, and others.
2. Experienced teachers and mentors. While it isn't important to me that a faculty member has made his or her living as a full-time teacher, I do look for writers who enjoy teaching and mentoring students, and who have been successful teachers either full-time, part-time, or as distinguished visiting faculty. Our faculty members have received numerous awards for teaching and mentoring, have dozens of years of teaching experience in graduate programs across the US and they have been distinguished visiting writers at numerous colleges, universities, and workshops.
3. I look for writers that I would have wanted to study with when I was a student. By that I mean I'm looking for individuals I respect as both writer, teacher, and as a colleague, writers who are committed to the art of writing and value the opportunity to share their knowledge of that art with others.

Residency/community

Jeffrey R. Schrecongost, student: During each residency, agents, editors, and publishers conduct panel discussions and question and answer sessions with students. Additional information on how to approach agents, editors, and publishers is provided by mentors during workshops, one-on-one conferences, and via correspondence throughout the semester.

Susan Tekulve, faculty: The daily schedule for the ten-day residencies is really intense. An average day begins at 9 a.m. and ends around 10 or 11 p.m. every night . . . I must say that I feel incredibly energized by this total immersion into a community of excited and accomplished writers and writing students. We have a really strong faculty that works really hard during the residencies and as mentors. The students see that the faculty members work hard and respect each other, and so they tend to model their own writing relationships the same way. The students share a mutual respect for the work they are all completing, and for each other. Additionally, the faculty members come to all of the student readings, and the students come to all of the faculty readings, so there is an overall strong sense of collegiality that grows out of this kind of atmosphere.

R. T. Smith, faculty: The actual time in workshop is my favorite. You never know what you'll learn from the students, what far-fetched suggestions they'll offer that will turn out to be canny and witty and right.

Format/study
Jeffrey R. Schrecongost, student: Each semester begins with a ten day residency, during which time students attend daily craft lectures, panel discussions, faculty and visiting author readings, and writing workshops. Students work one-on-one with mentors during the residency period, and an individual semester plan is created. After the residency, students return home and begin working on their semester assignments — a demanding and exciting combination of fascinating reading and creative and critical writing. These assignment packets are due approximately every three weeks via email or postal service, depending on the mentor's preference. The mentor evaluates the student's work, and then returns the packet with accompanying critiques.

Susan Tekulve, faculty: I think the Converse low-residency program offers a very serious and supportive community. In my residency workshop sessions, I see the students working just as hard on each other's drafts as they would on their own writing. They offer honest and insightful criticism to each other, but they are extremely sensitive to each other's feelings, so the atmosphere is at once productive and safe. Outside of workshop, the students and faculty mingle together, and there isn't a rigid hierarchy, just an informally professional rapport among faculty and students. When we are not in a residency session, I sense that we are all hunkered down, working. We keep in communication, especially around the time packets are due, but my students know that they can email me or phone me at any time they have questions.

Rick Mulkey, director: I'd say that all writing students in any program should focus on the writing first, focus on the work. It is more important than anything else they can do. If a student writer works hard at the writing every day, developing craft, reading other writers, then the degree part and the career part — especially the career part — will be manageable.

Having said that, however, the minute any of our faculty sees a student doing something exceptional, we're going to do whatever we can to make sure people know about this writer. This is why a number of our current students already have journal and book publications, have received regional and national awards and grants, have received such honors as the AWP Intro Award, among others. Our faculty want to be mentors who help a writer of talent become known. This, of course, is why it is important to have the kind of faculty we have here, instructors who are both good classroom teachers, but also active writers who have relationships with other writers and editors, and with a whole community in the writing and editing world. Some individuals might think if you come to a community like Spartanburg, SC, you are going to be cut off from that literary world, but because our faculty writers are so active in that national and international writing community, our Converse students have access to it also.

DREW UNIVERSITY
Poetry, Poetry in Translation
Madison, NJ
2 years, 5 residencies
www.drew.edu/grad-content.aspx?id=39651

The interviewees

Anne Marie Macari, director, is the author of *She Heads Into The Wilderness*, *Ivory Cradle*, and *Gloryland*. Her poems have appeared in *The Iowa Review*, *The American Poetry Review*, *TriQuarterly*, *Field*, and others.

Alicia Ostriker, faculty, has published twelve collections of poems, including *The Book of Seventy*. As a critic, Ostriker is the author of *Stealing the Language*, *The Emergence of Women's Poetry in America* and other books on poetry.

The program

Anne Marie Macari, director: The Drew MFA Program in Poetry and Poetry in Translation is unique because it includes translation as part of the curriculum. We offer an MFA in Poetry and we offer a Combined MFA in Poetry and Poetry in Translation. About a quarter of our student body officially translates and studies translation in the Combined MFA, but all of our students are exposed to translation lectures and guest translators during each residency. It is important to us that our curriculum not be insular and translation is one of the ways we give our students a broad education.

Alicia Ostriker, faculty: Be prepared for two kinds of intensity: the residency is ten days constantly living and breathing poetry, and bonding with fellow students, while the mentoring semester shifts to a one-on-one relationship with its own deeply personal interactions. Be prepared to work really hard. Be prepared to relate to a wide array of people and poems, and to connect with students who might be decades younger or older than you are.

Faculty/teaching philosophy

Anne Marie Macari, director: The Drew MFA faculty is comprised of award-winning poets. We are diverse in every way and we are committed to teaching; our faculty poets are known for their fine work and for their generosity of spirit. Most of the faculty poets have several books or more. No faculty member takes on more than four students at a time. Students and faculty work together to develop their programs of study.

Alicia Ostriker, faculty: Anne Marie is both warm and efficient — she plans well, she listens well, she troubleshoots, and she gets everyone, faculty and students, to feel that their concerns are heard and responded to. The fact that we offer just one genre, poetry, along with poetry in translation, is very appealing. In addition, the Drew administration has been extremely supportive.

Residency/community

Anne Marie Macari, director: Our residencies are intense experiences and take place on the beautiful campus of Drew University in Madison, New Jersey. They happen in early January and late June. We have workshops in the mornings, lectures in the afternoons, and readings at night. Students doing the MFA in Poetry must complete four semesters of correspondence work and attend five residencies. Students in the Combined MFA in Poetry and Poetry in Translation do an extra semester and an extra residency. One of the highlights of our program is that at every residency we have two internationally known poets, Jean Valentine and Gerald Stern, who meet individually with students and give workshops and readings. They are the spiritual center of our residencies.

Alicia Ostriker, faculty: We're a small program, and it's single-genre, so everyone knows everyone, and there's a great deal of bonding. Faculty and students mingle at meals, and there's a pub on campus for post-reading socializing. So students commonly become buddies with other students and correspond, sharing poems, etc., between residencies. I need to say also that we have a highly cooperative, non-competitive atmosphere, in which people care about each other.

We start the residency the first evening with faculty sharing a poem they love, and saying something about why, which psyches us all up. The morning workshops are small — four to five students. In the afternoon we usually have lectures by faculty and visiting poets — commonly one lecture each residency is about translation issues — on a wide range of topics. Evenings are readings. Each semester ends with senior panels and student readings. The stimulation is vibrant and exhausting, possibly too much to take in all at once — but CDs are available afterward, of all the talks and readings.

Format/study

Anne Marie Macari, director: The correspondence work happens by mail, not email — although students and faculty are in touch by email, and includes poems, revisions, and critical essays. Students work to learn the craft of poetry. They read deeply and extensively — about twenty books per semester — and they work closely with their poet-mentors. The program is rigorous and each student, working with their mentor, creates a program of study that speaks to their needs and interests. Although we are a low-residency MFA program, we try to offer our students some of the benefits of being high-res. For instance we have initiated a relationship with a nonprofit school in Trenton for high school students who have dropped out or for other reasons have not completed school and we will do a week-long residency there with one of our faculty and two student interns from the program. Drew University, which is the home to the archives from the Dodge Poetry Festival, is committed to poetry and to the MFA program in particular.

Alicia Ostriker, faculty: I have four students to mentor each semester; they each do four packets. While we are still at residency we plan the projects they will be working on: what craft issues they want to focus on over the next months, what reading lists of poetry books and critical essays will be meaningful for these projects, how they want to focus their critical papers. I like to get a cover letter with each packet of a minimum of three single-spaced pages, discussing whatever is important to them in their reading or issues around their writing. The packets are snail-mailed — I'm pretty strict about deadlines, though I'm not a monster — and I mail them back, with marginal comments as well as a minimum of three single-spaced pages of response, within a week. If there are urgent issues, we email or talk on the phone, but this is not the rule. We expect new poems every packet, but also revisions.

EASTERN KENTUCKY UNIVERSITY
Fiction, Poetry, Creative Non-Fiction
Richmond, KY
2 years, 2–4 residencies
www.english.eku.edu/mfa

The interviewee

Tasha Cotter, alumnus, served as the editor-in-chief of the inaugural issue of *Jelly Bucket*, the literary journal published annually by the Creative Writing program at Eastern Kentucky University. Her work has appeared or is forthcoming in *Sleet*, *Fogged Clarity*, and *Danse Macabre*.

The program

Tasha Cotter, alumnus: This program has been instrumental in my thinking about writing and the development of my skills as a poet. The program is small, around twenty-five students, and it is a very close-knit community of writers who genuinely want to see each other succeed. Perhaps one of the most valuable aspects of this program is the friendships that I've made and getting the chance to work with the incredible faculty. In short, the faculty and classmates have helped me in too many ways to count.

Faculty/teaching philosophy

Tasha Cotter, alumnus: The online workshop works really well. The program is always testing out different online meeting software to find out what works best. In the past we have tested out Skype, Ventrilo, and GoToMeeting. Class sizes are rarely, if ever, over ten people so you get a lot of individual attention, which is so valuable in a workshop.

The MFA coordinator, Dr. Young Smith, was incredibly helpful and showed a real interest in my manuscript.

Residency/community

Tasha Cotter, alumnus: The other members and I keep in touch pretty regularly, mostly via email and social networking sites like Facebook. In the past we have sent each other stories and poems to critique — outside of class and workshop — and that has been very helpful. We all want to see each other get better in our respective genre and we all work extremely hard at our writing whether it be non-fiction, fiction, or poetry.

Format/study

Tasha Cotter, alumnus: Eastern Kentucky University's program is designed so that students may choose to attend the required residencies in Lexington, Kentucky, or San Miguel de Allende in

Mexico. Each residency is two weeks long and fulfills three credits each — the program requires twelve credits of residency to graduate. The Mexico residency is somewhat unique in that students have the option of attending for four weeks at a time — therefore earning six credits.

FAIRFIELD UNIVERSITY
Poetry, Fiction, Creative Non-Fiction, Screenwriting
Fairfield, CT
2 years, 5 residencies
www.fairfield.edu/mfaonline

The interviewee
Michael C. White is the director of the Fairfield MFA. He is the author of six novels, including *Beautiful Assassin*, and was the founding editor of the *American Fiction* series.

The program
Michael C. White, director: I founded the program for three reasons. The first is because of the unique sort of school that Fairfield University is: a Jesuit university that valued the importance of the arts, lifelong learning, and non-traditional students, all of which are central to a low-residency MFA. Second, we are situated in wonderful place, just outside of New York, where I could have agents, editors, publishers, and guest writers come to our residency with ease. Third, I was allowed great freedom . . . in developing a program that would be first-rate. In the year since our founding we have grown to sixty-five students and have attracted a faculty of national reputation, including writers who have been a finalist for the National Book Award, the National Book Critics Circle Award, Four Connecticut Book Awards, and many other awards.

Faculty/teaching philosophy
Michael C. White, director: I look for three primary things in selecting our faculty. First, they must be very good writers with a strong publication reputation in their field. Second, they must be excellent teachers with a proven track record of superb teaching and mentoring of students. Third, they must be good colleagues who are committed to the low-residency model and are committed to helping students become better writers.

Residency/community
Michael C. White, director: Students rave about the tight-knit, supportive, and friendly writing community that exists both among students and between students and faculty. Since all students and faculty live, work, and eat together on the island, the bond that forms during the residency is extremely strong.

Format/study
Michael C. White, director: Students have several options for concentration. They can choose to concentrate on one of several genres — fiction, creative non-fiction, poetry, or screenwriting; they can have dual concentrations; or they can work in another genre outside of their main genre for one semester. They also can do an interesting third-semester option, which allows them to do internships in publishing houses or magazines, to teach in schools or in non-traditional teaching settings, or do a mixed-genre project such as writing a screenplay and filming it . . . Since Fairfield is two hours from New York City, for every residency we invite editors, agents, and publishers to join us.

FAIRLEIGH DICKINSON UNIVERSITY
Poetry, Fiction, Creative Non-Fiction
Madison, NJ
2 years, 3 residencies
http://mfa.fdu.edu

The interviewees
Martin Donoff, director, teaches dramatic writing and film studies at Fairleigh Dickinson University. He is the author and/or story editor of more than 125 network television scripts and plays including *Alf* and *Captain Kangaroo*.

Anne Harding Woodworth, alumnus, is the author of two chapbooks and three books of poetry, the most recent of which is *Spare Parts, A Novella in Verse*. She is a member of the Poetry Board at the Folger Shakespeare Library in Washington, DC.

The program
Martin Donoff, director: The hallmark of our MFA program is the very close working relationships that develop between students

and mentors. These relationships begin at the residencies where students and faculty work, take meals, and socialize together. We believe that learning should not be an experience reserved only for the classroom. So, along with the regular all-day activities, it is not unusual to find a student and mentor discussing a problem with the craft and form essay in one of the Wroxton pubs or debating issues of point-of-view over a 1 a.m. game of pool.

We are a close-knit writing and teaching community — one in which new students are welcomed and quickly find a home. The sense of belonging continues well past graduation. Many of our alumni return each August for special seminars, to meet current students and to attend graduation ceremonies.

Anne Harding Woodworth, alumnus: The fact that the January residencies would be at the Fairleigh Dickinson campus in England, I have to admit, was the real clincher. I knew I would get some poems out of a couple of trips to England, if nothing else. But believe me, there was a lot "else." I liked what I read about the program, its clearly defined requirements and the faculty, which I knew was a more or less permanent one.

Faculty/teaching philosophy
Anne Harding Woodworth, alumnus: The emphasis on craft is paramount in the Fairleigh Dickinson program, and that has stayed with me. If I had not done my literary thesis — called the Craft & Form paper — on W. D. Snodgrass's *The Fuehrer Bunker*, I probably would never have written my book, *Spare Parts, A Novella in Verse*, which I started shortly after finishing the program. My interest in the persona poem is still keen and very much a part of my writing.

Residency/community
Anne Harding Woodworth, alumnus: During the four semesters, I did two residencies in Wroxton, England, and one in Madison, New Jersey. Both places have excellent facilities, quite different in nature from each other, since the one in Wroxton is an old one-time abbey, later seventeenth-century manor house, on a beautiful sprawling piece of land near Banbury. And the one in Madison is more like a typical American college campus.

My mentor, Renée Ashley, a born teacher, was for both years

a caring and responsive guide. We had one-on-one meetings and small workshops. Renée always gave undivided attention to me and other students, and still managed to accomplish amazing things with her own work. There was always computer help, since so much of the program would be handled online. And there was always a warm spirit among the students, especially at Wroxton, where village pubs were within walking distance. We had guests at both campuses, such as Colm Toibin and Charles Simic.

I am in frequent contact with my mentor, Renée Ashley, and I am in touch with fellow students every so often. The MFA program sends out a newsletter periodically, so I keep up with readings, book tours, publications, and other achievements of alumni and faculty. FDU MFA alumni are always welcomed back to the August residency in Madison where special alumni readings and workshops are offered.

Format/study

Martin Donoff, director: [We use] a course system of eight modules that enables students to take one module in a different writing genre without reducing focus on their primary creative thesis.

Every student has the opportunity to work as a reader or reviewer for *The Literary Review*. On occasion, some students will have an opportunity to contribute to the review section. Additionally, there are first and second year graduate assistantships, with some tuition compensation, awarded on a competitive basis.

Anne Harding Woodworth, alumnus: Before I entered the program, I wanted to teach poetry, and I teach it now periodically. I think the MFA has been that extra plus in my credentials.

The experience forced me to read things I never would have read. During every module, I had to write oodles of annotations on books about writing poetry. We also had some elective courses. The most memorable for me was screenwriting, for which I had to produce a script for a twenty-minute film.

GODDARD COLLEGE
Fiction, Poetry, Creative Non-Fiction, Playwriting, Screenwriting
Plainfield, VT and Port Townsend, WA
2 years, 5 residencies
www.goddard.edu/masterfinearts_writing

The interviewees

Paul Selig, director, is the author of *I Am the Word: A Guide to the Consciousness of Man's Self in a Transitioning Time.*

Dawn Paul, alumnus, is the author of *The Country of Loneliness.* She teaches writing at Montserrat College of Art in Beverly, MA and runs a small literary press.

Ann E. Michael, alumnus, is the author of *The Minor Fauna* and *More than Shelter.*

Bridgette Mongeon is co-author of *Digital Sculpting with Mudbox: Essential Tools and Techniques for Artists.* She is a graduate of Goddard's MFA in Interdisciplinary Art.

Tina Broderick is a retired nurse, mother of three, grandmother of five, and a Goddard MFA student. Tina's poetry has been published in *Long Story Short* and *Pitkin Review.* She is currently working on a novel.

The program

Paul Selig, director: Our enrollment has more than doubled in recent years. I think this is due to the quality of education students are receiving and the word of mouth, which continues to be excellent. The program has been so successful that, thanks to a gift from an alum, we were able to launch a second residency location in Port Townsend, Washington.

Our visiting writers series has expanded to include nationally known publishers, agents and other industry professionals and we have developed a strong focus in playwriting and screenwriting that is thriving on both coasts. I suppose that I'm most proud of the community of Goddard teachers and writers. We attract extraordinary people, and the sense of community that evolves during a residency surpasses anything I've seen in a residential program.

Faculty/teaching philosophy

Tina Broderick, student: During my first two semesters I was mentored by Jan Clausen, who is a poet with a fine ear and knowledge of writing fiction, both genres I work in. Jan helped me to understand what I wanted to do at Goddard and how I could accomplish my goal of producing a cross-genre manuscript. I have a new advisor, Darcy Steinke, for my third semester who writes mainly fiction. Each advisor brings their unique talents and perspective to the writing process.

Paul Selig, director: I look for highly accomplished writers who are also gifted and generous teachers. When I get excited during an interview with a prospective faculty member and think, "Gee, I wish I could study with that person," I have to assume that our students will share my enthusiasm. We have an extraordinary faculty; wonderful writers who are also dedicated teachers of writing, committed to the student-centered model of teaching that is at the heart of a Goddard education.

Residency/community

Paul Selig, director: The level of community that evolves as part of a Goddard residency actually exceeds anything I experienced as a student in a residential program. The Clockhouse Writer's Conference, an annual meeting of program alumni that meets at our Plainfield campus every summer, was developed by our alumni so that they could maintain the sense of community that was born at Goddard. It's a warm community, a diverse and supportive one, and one that prizes the individual's work and process.

Dawn Paul, alumnus: I learned so much about craft from my advisors and in residency workshops. My writing career has benefited so much from the people I met at Goddard. There are several of us that stay in touch and try to meet at least once a year even though we are scattered all over the country. It's wonderful to have people looking at my work who know what I'm trying to do, who know my work. And we help each other in other ways: writing references for residencies, sharing teaching materials and ideas, reviewing query letters. I have local friends who are writers, great writers. But it's not the same as having this group that I can go to for inspiration and practical help.

Bridgette Mongeon, alumnus: The instructors are all of the highest caliber; everyone is supportive. It is extremely stimulating intellectually and there are times throughout the year that I wish

I could get a smidgen of that stimulation, but then I find things to incorporate into my study that do just that.

Tina Broderick, student: The residencies are packed with workshops lead by faculty, students, alumni, and visiting writers from all genres. Every aspect of the writing life and the writing process are discussed in these workshops and there is ample time to connect with other students and faculty socially. It feels like a blessing to be surrounded by a community of my peers and I have made some lasting friendships at residencies. The inspirational energy of the residency follows me home and fuels my independent study in a way that is difficult to describe.

Format/study

Paul Selig, director: A low-residency program like Goddard, which demands a completed book-length manuscript for a thesis and has a strong critical writing and teaching component, requires a real commitment from the student. It really is a program of rigorous, self-directed study. I have long been of the belief that students come to Goddard when their writing has become inevitable. We are all about transformational learning, and if the student is truly ready to engage with her work on a deep level, the experience can be extraordinary.

Ann E. Michael, alumnus: Getting published was not the focus of Goddard. Writing well was the focus: learning to revise, learning to push the personal expression, reading the work of other writers, and figuring out how to get the work to work for us.

Bridgette Mongeon, alumnus: My choice of Goddard was because it offered an MFAIA, Master of Fine Arts in Interdisciplinary Art. To me being able to focus on my two passions — writing and art — were very important to me. It is how my creative person is joined together.

GOUCHER COLLEGE
Creative Non-Fiction
Baltimore, MD
2 years, 5 residencies
www.goucher.edu/x1166.xml

The interviewee

Patsy Sims, director, is the author of *The Klan* and *Cleveland Benjamin's Dead*; her work has appeared in *The New York Times Book Review*, *The Washington Post Magazine*, *Texas Observer*, and most major American newspapers. Her most recent book is the anthology *Literary Nonfiction: Learning by Example*. She has received a National Endowment for the Arts fellowship and is associate editor of *River Teeth*, a journal of narrative non-fiction.

The program

Patsy Sims, director: I was primarily attracted to Goucher's program because of its focus on creative non-fiction. That focus signaled a couple of things to me: first, that the college, faculty, and students would share my enthusiasm — and passion — for what I consider today's most exciting genre; second, that it would allow us to concentrate all of our time and energy, both during our residencies and the semesters themselves, to CNF [creative non-fiction]; and third, it would enable us to assemble what I think now is probably the largest and strongest faculty devoted to CNF in the country. I was not wrong in my thinking. At our residencies, every workshop, lecture, and reading — literally every moment — is devoted to creative non-fiction, as is the students' work when they return to their home communities.

Faculty/teaching philosophy

Patsy Sims, director: I attempt to recruit the most accomplished practitioners in the genre who can both teach and inspire our students. I especially seek out individuals who excel as both writers and teachers of creative non-fiction, and who share a passion for the genre. The latter is important. I want them to convey an excitement both for writing and for the genre and to be warm and approachable. I also want folks who are willing go above and beyond the call of duty in helping their students become the very best writers they can.

Residency/community

Patsy Sims, director: Students are required to participate in three summer residencies on Goucher's Baltimore campus: the first two are two weeks in length; the third and final residency lasts five days and includes commencement. They must also attend two weekend mini-residencies at the beginning of each spring semester.

There is a strong sense of camaraderie in the program, which I think grows out of both the two-week residency and our focus on creative non-fiction. This camaraderie actually exists among the students, faculty, and our alumni. When I became director in January 2001, the two classes that had graduated by that point began emailing to ask if they could have a reunion. We planned a reunion for graduation weekend during that summer's residency — the middle weekend — and have had alumni returning for graduation weekend ever since.

We also have get-togethers at key conferences, like AWP [the Association of Writers & Writing Programs] and the Nieman Conference at Harvard, and the alumni and current students have the opportunity to meet and network there as well. I send out emails regularly with news of what the students and alumni are up to, as well as publishing and job opportunities, to everyone who has ever studied in the program. We have a listserv and a Facebook site as well. Because of all this, students and alumni form long, lasting friendships.

Format/study

Patsy Sims, director: Students must complete an internship of at least forty-five contact hours at a literary journal, a national or regional magazine, a daily or weekly newspaper, a recognized publishing house or a web-based publisher, or with a published writer, agent, or editor. The internship is intended to supplement the students' coursework at Goucher, and to offer them access and training in an area of CNF where they have no experience. A faculty member serves as Internship Coordinator to help students come up with appropriate internships. In the past, students have read manuscripts for literary agents, reviewed submissions at literary journals, assisted at writing conferences, written articles for newspapers and magazines, taught college courses, worked with professional writers as research assistants, and tutored writing students.

In their second year, students also have the option of participating in a two-day trip to New York publishing houses, magazines, and literary agencies. Students meet in small groups — no more than eight to ten students, sometimes smaller — with some of the leading editors and agents at such places as *The New*

Yorker, *Harper's*, *Paris Review*, Penguin, Random House, Norton, and the ICM and Creative Culture agencies.

HAMLINE UNIVERSITY
Writing for Children & Young Adults
Saint Paul, MN
2 years, 5 residencies
www.hamline.edu/gls/academics/degree_programs/mfa_cl/index.
html

The interviewee
Mary François Rockcastle is the Dean of the Graduate School of Liberal Studies at Hamline University. Her novel, *Rainy Lake*, was nominated for a Minnesota Book Award and selected as one of the New York Public Library's 1996 Books of the Teen Age.

The program
Mary François Rockcastle, dean: Hamline has always prided itself on its close attention to students and its commitment to each student as a whole person. Even with this as the university's mission, the Graduate School of Liberal Studies (GLS) stands out for the generosity shown to students and for the attention to community at every level. Students bond quickly and effectively over the course of each residency; they bond as individual classes, or cohorts, and they bind as a collective group . . . They keep in regular and close contact in-between residencies and after graduation. The community created is personal as well as professional: they read each other's work; support and cheer each other on; and offer help, advice, job and publishing connections. At each residency we offer an alumni weekend for our graduates to return, workshop with each other, attend lectures, and meet with an agent or editor.

Faculty/teaching philosophy
Mary François Rockcastle, dean: Hamline's program combines the best elements of the low-residency model with effective learning strategies learned from almost thirty years of teaching graduate-level creative writing. Thus, we developed a core curriculum that guides the planning and structure of each residency as well as the makeup and use of a required reading list. The

curriculum includes the major elements of the craft — each one applied to the picture book, non-fiction, and fiction; the writing process, forms of writing; the history of children's and young adult literature; the business of publishing; and the writer's life.

Residency/community

Mary François Rockcastle, dean: They can expect eleven exhilarating, informative, busy, fun, sometimes exhausting days. They will learn more in eleven days than they thought possible. They will learn from each other, from the faculty, from guest writers and editors, from the work on the page. They will make friends, advance relationships, and be constantly challenged. They will see their fellow students present work — via lectures and readings — that will blow their minds and inspire them to do the same. Residencies are hosted on Hamline's Saint Paul campus. In July, all students and faculty stay on campus in a modern, air-conditioned apartment complex. In January, events are held on campus but students and faculty are housed in the nearby Radisson Hotel and shuttled to and from campus.

Format/study

Mary François Rockcastle, dean: The low-residency model promotes regular, in-depth communication and interaction between and among students and faculty. During the residencies students attend faculty readings and lectures, interact with faculty informally during meals and breaks, work closely with faculty in daily workshops, and meet with faculty in groups and one-on-one. Midway through each residency, students are paired with faculty advisors, based on the nature and scope of the students' work and their own preferences for faculty, and meet with them to develop a semester plan. The semester itself is a close mentorship between student and faculty advisor.

CITY UNIVERSITY OF HONG KONG

Fiction, Poetry, Creative Non-Fiction
Kowloon, Hong Kong
2 years, 5 residencies
www.english.cityu.edu.hk/mfa

The interviewee

Xu Xi is the author or editor of eleven books, most recently the novel *Habit of a Foreign Sky* (2010), which was shortlisted for the Man Asian Literary Prize. She obtained her MFA in fiction from the University of Massachusetts at Amherst and is faculty chair at Vermont College of Fine Arts MFA in writing. As of March 2010, she became the first writer-in-residence at City University of Hong Kong where she helped establish an international low-residency MFA specializing in Asian Writing in English.

The Program

Xu Xi, faculty: For several years prior to the establishment of this program at City University of Hong Kong, I taught creative writing in English at cultural forums and other universities in Hong Kong, elsewhere in Asia, as well as in Europe. What was increasingly obvious was that English had moved beyond merely a *lingua franca* and was becoming a literary language for more than the Anglo-American native English speaker. In Hong Kong, especially, I could see that there was consistent and growing interest in the study of creative writing, although very little was offered in any kind of programmatic fashion. During this time, I would often say to my colleagues and contacts at various universities that a low-residency MFA model would be excellent for Asia, because the degree is still relatively new and unknown in this part of the world.

[The program offers] a high-quality MFA education, one that is comparable to established programs in the US, but one that places an emphasis on Asian cultures, languages, perspectives. The low-residency format was deliberately chosen to reach a broader universe of likely candidates for the degree.

Faculty/teaching philosophy

Xu Xi, faculty: We're new, progressive and open to evolution. Our focus on "Asian writing in English" is one that will be continually refined and redefined as the program develops. We are not rigid in outlook, but do believe in academic rigor and standards.

The critical writing is focused on writing craft as opposed to literary theory. Since an MFA is a graduate-level degree — or a "postgraduate" degree as classified in the Hong Kong education system — we believe our students should be able to write critically at a graduate level. Our program syllabus does clearly articulate our expectations. For example, the critical thesis aims at synthesizing students' awareness of the literary tradition(s) and genre(s) that inform their own creative writing, and to master the elements of writing craft in their own genre.

Residency/community

Xu Xi, faculty: Residencies will be hosted at City University's main campus in Kowloon Tong, although special events — visiting writer readings or talks — may take place elsewhere in the city. Activities include workshops, classes, lectures, readings, and engagement with Asia's literary culture through visiting writers, symposiums, and other programs.

While the university will provide some support in the form of information and recommendations for residency accommodation, including special rates at certain hotels or other accommodations, the ultimate responsibility for arranging and financing travel is that of the student's. However, the university will provide sufficient information and meet any legal requirements for students enrolled in our program. As with all travel visas, only the official government department that grants these has the final say, although City University will do everything within our power to assist our students in this regard.

We are offering a merit scholarship, which will be awarded to one candidate in the first class we enroll, and hope to offer further scholarships in future.

Format/study

Xu Xi, faculty: The ideal student is a talented creative writer in English who is serious about her or his writing, and for whom Asia occupies a significant space in her or his consciousness because it informs the writing, whether this be due to upbringing, ethnicity, location, life, language, literary heritage. Age, gender, profession, educational background, ethnicity, nationality, location are irrelevant to the profile of this ideal student. She or he just has to be a good writer with a strong commitment to the work and willing to search deep within the self to find that right creative voice. The ideal student is talented, but even more importantly, is disciplined and persistent in the quest for just the right word to use in a sentence for a story, poem, or essay. The ideal student writes, and just as importantly, reads as a writer and learns to do this well.

INSTITUTE OF AMERICAN INDIAN ARTS
Fiction, Poetry, Non-Fiction, Playwriting, Screenwriting
Scheduled to launch 2011
Santa Fe, NM
2 years, 5 residencies
www.iaia.edu

The interviewee
Jon Davis is the interim director of the IAIA MFA program. He has served as Writing Program Coordinator for the Fine Arts Work Center in Provincetown and edited the literary journals *Shankpainter* and *Countermeasures: A Magazine of Poetry & Ideas*.

The program
Jon Davis, director: The Institute of American Indian Arts' Low-Residency Program in Creative Writing began in response to requests from graduates of our BFA in Creative Writing. These former students, both those who continued on to succeed in graduate school and those who chose not to continue, expressed a real desire that IAIA provide advanced study continuing our tradition of an undergraduate program based on rigorous practice, literary study and attention to the development of craft. Many of those alumni who did not continue on to graduate school did not do so because of their desire to return home. IAIA is a multi-tribal college and our students arrive from over ninety different tribal nations in the US and Canada. A number of those who did not continue in graduate school are now teaching or working in other capacities in their communities. For these students an IAIA MFA program with a low-residency model was extremely attractive as it would allow them to participate in their communities, in their jobs and in their tribal nations' social and spiritual practices.

Once the new academic program received approval from faculty and administration, we surveyed our alumni for their opinions on what an IAIA MFA Low-Residency Program in Creative Writing should look like. The resulting program addresses many of their needs reflecting our mission of educating Native American students and encouraging them to strengthen their ties with their tribal communities. However, the program is designed for all students, regardless of ethnicity, who want to pursue excellence in their writing. I want to make it clear that, though we will exercise Indian preference in our decision-making processes, all students are invited to apply.

Faculty/teaching philosophy

Jon Davis, director: Grounded in Native American cultural values, but contemporary in its outlook, the IAIA MFA program provides, for both Native and non-Native students, a solid foundation and the freedom to explore that comes from operating with historical and literary knowledge and depth.

Probably what marks a Native American community such as IAIA most is the feeling of being a part of a community — eating together, making decisions together, celebrating our triumphs and sorrows together. Our alumni really are part of an extended family. That approach may not be for everyone — community also implies responsibility for each other — but many students thrive in that situation. What also happens in that situation is that diverse styles thrive. An experimental poet, for example, might be a close confidante with a traditional narrative poet. Or a screenwriter might be providing close reading and guidance to a novelist — and vice versa. Such things happen all the time at the undergraduate level at IAIA; we expect such alliances to occur in the MFA program as well.

Residency/community

Jon Davis, director: Residencies will take place on the campus of the Institute of American Indian Arts on the south side of Santa Fe, a gorgeous location with 360 degree views of the Sangre de Cristo, Ortiz, Sandia, and Jemez mountain ranges with easy access to outdoor activities of all kinds, hiking, fishing, rafting, biking, skiing, and so on. Santa Fe is renowned as an artists' and writers' community, and residencies will include access to literary, visual, and musical events and, when appropriate, the nearby pueblos' cultural activities. The residency itself will include workshops, lectures, readings, open mics, social events, and cultural activities.

Format/study

Jon Davis, director: We hope to offer fiction, poetry, non-fiction, playwriting, screenwriting, and mixed-genre tracks. Other areas, such as performance, collaboration, and traditional storytelling, will be addressed in workshops during the residency. Other specialty tracks may evolve, but for now, the interest has centered on the traditional literary genres. Over half of our faculty will be Native American; the remaining faculty will represent diverse ethnicities and cultural backgrounds. Our goal, as in our undergraduate program, is to provide an extremely rigorous program of readings and craft study, as well as encourage experimentation and freedom. Most programs tend to emphasize either craft or experimentation but rarely both. We believe that a deep familiarity with literary history and craft positions the emerging author to experiment freely. Finally, we will strive to keep costs down for the students while providing high quality instruction; we expect to be among the most affordable MFA programs in the country. While we considered all the various models and find online workshops and lectures attractive, we want, at least initially, to be as flexible as possible. Given that many of our students will be working from reservations, some with limited internet access, we will allow students and faculty to choose the most expeditious method of exchanging work — either through mailed packets or via email. While we will encourage a range of contact methods — telephone, Skype, audio recordings, whatever works best for the student — written critiques will be required and will be at the center of the professor–student relationship.

UNIVERSITY OF KING'S COLLEGE, HALIFAX

Narrative Non-Fiction
Scheduled to launch 2012
Halifax, NS
2 years, 5 residencies
www.ukings.ns.ca

The interviewee

Stephen Kimber is the Rogers Communication Chair in Journalism at University of King's College, Halifax, in Nova Scotia, Canada. Together with Don Sedgwick, a former president of Doubleday, Stephen prepared the proposal for the MFA program.

The program

Stephen Kimber, faculty: We hope to accept our first students in the summer of 2012. The program proposal is still working its way through the various approving bodies: at our university, Dalhousie University's Grad Studies Department — our larger sister institution which will administer the program — and the Maritime Provinces Higher Education Commission. We're confident the program will get approval but it is, of course, pending until we get the formal OK.

Faculty/teaching philosophy

Stephen Kimber, faculty: We're looking at a combination of small group online forums, packet exchanges, and one-to-one communication between mentor and student.

Residency/community

Stephen Kimber, faculty: There will be two residences each year: a two-week summer residency at King's in Halifax, probably in early August, and a one-week residency alternating between Toronto and New York that will feature meetings with agents, editors, publishers, and so forth.

Format/study

Stephen Kimber, faculty: Partly because of the fact that we're a journalism school, the program's exclusive focus will be on narrative non-fiction, including all its many and various offshoots — from memoir to literary journalism to travel writing to biography to historical non-fiction.

Though our focus isn't exclusively journalistic, we think the program will appeal to many mid-career journalists looking to make the transition to larger projects and longer-form storytelling.

We hope to have a program-specific website up by spring 2011. In the meantime, anyone interested can email me (stephen.kimber@ukings.ns.ca) for more information.

LANCASTER UNIVERSITY
Master of Arts (MA) in Creative Writing
Lancaster, UK
2 years, 1 residency
www.lancs.ac.uk/fass/english/postgrad/creativewriting

The interviewee

Lee Horsley, alongside Graham Mort, is the Co-Convenor of the Distance Learning Master of Arts (DLMA) offered by Lancaster University.

The program

Lee Horsley, co-convenor: The program is unique in its international configuration and its links to Lancaster's Centre for Transcultural Writing and Research. We receive many more applications than we can possibly accept, so the standards are high and competition is tough.

Faculty/teaching philosophy

Lee Horsley, co-convenor: The program has no set curriculum, but is student-centered and conceived as an MA by personal research rather than a taught program. Each student has a personal tutor who helps them to develop their work through detailed written reports in the context of wider student interactions such as the Summer School and online conferences. We also provide online research training.

Residency/community

Lee Horsley, co-convenor: The Summer School provides a week of intense writing workshop activity by day, followed by a relaxing candle-lit dinner and readings by tutors and students. Throughout the week there are personal tutorials with tutors and visits from publishers and agents.

The course creates a very strong sense of identity among its participants through the lively exchanges in our virtual learning environment, both in the informal chat rooms and in the conference groups. This atmosphere is reinforced after they all meet one another at the Summer School. Members of staff remain available for advice after the course.

Format/study

Lee Horsley, co-convenor: The Lancaster University Virtual Learning Environment offers a highly developed context for interactions among students and tutors: each site provides a meeting place for sixteen to twenty students and four tutors. Each student has a member of faculty as a personal tutor, and additionally meets all of those involved with the DLMA at the Summer School.

The connection between creative work and online study is seamless. Students can organize their own time around the tutorials and online conferences. They are able to test their own work in English against the responses of a truly international community working in English.

LESLEY UNIVERSITY
Fiction, Poetry, Non-Fiction, Writing for Stage and Screen, Writing for Young People
Cambridge, MA
2 years, 5 residencies
www.lesley.edu/gsass/creative_writing/index.html

The interviewee
Steven Cramer, director, teaches poetry and criticism. His published works include *Goodbye to the Orchard, Dialogue for the Left and Right Hand, The World Book*, and *The Eye That Desires to Look Upward*.

The program
Steven Cramer, director: Lesley's Interdisciplinary Studies (IS) component constitutes the program's key distinction. A single question underpins it: What feeds an apprentice writer's work? Careful, challenging feedback, of course, and a diet of reading that nourishes imaginative and technical growth. But something individual and often eccentric also feeds a writer's work; or, as is often the case with the graduate student, that writer's aspirations to work in a literary field after graduation. The Interdisciplinary Studies component honors how widely that "something" can vary.

Faculty/teaching philosophy
Steven Cramer, director: I look for passionate writers who are also passionate teachers. Keeping with the studio arts model, MFA creative writing faculty are active, public practitioners of the art they teach. Beyond those bedrock criteria, I think a faculty should be diverse — memoirists and literary journalists; traditional narrative and experimental fiction writers; masters of free verse and "received" poetic forms; writers who know what clicks

with young people in a picture book or young adult novel; expert practitioners in dramatic writing from the ten-minute play to the full-length screenplay.

Residency/community

Steven Cramer, director: The workshops are of course the hub of the residency. At Lesley, there are two kinds: workshops with no more than ten students orchestrated by two or more faculty, and groups of no more than five. The faculty mentor conducting the smaller workshops will also work with those students for the semester.

For their craft component, many low-residency programs — by no means all — rely on a mixture of faculty and graduating student lectures and visiting presentations. We've opted for small-group, faculty-taught craft seminars, creating a logistically complex but pedagogically rich curriculum. By the end of a residency, students will have witnessed close-up the teaching style of as many as ten different faculty members. Over the course of two years, the curriculum offers students increasingly sophisticated techniques for mastering the writer's craft.

Every residency, of course, has readings — by faculty, visiting writers, and graduating students. Writing for Stage and Screen and Writing for Young People have enlivened our evening events with staged readings and visual presentations of illustrated books.

Format/study

Steven Cramer, director: Broadly speaking, Interdisciplinary Studies projects fall into two categories: those that intrinsically enhance students' ongoing writing and those that serve their goals to work as public writers in the future ... The Interdisciplinary Studies projects have resulted in interviews published in the AWP *Writer's Chronicle*, teaching in public or private schools and colleges, and designing writing workshops for special populations. Interdisciplinary Studies online courses can focus on pedagogy, book reviewing, and specialized tools of the craft such as diction and syntax. Students with promise in a genre other than their concentration may use some or all of their Interdisciplinary Studies credits to explore that other genre. In a nutshell: the Interdisciplinary Studies component is designed to enhance, not distract from, each student's devotion to writing.

Because Lesley MFA students receive academic credit for internships, they are very reliable interns. No reliability, no credit. Internship supervisors like that. Again, it's our Interdisciplinary Studies component that offers these opportunities, and many of them: independent studies in editing; work as tutors at university writing centers; office and online internships at *The Adirondack Review*, *Beacon Press*; Cleveland Museum of Art; *Harvard Review*, *The Hornbook*, Lark Books in Asheville, NC; PEN/New England; the Perseus Books Group, *Poetry Northwest*, *Post Road*, and other literary magazines around the country.

MURRAY STATE UNIVERSITY
Fiction, Poetry, Creative Non-Fiction, Writing for Children & Young Adults
Murray, KY
2 years, 4 residencies
www.murraystate.edu/chfa/english/mfa/index.htm

The interviewees
Ann Neelon, director, is the author of the book *Easter Vigil*. She has been a Wallace Stegner Fellow as well as a Jones Lecturer in Poetry at Stanford University. Ann's poems and translations have appeared in many magazines, including *The American Poetry Review*, *Ironwood*, *The Gettysburg Review*, and *Manoa*.

Squire Babcock, former director, is Associate Professor at Murray State University, where he has taught English and creative writing for sixteen years. He is the author of *The King of Gaheena*.

Leah Stewart is the author of the novels *The Myth of You and Me*, *Body of a Girl*, and *Husband and Wife*. Leah is a former faculty member of Murray State and was the recipient of a 2010 NEA Literature Fellowship.

The program
Ann Neelon, director: In July 2010, we celebrated our fifth anniversary as a program. It is gratifying to me to note how many milestones we have achieved in such a short time. We now have alumni all over the South and Midwest, even a few in states far

afield like Oregon, Nevada, and New York, and we find ourselves designating a spot in each residency for alumni to come back and read from their publications. [The program's literary magazine] *New Madrid* has published writers of distinction from thirty-two states and numerous foreign countries, including Canada, Russia, Germany, Spain, Mexico, India, and Nigeria. People we respect highly are also stepping forward to support what we are doing: a recent generous donation from Michael and Marilyn Denington will allow us to offer fellowships to a number of worthy MFA students.

Faculty/teaching philosophy

Ann Neelon, director: Our faculty combines the best of both worlds in the sense that we have writers who teach full-time at Murray State and provide something resembling institutional authority, as well as writers who teach full- or part-time in many other universities and who provide a necessary challenge to that authority. The dynamics of inside and outside are essential to the richness of our program. We have been very lucky to have been able to hire faculty who are not only accomplished writers and excellent teachers, but also generous — and fun — human beings.

Residency/community

Squire Babcock, former director: Students can expect an invigorating nine days of intense literary energy generated by stimulating readings and talks by visiting writers, great discussions in workshops and seminars, deeply helpful one-on-one meetings with mentors, relaxed and fun social time with a diverse group of peers and faculty, and quiet reflective time, all of which will ultimately send them home fully charged and raring to write.

The bonds that students form during the residencies sustain them throughout the semesters of their stay in the program and beyond. We understand that writers need community and we structure our residencies to encourage many opportunities for community interaction. When not in residence, students interact with each other through online social networking or by finding ways to meet in person if they are geographically close enough. These communities often last and sustain our writers well after they are done with their degree programs.

Leah Stewart, former faculty: Murray State faculty are very accessible, and the residencies had a congenial, supportive atmosphere ... There was a strong social element, with multiple readings, panels and receptions, including student readings.

Format/study

Squire Babcock, former director: Murray State is unique for our diverse and gifted faculty, our field study requirement, our supportive and dedicated administrative staff, our affordability, and our location in a uniquely beautiful geographic region.

As part of our curriculum, all students must complete a three-hour field study that, for most, comprises a semester of working on the editorial staff of our national literary magazine, *New Madrid*. This experience is eye-opening and invaluable to aspiring writers in any genre.

Ann Neelon, director: As the editor of *New Madrid*, it has been my privilege to work with dozens of inspired MFA interns. Each issue we put together grows out of its own idiosyncratic process. The great thing is that the high quality of the editorial community remains constant.

NAROPA UNIVERSITY
Jack Kerouac School of Disembodied Poetics
Fiction, Poetry, Non-Fiction, Translation
Boulder, CO
3 years, 2 residencies
www.naropa.edu/academics/graduate/writingpoetics/mfalowres

The interviewee

Junior Burke, department chair and director, is a prose writer, dramatist, and lyricist. His published works include the novel *Something Gorgeous*. He received his MFA from the Jack Kerouac School at Naropa University and teaches fiction and dramatic writing workshops and courses in literary studies.

The program

Junior Burke, director: Writing & Poetics at Naropa has always been singular. First off, it's not an English department. The emphasis is on creative poetics and prose, alternative publishing, and public engagement through performance. There is also a solid activist tradition, as well as proximity to contemplative, Buddhist-inspired teachings. While there are rigorous academic standards and practices, the instructors are not traditional academics, but rather working writers who have established themselves within their chosen form(s).

Faculty/teaching philosophy
Junior Burke, director: The faculty members are active, published writers. Each has an expertise regarding both the creative form(s) they workshop, as well as the literary modes they choose to teach.

Residency/community
Junior Burke, director: Our low-res community is quite strong. Because the Summer Writing Program is built into both the residential and low-res degrees, there is ample opportunity to fuse relationships that are then further deepened during the online seminars and workshops.

The Summer Writing Program is available for graduate and undergraduate credit, and for non-credit. It is built into both the residential and distance graduate degrees, representing effectively a third of the credit hours for each. For our low-res students, the Summer Writing Program represents the residency portion of their degree. The instruction is incredibly diverse, as each week a student will be in workshops with a different instructor. The Summer is total immersion, with more than five hundred events included within the four weeks: workshops, lectures, readings, panels, interviews, and visual presentations. Intense community-building takes place. Naropa is confident in saying that as an experience for a writer at any level, there is nothing else like it.

Naropa's Summer Writing Program includes a housing option. Our low-res students also sublet and organize shared housing for the summer session. There's a great café here on campus that offers low-cost healthy meals, and we host a catered book signing each Friday afternoon at which students can mingle with faculty and get their books signed.

Format/study

Junior Burke, director: We feel that the online courses reflect, as effectively as possible, the standards and practices that have defined Writing & Poetics at Naropa. When the distance degree was designed and implemented, a great deal of care went toward ensuring that in no way would the experience be diluted.

Over the past few years, Writing & Poetics has transitioned *Bombay Gin* into a periodical with national distribution. We have a faculty member who serves as editor-in-chief, but the board is comprised of students. There is a graduate assistantship for the journal as well.

The online magazine *not enough night* has, from its inception, published excerpts from the final manuscripts of graduating students. The thought is that this will provide a gateway for continued publication and professional engagement.

NATIONAL UNIVERSITY
Fiction, Poetry, Non-Fiction, Screenwriting
La Jolla, CA
2 years, 0 residencies
www.nu.edu

The interviewee

Frank Montesonti, lead faculty, has published poems in journals such as *Black Warrior Review*, *AQR*, *Cream City Review*, and *Poet Lore*. He also coordinates the student literary journal, the *GNU*.

The program

Frank Montesonti, faculty: At National University our student population is very diverse. I find that this makes for very exciting writing. In any given class, I may have a doctor, a soldier, and a former lawyer; someone writing about the deep winters in Alaska or the sunny shores of Guam. It is always exciting to work with students who have such a variety of life experience.

Faculty/teaching philosophy

Frank Montesonti, faculty: Since we are a completely online program, we can select the best faculty from around the country. We have faculty who have many books and some who have one or two. Often times we hire up-and-coming writers because we feel they have more time to dedicate to their students and can better relate to the struggles of putting together a first book. In our entire faculty, a dedication to teaching is essential.

Residency/community

Frank Montesonti, faculty: National is a no-residency program. The vast majority of our students are those who are busy with careers, children, and all of life's other demands. They are so busy that they can't afford or find time for even a brief residency requirement. Our program lets the students work from home while joining a community online. Our classes have lectures, workshops forums, discussion questions, and activities. Though the classes are online, they function very much like on-ground creative writing classrooms. Though some of our students never meet face to face, I have found that many close friendships have been made. We also hold a reading series in Los Angeles and many students often meet up at the yearly AWP conference.

Format/study

Frank Montesonti, faculty: All classes are online and all are asynchronous — meaning that there is no specific time every day where you have to be in front of your computer screen. Our classes are accelerated, so you take one class at a time. Because of our low overhead, National University is also a very affordable program. In our program, students are required to explore in genres other than their focus, so you will get experience in writing fiction, non-fiction, poetry, and screenwriting.

Students may volunteer to work on our biannual student literary journal, the *GNU*. Positions for Editor-in-Chief and Designer are open yearly. Any student may volunteer as a reader for the journal. Some of our students can get internship credit for working on the *GNU*. Other students may get internships working at our online writing center. Still other students can get credit for literary projects they do in their own communities.

UNIVERSITY OF NEBRASKA
Fiction, Poetry, Creative Non-Fiction, Playwriting
Omaha, NE
2 years, 5 residencies
www.unomaha.edu/unmfaw

The interviewees

Richard Duggin, director, received his MFA degree in fiction writing from the University of Iowa Writers' Workshop and has taught fiction writing at the University of Nebraska at Omaha for the past forty years. He is the founder of the UNO Writer's Workshop, a BFA degree program in creative writing, and the University of Nebraska MFA in Writing Program. His published work includes the novel *The Music Box Treaty*.

Kate Gale, visiting faculty, is managing editor of Red Hen Press. She is a librettist, poet, and novelist with five books of poetry, one bilingual children's book, and five librettos. She is also the editor of four anthologies.

Tim Black, alumnus, has had poetry published in several journals and magazines, and is the recent winner of an American Academy of Poets prize.

Stephanie Austin is a student whose short fiction has most recently appeared in *Fiddlehead* and *American Short Fiction*. She will graduate from Nebraska's fiction program in 2011.

The program

Richard Duggin, director: I am the founder of the University of Nebraska MFA in Writing program, which opened its doors to its first low-residency graduate students in August of 2005. I became attracted to the low-residency model for graduates by the success of those undergraduate BFA students of mine who went on to do their graduate work in similar low-residency MFA programs. I became convinced that this was the way to organize and conduct the development of writers on a graduate level.

The major quality of the Nebraska MFA that seems to draw students to it, and to retain them even after they have graduated, is the personal attention mentors provide the student's work and the effort the mentors put out to encourage the success of the student in accomplishing their goals for their writing.

Faculty/Teaching Philosophy

Tim Black, alumnus: My first mentor, Jim Petersen, is a Zen master — at least that's what the wife and I call him. He helped me to see the energy of my work. My second mentor, Teri Grimm, allowed me to continue to experiment, which was great; I thought I would be asked to "settle down and write normally" but Teri really let my experimentation grow, and because of that I've developed a more contemporary style. It was under her tutelage I won an Academy of American Poets award.

Stephanie Austin, student: I am involved 100 percent in my study plan. My mentor and I sit down each residency and just have a long discussion about what I like to read and write and what they like to read and write and we each throw ideas on the table. It's a mutual decision.

Richard Duggin, director: We look for writers who are actively writing and publishing their work and have a keen desire to pass on the experience of their process to aspiring writers and other colleagues in a community of shared aspirations and encouragements.

Residency/community
Kate Gale, faculty: It's the most wonderful writing community. The directors Richard and Jenna, first of all, make you very welcome. They are not standoffish or full of themselves, so that sets the tone for the faculty. It's about us writers working on our craft, our business, our stuff. There's not a lot of "us and them" going on, nor a lot of slackerdom, but yet people are having fun. I like the feeling of being there, like being in a house with no windows and no doors . . . and it does rain, but you just happen to be the kind of person who likes being wet. By that I mean, mistakes happen, you might find you don't have the right packet or the right this or that, but everything is going to be okay, because the tone is set that the dance goes on anyway.

Tim Black, alumnus: Upon going through my first residency, I was glad I chose Nebraska due to the staff; the mentors were very open and willing to help . . . The instruction is top-notch. I even went to the fiction lectures since they help so much in my poetry. I could tell, after my first residency, I was a much better poet. Actually, I was much better after the first day. The energy there is so high, you can't help but step up your game.

Stephanie Austin, student: I love residencies. It makes all that hard work during the semester worth it. They are like a super-conference. All the students and faculty come together for ten days of intense study. You live, eat, breathe with these people and by the end, you've formed these amazing bonds. In Nebraska, we stay at the Lied Lodge, which is like a great big tree house and we're all in the same club. Most people who come into the low-res program are like me. They are students who love reading and writing and advancing themselves but at the same time have work and family obligations. We all come from different places but have ended up together. It's truly amazing.

I am in daily contact with my friends from the program — both those who have graduated and those still in it. I was looking for a writing community and I found one. We all have email chains, Facebook threads, phone calls on a weekly basis. It's a great support. When we come together, we're like long lost friends.

Richard Duggin, director: There are alumni who return to Nebraska City each residency just to renew personal friendships they have made while they were students with us. Mentors keep in touch with former students, advising and encouraging them long after they have worked with them in the program. The setting for our residencies — a resort lodge with fine dining and lodging amenities that cater to the comfort of their guests — lends itself to this atmosphere of a family of friends and colleagues.

Format/study
Stephanie Austin, student: Most of the time I communicate with my mentor via email and regular mail. I email my work and he prints it out, makes suggestions and mails it back to me. Last semester, my mentor used track changes and emailed my work back to me. I can communicate with him as often and as much as I like. I have certain deadlines I have to meet, but if in the meantime I have questions or concerns, I'm free to make as much contact as I want. I know of students and mentors who, if they live in the same town, will meet once a month for coffee.

NEW ENGLAND COLLEGE
Poetry
Henniker, NH
2 years, 5 residencies
www.nec.edu/graduate-and-professional-studies/mfa-in-poetry

The interviewees
James Harms, director, is the author of *After West*, *Freeways and Aqueducts*, *Quarters*, *The Joy Addict*, and *Modern Ocean*. His poems, stories and essays have appeared in *Poetry*, *The American Poetry Review*, *The Kenyon Review*, *The Gettysburg Review*, *TriQuarterly*, *Ploughshares*, and others.

Mariela Griffor, student, is the author of *Exiliana* and *House*. She is also the publisher of Marick Press.

The program
James Harms, director: We're the first poetry-only low-res program, and the only one that offers concentrated study in translation, new media, and performance. We're proud of our diversity, and our ability to create individualized curricula, and we're committed to being a program that recognizes and participates in the innovative practices of contemporary poetry. We think of ourselves as a program where tradition meets innovation, and where both are respected and nurtured.

Faculty/teaching philosophy
James Harms, director: Our program has several concentrations, so it's essential that our faculty be able to contribute in more than one way. All are award-winning poets, but they're also renowned translators, performance artists, and multimedia specialists. And every one of them must demonstrate a commitment and a talent for teaching. We're very careful to hire only the most passionate and generous poet-teachers.

Mariela Griffor, student: The folks at NEC are creating a culture in addition to teaching a curriculum . . . To create a culture behind a program is something that doesn't happen from one day to another and it is created in a complicated way, but most of all are the people behind it with a vision or idea that can shape something like this.

Residency/community

James Harms, director: NEC's commitment to creating a supportive, collegial environment has really worked, and the students feel both challenged and respected. We insist on a supportive, respectful atmosphere, and in every possible way we work to create a community where each and every member has responsibility for the success of every other member. There is very little of the cutthroat competitiveness that you find at many MFA programs, low-res or not; the faculty and students genuinely care about each other as people as well as artists. I can say with all honesty that our residencies are feel-good events, and that students respond by producing remarkable work.

Format/study

James Harms, director: The opportunity to work closely with a single poet over the course of a semester, and to develop an individualized plan of study that includes a comprehensive reading schedule, these things just can't be over-valued. Low-res programs such as ours supply developing writers with extensive feedback on their work, a coherent and thoughtful reading list that changes and expands each semester, and the opportunity to join a community of like-minded artists. It preserves the solitary nature of the writing process while offering the lifeline of fellowship with other writers. Our students feel less alone with their devotion.

We encourage our students to take advantage of teaching opportunities at New England College, though not all are able to do that. As a result, we offer all students the chance to design and teach workshops in their final residencies, and help them create teaching opportunities for themselves in their communities.

UNIVERSITY OF NEW ORLEANS

Poetry, Fiction, Non-Fiction, Playwriting, Screenwriting
New Orleans, LA
2 years, 3 residencies abroad
http://lowres.uno.edu

The interviewee

Bill Lavender, director, is managing editor of UNO Press. His most recent book of poetry is *transfixion*.

The program

Bill Lavender, director: The program at UNO actually grew out of our groundbreaking summer writing program in Prague, which we began twenty years ago. There are several programs now in Prague, but ours was the first. We believe the most important part of our program is the summer residencies abroad. The value of immersion in a foreign culture is simply inestimable for a young writer. We have hundreds of testimonials to the effectiveness of these residencies.

Faculty/teaching philosophy

Bill Lavender, director: [We seek faculty with] publications, teaching experience, and a publication record from former students.

During the fall and spring semesters, our program is modeled after a normal, resident, program, rather than the old correspondence courses. We have virtual classrooms where students and faculty alike chat with each other and exchange ideas via a Discussion Board interface.

Residency/community

Bill Lavender, director: The [international residencies] last four weeks, and after the first week you feel like you've been there a month, and after the month you feel like you just got there. At first you are confused, bewildered, lost, but you gradually get your cultural legs under you and come out the other side with new confidence and you new identity as a writer.

Format/study

Bill Lavender, director: Unlike in "mentor and packet" programs, our students form a strong community via our online interactive classes during the regular semester, a community that is only bolstered by the intense bonds formed during the summers abroad. During the regular semester, our students don't work only with a mentor, they interact with each other in virtual classrooms. They read each other's work and comment on it, just like in an on-campus workshop, and we facilitate all sorts of social interactions via new social media like Facebook and also by sponsoring get-togethers at conferences like AWP. By the end of our program, I think our students have formed as close a community as any students will in a resident program.

NORTHWEST INSTITUTE OF LITERARY ARTS
Whidbey Writers Workshop
Fiction, Poetry, Creative Non-Fiction, Writing for Children and Young Adults
Freeland, WA
2 years, 5 residencies
www.writeonwhidbey.org/mfa

The interviewees
Wayne Ude, director, is the author of *Becoming Coyote*, *Buffalo and other stories*, and *Maybe I Will Do Something: Seven Tales of Coyote*. His stories have appeared in *North American Review* and *Ploughshares*, among others.

George Shannon, guest faculty, began his professional work with children in 1973. He is the author of thirty-eight books, including twenty-seven picture books. His publications include *Lizard's Song*, *Dance Away*, *Climbing Kansas Mountains*, and *Busy in the Garden*. In 2010, he presented a number of sessions during the NILA residency — his first personal experience with MFA programs of any kind.

FeLicia A. Elam, alumnus, is a native Tennessean who lives in Portland, Oregon. She has attended workshops at Hurston/Wright, VONA, and Tin House. Her work has appeared in *The Sounding Review*, *Eugene Magazine*, *VoiceCatcher3: Women's Voices of Portland*, and other publications.

Stefon Mears, student, has worked as a writer and editor in technology, the law, and various other fields, most recently development. To date, he has published mainly in the role-playing game industry, such as the adventure sourcebook *Heart of the Machine*. He expects to graduate from the Whidbey Writers Workshop in August 2012.

The program

Wayne Ude, director: We wanted to bring to our students a focus on three things: writing; learning about the profession of writing in terms of working with agents and editors as well as continuing to produce new work; and becoming part of the local, regional, and national community of writers. We later realized that implicit in our mix of workshops, courses on craft within each genre, and directed readings was another goal: to produce writers who could articulate their understanding of writing.

And, of course, a thesis requirement of a book-length manuscript of publishable quality places us in the mainstream of what residential MFA programs have always done. We've sought to combine the best features of traditional programs — workshops, separate craft and reading classes, a final thesis project — with those of low-residency programs: the intense community and variety of guest faculty offered by the residency, with the majority of the semester taking place from the student's home.

Faculty/teaching philosophy

Wayne Ude, director: We offer individual five-credit courses, which allow students to take one, two, or three courses each semester. Except for the Profession of Writing course, all courses begin at the residency and continue online. Faculty and students are required to participate in their online courses at least three times a week, but most find themselves wanting to check in on the discussion at least once a day to see what's going on. We're very flexible; students may take from two to six years to complete the program.

The Profession of Writing course focuses on all aspects of the professional side of writing. This course is taught only during the residencies and requires a minimum of five residencies to complete. We provide twenty-four to twenty-seven hours of instruction in professional matters in each residency. In a typical residency, that course will include four visiting agents or editors, five visiting writers, and one or two specialists — perhaps a publicist or an expert on blogging, for example. The Profession of Writing concludes at the students' graduation residency in August with five hours of instruction in building a publication record as a writer of poetry or short prose focusing on literary magazines and presses, and five more on pitching manuscripts to commercial presses.

George Shannon, guest faculty: To write well for children — to write books that engage them and stretch their minds — one needs to play. To explore. One needs to remember that stories must first and foremost entertain, and that each audience member will receive the themes he or she is ready to receive when the time is right. Until they do, there is always the delight of the story itself.

FeLicia A. Elam, alumnus: A fiction teacher, who was not my advisor, requested a conference with me. She wanted to tell me that she felt a short story of mine was really a novel and that I should collect my short stories for publication. She felt that I could have two works ready for publication not long after graduation and took the time to tell me despite not being my own advisor.

Residency/community
Wayne Ude, director: We place a great deal of emphasis on community. After the first couple of days of each residency, it's impossible to tell new students from returning students. Mornings at the residency are devoted to the first nine days of classes that will continue for sixteen weeks online. Afternoons feature guest speakers: agents, editors, publicists, social media experts, and writers speaking about the professional side of writing. Most evenings see faculty and students giving public readings from their work.

George Shannon, guest faculty: I was an MFA virgin. Years ago when I wondered about working toward an MFA there were no programs that even acknowledged writing for young people. Thus I was delighted to contribute to a program and work with students who also value literature for younger readers. I was impressed with the mutual support between students and faculty. I had no expectations as to the number of students in the program or their ages. It was encouraging to work with students ranging in age from twenty-something to retired.

Stefon Mears, student: I was amazed at how welcome I felt from the moment I arrived. The atmosphere was so relaxed and congenial that I had an easy time talking with everyone, from students, to alumni, to faculty, to guest speakers, to members of the board of directors. Every meal was a convivial mixture of faculty, students, and visiting speakers. Sometimes it was general socializing, about lives and current events and the like, sometimes we spoke about writing, and sometimes the faculty and guest speakers spoke about the state of publishing, changes taking place right now, and how they are adapting to the times.

Format/study

Stefon Mears, student: I'm still at the beginning of the program, but already I've learned a lot about the craft and seen ways to improve my writing: both the projects I have finished and those I am developing. I'm having an easier time looking at the structure of what I write, seeing where it is strong and where it is weak. What's more, I'm coming to understand how to strengthen what is weak.

Wayne Ude, director: NILA is very committed to the workshop method of teaching creative writing, and we support the workshops with semester-length craft classes and directed reading classes in each genre. Faculty work very closely with students in those courses and in the final thesis project, which is a mentoring situation.

FeLicia A. Elam, alumnus: The afternoon seminars give me the inside view of what publishers, editors, and agents want that I have never received in any workshop or class I've previously attended. During one residency, we were walked through how book publishers decided on what books to accept. We had to pitch our books to the "pub board," made up of teachers, and that was a lesson I don't think I could have learned elsewhere.

I am much more confident with my writing, spend less time revising and have the support of my classmates. Instead of looking for other people to answer my writing questions, I now have the ability to do so myself.

OKLAHOMA CITY UNIVERSITY
The Red Earth MFA
Fiction, Poetry, Non-Fiction
Scheduled to launch 2011
Oklahoma City, OK
2 years, 5 residencies
www.okcu.edu/english

The interviewee

Danita Berg holds an MFA in Creative Writing from Goddard College and a PhD in English from the University of South Florida. She currently works as an assistant professor of writing at Oklahoma City University, where she teaches composition and creative writing and chairs the annual Creative Writing Festival. She has published creative work in *Redivider*, *Southern Women's Review*, and the *Press Pause Now Anthology for Women*, among other publications.

The program

Danita Berg, faculty: The Red Earth MFA in Creative Writing at Oklahoma City University offers graduate-level study in creative writing. Students work with faculty mentors to create a manuscript-length work of creative prose in fiction, non-fiction, poetry, or another creative genre with approval of the program director. Students also concentrate on academic work in literary criticism and analysis of writing craft. Students can elect to pursue strands in pedagogy or professional writing.

Faculty/teaching philosophy

Danita Berg, faculty: Students pursue creative writing tracks according to a curricular plan co-devised with their academic advisor, with options for pursuing strands in pedagogy and professional writing. While emphasis is placed on creative writing, students will also have the opportunity to pursue strand work in creative writing pedagogy and professional writing in order to prepare for careers in publishing, editing, writing, and teaching. Learning outcomes will strengthen and fulfill each student's stated goals, which may vary from personal enrichment to career development as teachers, editors, or authors.

Residency/community

Danita Berg, faculty: This is a two-year program which includes five residencies, one each summer and each winter, plus one at the end of the program, for periods of approximately ten days. At the residencies, students not only attend classes but also work with a faculty mentor within small workshop groups with their peers.

Format/study
Danita Berg, faculty: Students will complete twelve hours of course work each fall and spring semester for two years, for a total of forty-eight hours. Students finish four semesters of off-campus study by completing both packet work with their individual mentor as well as participating in online workshops, fostering a community of writers that is sustained beyond the residencies. The final residency will include a public reading and defense of the thesis.

OXFORD UNIVERSITY
Master of Studies (MSt) in Creative Writing
Oxford, UK
2 years, 3 residencies
http://awardbearing.conted.ox.ac.uk/creative_writing/mstcw.php

The interviewee
Rebecca Rue is the program administrator of the Oxford University MSt in Creative Writing.

The program
Rebecca Rue, administrator: The emphasis of the course is very much on widening students' sense of what is possible in their own creative output, and on cross-genre exploration in their writerly practice as well as in their critical investigations. In Year One particularly, students are encouraged to experiment as widely as possible beyond the limits of what they have hitherto felt their writing might be aiming to do, while in Year Two they work on material and genre-specialization of their own choosing.

Faculty/teaching philosophy
Rebecca Rue, administrator: Teaching during the residences includes writing workshops, critical analytical seminars and talks from visiting writers and professionals in the field, such as agents and publishers.

Students are expected to undertake a significant amount of private study, but are assigned supervisors for their Year Two Final Project and Extended Essay, who guide the development of this work. Students are also assigned tutors/supervisors to help guide the development of their Year One Portfolio and Extended Essay. The course is not a "distance-learning" course, and tutors, while being happy to help with questions or problems, do not offer regular weekly "office hours."

A dedicated course website provides a vibrant interactive forum for dissemination of information and channeling of guidance and support in periods between Residences and Retreats. Students use the site not only to discuss work but also to encourage each other, announce student successes, and organize get-togethers.

Residency/community

Rebecca Rue, administrator: Workshops and seminars in the residences are divided between creative and critical studies. All critical investigations undertaken by students are designed to support their own creative explorations. We focus on a range of writers and critics in all genres, both contemporary and canonical. Oxford always employs a variety of styles and approaches, whether in creative teaching or in other humanities subjects. We aim to facilitate the development of the individual writerly voice by opening doors and providing guidance and support, including rigorous feedback from tutors and the student group.

Students receive full accommodation, including all catering, at Rewley House in central Oxford for five blocks of three days, plus the induction afternoon and evening. The days are full and intensive, and contact hours provision amounts to around 130 hours including the in-house placement learning experience. The high number of contact hours in the MSt are concentrated into these residences and retreats. Students would also be expected to come to Oxford in order to matriculate, and the research placement — usually of one week's duration — is generally in February of Year Two.

Format/study

Rebecca Rue, administrator: The MSt is offered part-time but is a very intensive course. We feel that the structure of the course . . . is an excellent way to develop each writer's individual voice and also to prepare for the "real world" of being a professional writer — where writers have to spend a lot of time wrestling with the challenges of their craft.

PACIFIC LUTHERAN UNIVERSITY
Rainer Writing Workshops
Fiction, Poetry, Creative Non-Fiction
Tacoma, WA
3 years, 4 residencies
www.plu.edu/mfa

The interviewees
Stan Sanvel Rubin, director, served for over twenty years as director of the Brockport Writers Forum and Videotape Library (SUNY), a multi-faceted literary arts program. He holds the SUNY Chancellor's Award for Excellence in Teaching. His publications include *Lost and Midnight*, *On the Coast*, and *Five Colors*. Stan is the current chair of the Low-Residency MFA Directors' Caucus, which meets annually at the Association of Writers and Writing Programs annual conference.

David Biespiel, faculty, is the author of four collections of poetry, most recently *The Book of Men and Women*. He is the founding director of the Attic Writers' Workshop in Portland, Oregon.

Natalie Haney Tilghman is currently a student in the MFA in Creative Writing program at Pacific Lutheran University. Her work has appeared in publications such as *Santa Clara Review*, *Red Clay Review*, and *South Loop Review*.

The program
Stan Sanvel Rubin, director: Everything in our program is collaborative and process-oriented. The attention is personal. Participants make many of the choices that drive their progress. We make no attempt to force an esthetic on anyone; we challenge yours to grow. Our extended mentorships are unique — and they make for a deep and meaningful experience.

Natalie Haney Tilghman, student: Rainier Writing Workshops (RWW) encourages work in multiple genres, and as a poet and fiction writer, I appreciated that I didn't have to choose to work only in one genre. The program offers individualized attention and challenges and supports writers to reach their fullest potential. Through RWW, I have had career-altering opportunities that I might never have had otherwise. For me, RWW has not just been school — it's been an experience.

Faculty/teaching philosophy

Stan Sanvel Rubin, director: Our faculty are writing partners for our participants. They are established writers who are as passionate as they are professional about good writing . . . [They demonstrate] enthusiasm, experience, achievement, plus commitment to the individual growth of their students.

Natalie Haney Tilghman, student: My mentors have been fabulous. The faculty members at RWW are not just talented writers, they're also talented teachers, who provide guidance, advice, instruction, and support by sharing their seemingly bottomless knowledge of craft. Through my mentorships, I have been challenged to stretch and grow and experiment. As a result, I developed my own unique voice as a writer. Perhaps this is the greatest gift that my mentors have given me.

Residency/community

Stan Sanvel Rubin, director: Residencies offer workshops, including a mixed-genre workshop. High-energy participation. Courses in all genres on a wide range of topics that are stimulating and interactive. A lot of smart conversation that never ends. You will leave with new friends and a sense of community to support you.

David Biespiel, faculty: The residencies are rewarding and exhausting. There is little downtime between conferences, readings, lectures, and classes. Then there is the pressure to stay up late and chat. For introverts, it's tough. For extroverts, it's heaven. It's a wonderfully supportive community that values every writer's success.

Natalie Haney Tilghman, student: One of the unique things about residencies at RWW is that while one workshop is in the student's primary genre, the second can be in whatever other genre the writer works in. In addition, many of the faculty members work in multiple genres as well. The class offerings are always rich and inspiring, allowing for stimulating discussion. At the community dinners and readings, faculty and students mingle.

Format/study

Natalie Haney Tilghman, student: From the beginning, I was welcomed into the supportive RWW community of faculty, students, and alumni. Though we are scattered all over the country, the group is like an extended family. I have exchanged manuscripts with other students and alumni for feedback, and learned of publishing or career-related opportunities from my peers. Some of my closest friends are RWW students. The culture is one of collegiality, mutual respect, and encouragement, and a shared love of literary arts. There is a generosity of spirit in this writing community.

Stan Sanvel Rubin, director: We make a very personal commitment to every writer we admit. We look for that sort of commitment to the program on their part. We cultivate an intense, joyous, and supportive community.

Everything about our program is collaborative and process-oriented, [and] meant to model a writer's life. Our goal is literary achievement, but a sustainable writing life whether there's quick success or not. For us, the degree is a transition, not an ending or a prize.

PACIFIC UNIVERSITY
Fiction, Poetry, Creative Non-Fiction
Forest Grove, OR
2 years, 5 residencies
www.pacificu.edu/as/mfa

The interviewees

Shelley Washburn's articles and short stories have appeared in various publications, including *DoubleTake* magazine and two anthologies by the Crossing Press. She is the director of the Pacific University MFA program.

Marvin Bell has authored more than twenty books including *Mars Being Red*. Long on the faculty of the Iowa Writers' Workshop, and Iowa's first Poet Laureate, he teaches now for the Pacific University brief-residency MFA based in Oregon.

Peter Sears has been a faculty member in the Pacific University MFA in Writing program since the beginning. He teaches poetry.

Jennifer Singleton Miller, alumnus, was in the creative non-fiction program. She is currently teaching.

Robert Peake studied poetry at UC Berkeley and in the MFA program at Pacific University, Oregon. His poems have appeared in *North American Review*, *Poetry International*, *Rattle*, and two anthologies of Southern California poets.

Nomi Morris has been a journalist for twenty-five years. She has written for *Time*, *Newsweek*, and the *Los Angeles Times*. Morris will graduate from Pacific University's MFA program in non-fiction in January 2011.

The program
Shelley Washburn, director: I am most proud of the community we have created here. It is a safe place to be wild, to take a chance, to jump over the line. We are saying yes to art. No one esthetic rules. You've got this crazy group of writers from all over the country who share a love of teaching, but in their writing span a wide spectrum of styles, topics and themes. Students have repeatedly told me that they are inspired and enriched by these diverse ideologies and teaching styles.

One result of this community is that we are fostering a national, literary dialogue. Our faculty members attend each other's craft talks and comment on them. For example, the poet Dorianne Laux, who lives in North Carolina, might say something about music and meaning in her morning talk, and then later in the afternoon fiction writer Jack Driscoll, who lives in Michigan, might reply to her comments in his craft talk on story line. Over the course of a residency — in a playful back and forth — the writers come to ideas that might not have emerged without the group dynamic. Everyone seems to understand that we are all in this together.

Faculty/teaching philosophy
Shelley Washburn, director: We look for accomplished writers who teach as well as they write, who share a sense of joy around the work. We hire hardworking, productive writers who give their all to students. I especially like the ones with an edge to them, who see the world upside down, sideways, off-kilter. We look for

people with diverse writing styles and those who can bring new voices to the mix.

Marvin Bell, faculty: [I aim to offer] the confidence to write with abandon, the permission to be different, how to read as a writer, analysis when useful, the cheap tricks of the best poets, and ways to become someone who thinks of himself or herself as a writer every day. When necessary, I fill in the blanks. I hope, also, to confirm for them why and how poetry is a survival skill, and that the person who gets the most from a poem is the one who writes it.

Peter Sears, faculty: In responding to student work, I do not write on the poems or commentaries I am sent. Instead, I write about them and mail back just my comments, within a week. This forces me to be clear and full in commenting about poems; it also ensures legibility. In my typed comments, I point out precisely where I think the student can improve the poem or where I have a question, and I relate these specific issues to the overall strategy of the poem, as I understand it. This response gives them, I hope, something to respond to. For example, if I have misread the poem because of a lack of clarity in the basic situation of the poem, the student has reason to revise, to send me a revision, and thereby straighten me out about my misreading. I am all for that.

Robert Peake, alumnus: People often say that with MFA programs, and especially the workshop aspect of being barraged with feedback, the consensus sum of which often whittles the piece back to mediocrity, ends up stamping one with a cookie-cutter style. Particularly in studying with Marvin Bell, I found that this did not have to be the case. In fact, he would often introduce his workshops with the idea that the best revision of a poem might be simply to keep writing with abandon, rather than taking every bit of feedback as truth from on high.

Residency/community
Marvin Bell, faculty: Some students become pals and stay in touch, of course. Those from the Portland, Oregon area are likely to get together. Some faculty members are friends who keep in touch. There is an online community presence and a magazine. The director sends out periodic updates and news, and the faculty

exchanges emails throughout the year to make suggestions and decisions, as well as to evaluate applications.

Robert Peake, alumnus: Five elements struck me about the residencies: the staff are incredibly helpful in a genuine way; the faculty seem to really like each other; the atmosphere is laid-back, yet sincere; the people are really enthusiastic about good writing; there is a minimum of extraneous nonsense going on.

Jennifer Miller, alumnus: Pacific has two different residencies. Residency for the winter semester is held on the Oregon coast, in Seaside, while summer residency is held on campus at Forest Grove. Everyone has a favorite. Winter on the Oregon coast means big ocean swells, rain, and gusting winds. It seems so natural to settle in the hotel lounge or a local coffee shop for long conversations about writing. Forest Grove has more of a college feel. You're back in a dorm, with roommates. Some people go out to the local pub, while others stay awake until the early morning hours writing, reading, and talking.

Pacific's faculty is fabulous. They hang out after lectures, workshops, and readings. It's easy to get one-on-one time. All you have to do is ask. If you're too shy, that's okay. They'll pull up a chair at lunch, or see you at a coffee shop and sit down for a few minutes just to chat and see how things are going.

Nomi Morris, student: The residencies are the highlight of the program for me. The level of writers at Pacific is so high that the craft talks, readings, and workshops are incredibly stimulating. There is also a great feeling in this program. The professors set the tone by not being at all hierarchical. They consider anybody who was good enough to be accepted into the program to be a colleague and they treat us as part of their community of writers.

Format/study

Shelley Washburn, director: I should say that our program is first and foremost about the art of writing. Our faculty members believe that writing and teaching are distinct skills, and we have chosen to put the writing first. It is our thinking that four semesters and five residencies are barely enough time to master a genre, let alone the art of teaching as well. That said, at most of our residencies we do offer a limited number of classes on pedagogy and the nature of university teaching. We encourage and facilitate job shadowing, internships, and teaching assistant positions for our students both locally and around the nation. Pacific offers several paid teaching associate positions on campus that are open to MFA alumni and current students in their third and fourth semesters. Many of those who have taught at Pacific have gone on to teach at other colleges.

Robert Peake, alumnus: Overall, throughout my two years in the program, I became less "precious" about my work, and more confident in my ability to keep writing, developing, and improving over time. More than anything, the program gave me this kind of confidence in myself as a writer. I studied under some tremendous writers who had dedicated their lives to writing. Just being around them, studying under them and talking about writing, was a privilege. It felt like I had found my people — individuals just as serious about writing, and the power of art, as I am. And by being around such great models of the traits required to sustain a life dedicated to art, I would like to think that some of it rubbed off.

Jennifer Miller, alumnus: I cannot say enough good things about my advisors and the correspondence semesters. They have all been extremely kind and quick to praise what was working in a piece. When something was not working, they did not tell me how I should fix it. Instead, they offered suggestions of other authors I could read whose particular technique might benefit my writing.

Nomi Morris, student: Although some of the faculty do accept communication by email, Pacific's MFA is not an online program. We are paired with a writer for the semester and exchange five packets during each semester. Each packet contains a letter, twenty pages of creative writing, and commentaries on the twenty books per semester we are required to read. It is a literary conversation between faculty writer and student writer . . . It is very exciting to receive that packet back in the mail and open it up for comments and notes.

PINE MANOR COLLEGE
Solstice Creative Writing Programs
Fiction, Poetry, Creative Non-Fiction, Writing for Children and
Young Adults
Chestnut Hill, MA
2 years, 5 residencies
www.pmc.edu/mfa-program-overview

The interviewee
Meg Kearney's poetry books include *Home By Now* and *An
Unkindness of Ravens*. For eleven years, she was associate direc-
tor of the National Book Foundation — sponsor of the National
Book Awards — based in New York City. Kearney is founding
director of the Solstice Low-Residency MFA in Creative Writing
Program at Pine Manor College as well as director of its Solstice
Summer Writers' Conference.

The program
Meg Kearney, director: We can probably boast the most diverse
faculty in the country, but I think another thing that makes us
unique is our interest in community involvement and how students can be active as writers in their home towns. We provide
elective sessions that give students ideas about how they might
start a writing group or reading series, how they might launch an
online journal, how they might get involved in teaching writing
in alternative settings like prisons or organizations for at-risk
youth. Students in their third, critical-essay semester also have
an option of taking on an internship in publishing, pedagogy, or
community outreach in order to add experiential knowledge to
their essay topics.

Faculty/teaching philosophy
Meg Kearney, director: Our faculty members reflect the faces
one sees across America — they represent different ethnicities,
religions, and sexual orientations; they come from middle-class
and working-class backgrounds; they hail from ten different states.
What they have in common is their success as writers and their
attitude about teaching.

   They are generous in the classroom and in their one-on-one
mentoring of students. They don't impose their own esthetics

onto students' work, but want students to develop their own unique voices. I guess what I'm saying is that our faculty members are friendly, approachable people who work hard on behalf of students.

Some of our faculty members teach only at the summer residency/fall semester; others teach only winter/spring. A few teach year-round.

Residency/community

Meg Kearney, director: Residencies are pretty intense. Each morning, students spend three hours in workshop. We break for lunch, and then our Craft, Criticism, and Theory Classes and Elective Seminars and Studies Sessions take up the afternoon. There's a reading each night, including a student reading that's run by the students themselves.

In between classes and often at meals, students and faculty mentors mix informally; late in the residency, once mentors have been assigned, they sit down to discuss each student's semester plan and goals. By the time our students head home, they know which faculty member they'll be partnered with for the coming months, and they'll have a solid sense of what they'll be reading and working on writing-wise. They're also pretty exhausted, but energized at the same time!

In addition to our diversity and non-hierarchical atmosphere, students and faculty are very supportive of each other. We celebrate each other's literary successes, and see each other through our disappointments. If a student is looking for a fiercely competitive atmosphere, they won't find it at Pine Manor College. The outside world — especially when it comes to publishing — is difficult enough! While our admissions process is competitive, once students are accepted and land on campus, they're welcomed into a community that's friendly, smart, respectful, fun-loving, and tightly knit.

Format/study

Meg Kearney, director: Another feature unique to our program is that students are able to work in a different genre in their second semester, if they so choose. We've had a few students so far start off writing fiction or non-fiction for adults, for example, and then try writing for young adults in semester two. At the end of the second semester, the student makes a choice to remain in the new genre or to return to their original focus.

The different genres mix quite often and easily in the Solstice Program. While the workshops are separate groups, our craft, criticism, and theory classes and elective seminars and studies sessions see a mix of poets, fiction writers, non-fiction writers, and students who write for young people. And speaking of writing for young people — we're one of the few MFA programs to offer this concentration, but we don't separate those students from the rest of the group, as some programs do. We all have something to teach each other.

QUEENS UNIVERSITY OF CHARLOTTE
Fiction, Poetry, Creative Non-Fiction, Writing for Stage and Screen
Charlotte, NC
2 years, 5 residencies
www.queens.edu/graduate/programs/creative_writing.asp

The interviewees

Michael Kobre, director, teaches literature at Queens University of Charlotte. His critical writing and fiction have appeared in *TriQuarterly*, *Tin House*, *West Branch*, *Critique*, and other journals. He's the author of *Walker Percy's Voices*.

Daniel Mueller has been on the fiction faculty since 2005. His work has been published in journals such as *Story*, *Story Quarterly*, *Mississippi Review*, *CutBank*, and *Prairie Schooner*.

Jessie Carty, alumnus, has had poems and non-fiction published in *The Main Street Rag*, *Iodine Poetry Journal*, and *The Northville Review*. She is the author of two chapbooks and a full-length collection of poetry, *Paper House*.

Melanie Faith's poetry chapbook, *Bright, Burning Fuse*, was a finalist in the 2008 Keyhole Magazine Chapbook contest and was published by Etched Press. Her articles about creative writing have appeared most recently in *The Writer* and *Writers' Journal*. She is a graduate of the Queens University of Charlotte MFA program.

Clifford Garstang, alumnus, has published work in *The Tampa Review*, *Los Angeles Review*, *Cream City Review*, and elsewhere. He is the author of a short story collection, *In an Uncharted Country*.

The program

Michael Kobre, director: We believe the workshop model has some significant benefits. First, of course, by continuing to exchange submissions and comment on one another's work throughout the semester, our students deepen the friendships they form during residencies. The workshop model goes a long way to fostering the sense of community that all writers need.

Moreover, because our student–faculty ratio is so small, never exceeding four-to-one, Queens MFA students get the benefits of both a workshop model and the close attention of a faculty mentor ... We also differ from some other low-residency programs in that we don't devote an entire semester to an extended piece of critical writing.

Melanie Faith, alumnus: Queens is a beautiful campus and I found the students and professors to be inclusive and dedicated writers themselves, in all respects. Queens is truly a community of writers within the classroom as well as during distance learning and beyond into the post-graduation years.

Faculty/teaching philosophy

Clifford Garstang, alumnus: I had some terrific teachers. I will always remember working with Elizabeth Strout and her focus on writing true sentences without extraneous elements, which she calls "twigs." When I edit my own work, I think about her.

Michael Kobre, director: As any glance at the Queens faculty roster will clearly indicate, the breadth and depth of accomplishment of our faculty include bestselling books, among the highest honors in literature and publishing, and work that regularly appears in the very best magazines in the country. We've been very fortunate to attract a pretty stellar level of talent to Queens.

We also look for a range of esthetics and diverse backgrounds, so that we can be sure that every student over four semesters of coursework has an opportunity to work with different kinds of writers, including some who might be immediately sympathetic to the student's own esthetic approach and some who will challenge that approach.

Residency/community

Michael Kobre, director: One of the things I'm proudest of about the Queens MFA program is the extraordinary community we've fostered. In part, this is the deliberate result of specific curricular decisions, most notably our use of the workshop model, which requires continual and intense interaction between students. But the Queens MFA community also simply reflects the way our culture has developed informally.

This community is manifest in many ways. During residencies and in our distance learning workshops, of course, many strong friendships are established. But the community that takes physical form during the residencies continues online and after graduation too. Perhaps because the workshop system is so ingrained in them, many of our alumni go on to form their own critique groups after graduation.

Daniel Mueller, faculty: During the week-long residencies, students and faculty dine together, attend craft seminars and readings together, and socialize with one another in the evenings. Because the residency is as much a retreat for faculty as it is for students, both groups avail themselves to each other more freely than they do in more traditional programs where faculty reside in the city or town to which most graduate students have had to move. While I'm loathe to compare the week-long residency to a pleasure cruise, closeness between faculty and students is engendered by a mutual sense of adventure that extends into the months of online learning, when students are submitting their work to one another and their instructors and receiving written feedback.

Jessie Carty, alumnus: I didn't know what to expect when I started the low-residency program at Queens. I was frankly overwhelmed during the first residency but I was also in love with being in such a rich community of writers . . . The first four residencies are comprised of daily morning seminars, [for] which you have had course material to read prior to attending the residency. At Queens you take more classes in your genre but you will also take at least one seminar in each genre during each residency. After lunch there are often panel discussions on things such as publishing before the workshops take place. Besides the panels there were also graduating student seminars to attend.

Clifford Garstang, alumnus: The residencies were a blast, very much like the best writers' conferences. They always began with a kick-off reception on the day of arrival, which was part reunion and part orientation for new students, because new MFA candidates joined us each semester. The receptions were in an elegant room in one of the historic buildings on the Queens campus, setting an appropriately academic tone for the week.

The residencies focus on workshops, so there's actually a lot of work to be done — reading peer submissions and preparing critiques for discussion. During the course of the workshop, writers bond with the others in their group, which will be together for the whole semester, as well as the instructor. Because the groups are so small, the writers get to know the instructors very well, and that carries over to time outside the classroom and workshop. In addition to the workshops, each residency has a series of craft lectures, too, for which the extensive reading is assigned well in advance.

Melanie Faith, alumnus: Coming from a small, largely non-literary rural community, it was vital and encouraging to meet fellow writers who dedicated so much of their passion and devotion to the craft of writing. In general, I found that most students at residencies were enormously respectful of other students' work within the workshop setting.

Format/study

Jessie Carty, alumnus: The whole idea of a thesis was a bit overwhelming. I was working with very old revised material and new poems on what seemed to be such scattered topics. I wanted my thesis to be a cohesive book of poems. After my third residency I had the difficult decision of who to select as my thesis advisor. I had worked with so many good writers. Who to pick? Then I also had to select two readers. I chose two people I had not worked with as my readers.

I sent my thesis advisor about sixty poems in the first draft. She sent fantastic comments back and even agreed to review fifteen newer poems to see how they might merge into the thesis. Each advisor is different but I emailed and mailed my advisor copies of the thesis and I received my comments back in both formats . . . I was very pleased with the comments I received and a somewhat different version of that thesis is my first full-length collection, *Paper House*, published March 2010 by Folded Word.

Melanie Faith, alumnus: I loved the online workshops. Each month between residencies, students sent four or five poems for the other students in assigned groups to critique. We had been given a thorough and helpful seminar at the beginning of the program on critiquing someone else's work justly, and I found that most students followed these guidelines with good will and honestly wanted to point out both the weaknesses and strengths of a piece. Groups were composed of between three and five students, which I found to be a perfect number, as we could all get to know each other's talents and struggles as writers and could also ask the instructor individual questions and get personal attention from both professors and fellow poets.

Michael Kobre, director: All of our students are required to compose 300- to 500-word formal critiques on each submission they receive during the semester from their colleagues in their workshop. This core requirement of our curriculum insures that serious and substantive discussion takes place in the workshop, but it also fosters the self-critical skills that any writer needs too. If you work that hard to assess and articulate the strengths and weaknesses of someone else's manuscript, you'll also bring a sharper perspective to your own work.

SEATTLE PACIFIC UNIVERSITY
Fiction, Poetry, Creative Non-Fiction
Seattle, WA
2 years, 5 residencies
www.spu.edu/prospects/grad/academics/mfa

The interviewee
Gregory Wolfe, director, is the publisher and editor of *Image: A Journal of the Arts and Religion*. He is the author of *Intruding Upon the Timeless: Meditations on Art, Faith, and Mystery, Sacred Passion:*

The Art of William Schickel, and *Malcolm Muggeridge: A Biography*;
he is also editor of *The New Religious Humanists: A Reader*.

The program

Gregory Wolfe, director: Our acceptance rate hovers around
20–25 percent. The single most important part of an application
is the creative manuscript — it's what tells us where you are as a
writer — what understanding you have of the basic elements of
craft in your genre.

Faculty/teaching philosophy

Gregory Wolfe, director: SPU approached me because I am the
editor of *Image*, a journal that features contemporary writing and
art that grapple in some way with the Judeo-Christian tradition.
Then chair of the English department, Mark Walhout, suggested
to me that an MFA could share the same concerns as *Image* and
that the journal would provide instant credibility for the program.
The goal was not to produce pious or didactic literature — quite
the opposite. We believe that great writing must above all be
incarnate in flesh and blood — and that's a messy, ambiguous
place. But it is also a place beyond the autonomous self, which is
where so much contemporary literature is stranded.

Residency/community

Gregory Wolfe, director: When we started the SPU MFA
we pondered where to hold our residencies and it just naturally occurred to us to run one residency alongside *Image*'s Glen
Workshop program in Santa Fe. That way the MFA students
automatically get a dozen world-class visitors — from the great
illustrator Barry Moser to the band Over the Rhine to writers like
B. H. Fairchild, Marilyn Nelson, and Melissa Pritchard.

   The Milton Center is *Image*'s writing-specific program: it
brings a postgraduate fellow to campus for a year to work on a
first book and that fellow runs a workshop which MFA students
are automatically invited to join.

Format/study

Gregory Wolfe, director: An essential part of our program is
known as the Common Reading, which involves texts that everyone in the program reads together, regardless of genre. Recent

Common Reading texts have included Augustine's *Confessions*, Dante's *Inferno*, Erasmus's *The Praise of Folly*, Dostoevsky's *The Brothers Karamazov*, Simone Weil's *Waiting on God*, and the poetry of Denise Levertov. We study these works together in [the course] Art and Faith. Sometimes we will also step back and think about what I call literary esthetics — and here the essays of T. S. Eliot and Flannery O'Connor have been invaluable.

SETON HILL UNIVERSITY
Popular Fiction
Greensburg, PA
2 years, 4 residencies
www.setonhill.edu/academics/fiction

The interviewees
Albert Wendland is the director of Seton Hill's Writing Popular Fiction program. His publications include *The Man Who Loved Alien Landscapes* and *Science, Myth, and the Fictional Creation of Alien Worlds*.

Shelley Bates, alumnus, writes as Shelley Adina and has published *The Chic Shall Inherit the Earth* and *Tidings of Great Boys*. She is adjunct faculty at Seton Hill University.

Heidi Ruby Miller, alumnus, is the Educational Marketing Director for Frank Lloyd Wright's House on Kentuck Knob and adjunct creative writing faculty at Seton Hill University.

Jason Jack Miller, alumnus, instructs students about Earth and Space Science at the high school level and about creative writing at Seton Hill University.

Nicole Taft, alumnus, works as a freelance writer and is seeking a publisher for her novel.

Matt Duvall, student, has been published in a number of venues, including *The Palace of Reason*, *Dark Krypt*, and *Chizine*. He will graduate from the MFA program in 2011.

Natalie Duvall, student, met her husband [Matt Duvall] during the residencies at Seton Hill. She is a fiction author and is focusing on Regency historical romance. Natalie will graduate from the MFA program in 2011.

The program
Albert Wendland, director: We're different from other graduate writing programs because of our emphasis on popular or genre fiction. Much talk of genre in the teaching of writing refers to poetry, plays, fiction, non-fiction. But we emphasize market or publishers' genres — mystery, romance, science fiction, fantasy, horror, children's lit, young adult. This is the fiction that most of us read for pleasure, and what many of us really want to write.

Faculty/teaching philosophy
Albert Wendland, director: We believe that popular fiction, like all forms of mainstream fiction, can be either "bad" or "good." We encourage and ask of our students the best in genre writing, the writing that provides reader expectations but that does not repeat worn clichés, that is innovative and thus interesting and not just repetitive of genre habits, that still provides a high standard of all the needs of fiction writing — character, plot, theme, style, setting. We want our students to provide the needs of their genre and what's expected of its readers, but to do this always in new and provocative ways, and at the same time to write strong and worthwhile stories that satisfy all the standards of fiction.

Heidi Ruby Miller, alumnus: I was fortunate to have two wonderful mentors who helped me with different aspects of my writing, horror guru and multiple Bram Stoker Award-winning author Thomas F. Monteleone — just Tom when he's filling the margins of your manuscript with brutal honesty — and *New York Times* bestselling science fiction author Tobias S. Buckell.

Tom taught me how to construct a story. I'm not talking about the grammar and mechanics, but how to keep tension high, avoid redundancies, and trust your reader. Toby helped me with the rewriting and polishing of my thesis novel, which was dark science fiction. His first book had just been released so I also used him for all of his recently acquired wisdom about how to break into the business, then how to deal with everything once you're there.

Nicole Taft, alumnus: Faculty members are always willing to chat with students and I had a really positive experience with my two personal mentors while writing my thesis. Their feedback on my work was invaluable, helping me to become a much better writer than I was a mere two years ago. They bring their experience into the program, which is great for beginning writers looking to improve.

Matt Duvall, student: The mentors at Seton Hill are, for the most part, well-published writers in their specific genre of popular fiction. During my time, I worked with award-winning science fiction author Nalo Hopkinson and award-winning horror author Gary Braunbeck. There is no way to measure the value of advice from an actual working writer, and I found both mentors to be supportive and insightful.

Residency/community

Albert Wendland, director: The extent of mutual support and interaction is most rewarding and useful — we expected some of this when we designed the program but not to the extent it actually developed. Our alumni are the most in touch of any graduate program on campus, and they regularly get together and have writing retreats of their own. The thesis readings are memorable for their inspiration and skill, and the guest speakers — which we have each residency — share their own experiential learning and excite students with their creative suggestions. Workshops are conducted in both mixed and genre-specific groups. We encourage critiquing in both other genres and more intensively in one's own genre.

Jason Jack Miller, alumnus: Some of the people I met at Seton Hill are some of the best I know. To go through a program with people who share a common interest creates a rare bond. When somebody knows you through your writing and sees how you've grown as a writer, they have an understanding of you that family and non-writing friends don't. Many times after a residency I would dread the return to the real world because on the outside, people just didn't get it.

Nicole Taft, alumnus: The residencies were a blast. Everyone there is ready to have a good time and learn new things to make their writing better. You quickly make friends — even if you're somewhat reserved like me. Everyone has so much in common, you feel at ease surprisingly fast. Everyone writes popular fiction, so if you've never been around other people who write in those genres before, suddenly you realize you aren't the odd duck out anymore.

Natalie Duvall, student: Residencies are amazing blurs of action, writing, reading, and sleeplessness! The intellectual stimulation of one week keeps me going for a year. Critique sessions, craft workshops, lectures from famous authors, pitch sessions — each piece is like eating a creamy milk chocolate bar that doesn't have any calories. The week is so exciting and enjoyable that it's only the day you get home that you realize how much is packed into it.

Networking at Seton Hill is by far the best thing that happened to me. It was during a pitch session at an MA alumni retreat that I met my current agent. Though he rejected what I pitched at the time, it opened the door for our current relationship.

Format/study

Albert Wendland, director: Every other year we have a panel of practicing editors and agents give presentations and pitch sessions for our students. All students are required to take modules on "The Business of Writing" and "Current Markets and Recent Trends" in their own genre. Graduating students get a special session on the writing career. All of our mentors, who oversee the student novels, are encouraged to get that manuscript to as close as market-ready as possible — to make sure that it does have market appeal. Students can elect to take modules in such practical subjects as "Marketing Your Work," "Online Presence," "Successful Book Tours," "Finding an Agent," "Crossing Genres," and "Webpages for Writers." We also stress, for further practical reasons, experiencing the teaching of popular fiction and various non-fiction markets in writing about popular fiction.

Heidi Ruby Miller, alumnus: One of the most important things I learned at Seton Hill is that writing doesn't have to be a lonely pursuit. Having a support group that continued even after I received my degree keeps me motivated and excited about writing and publishing. The idea that there is strength in numbers is especially true when you're trying to promote a book!

Shelley Bates, alumnus: When I entered the Writing Popular Fiction program in 2000, I was published in short fiction with a small press, and had five rejected full-length novel manuscripts under my bed. Through the modules, critique process, and working with an experienced mentor, my skills improved to the point that, eight months after graduation in 2002, I sold my romance thesis to Harlequin. It subsequently became a double finalist for the National Readers' Choice Award . . . Needless to say, the Seton Hill MFA program prepares its students well for the realities of the publishing industry.

SEWANEE: THE UNIVERSITY OF THE SOUTH
Sewanee School of Letters
Fiction, Poetry, Creative Non-Fiction
Sewanee, TN
5 years, 4 residencies
www.sewanee.edu/SL/SLHome.htm

The interviewee
John Grammer, director, teaches English at Sewanee: The University of the South. His essays and reviews have appeared in *American Literary History*, *The Southern Literary Journal*, and other journals.

The program
John Grammer, director: Sewanee has a long-standing reputation as a place for writers and literature, dating back to the founding in 1892 of *The Sewanee Review*, the oldest continuously published literary quarterly in the country. More recently, it has been the home of the Sewanee Writers' Conference, which — thanks to a large monetary bequest from Tennessee Williams — quickly established itself as one of the top summer writers' conferences.

I should add that Sewanee's program is not a typical low-residency program but thinks of itself as an alternative to those programs *and* to traditional residential programs. Our students are "in residence" for six solid weeks each summer, for four summers, during each of which they take a workshop and a literature class. Outside the six-week sessions, our students have no formal obligations to the program: no exchanging packets with faculty by mail. Only thesis work, undertaken after four residential summers, can be done by correspondence.

The other principal difference between our MFA program and others is that it shares space each summer with an MA program in English and American literature, and our MFA students take literature classes taught by a very good graduate literature faculty, as well as workshops taught by accomplished writers. In this respect it is more like a traditional program housed in a university English department.

Faculty/teaching philosophy

John Grammer, director: I'm most interested in faculty who love teaching and are good at it. We've been lucky to engage faculty with distinguished records of publication, but their bibliographies aren't running the workshops. I also look for nice people whom I will enjoy being around for six weeks each summer.

Residency/Community

John Grammer, director: Between the workshop and the literature class most students take each summer, students spend several hours a day in class and many, many hours writing and reading outside of class. Yet spirits are high, naturally enough since most of our students are giving themselves the experience as a gift and a kind of vacation from lives that normally revolve around other things than literature.

Format/study

John Grammer, director: The Sewanee program, by largely eliminating the correspondence element, assures that almost all teaching is done face to face. On the other hand it demands a significantly greater residential commitment from its students. It works well for people who can find six weeks in the summer to attend, but would no doubt be impossible for others.

SOUTHERN NEW HAMPSHIRE UNIVERSITY
Fiction, Non-Fiction
Manchester, NH
2 years, 4 residencies
www.snhu.edu/5749.asp

The interviewee

Robert Begiebing, director, teaches fiction and non-fiction. He has written twenty critical and freelance articles, two books on contemporary novelists, a critical anthology of nature writing and a trilogy of historical novels set in New England. His novel *Rebecca Wentworth's Distraction* won the 2003 Langum Prize for historical fiction.

The program

Robert Begiebing, director: I became director when the university started pursuing — in collaboration with the NH Writers' Project — a low-res MFA. The VPAA and the President — a former Houghton Mifflin VP — asked me to direct the program.

My students tell me the low-residency model is perfect for working adults who don't really want a campus experience anymore anyway. They can meet monthly deadlines by working around their own employment and family schedules.

Faculty/teaching philosophy

Robert Begiebing, director: I've been fortunate in that all of the faculty I originally hired five and four years ago are still with us and teaching every semester. I looked for that kind of commitment and that kind of delight in our program. I also told each faculty member walking in the door: "No high maintenance people, please, no prima donnas; check your egos at the door with mine." We are a very non-hierarchical program.

Residency/community

Robert Begiebing, director: Our residencies are no doubt quite typical: faculty craft workshops, peer manuscript workshops, visiting writers' master classes and readings, faculty readings, student open mics and graduate readings, and a day spent with our advisory board — agents and editors — where students take board workshops, eat lunch with the board, and have small group and one-one-on sessions to discuss their work. We are a very social group and there are all kinds of informal gatherings and convivial events.

Format/study

Robert Begiebing, director: We offer internships with the NH Writers' Project on campus and with the university literary magazine, *Amoskeag*, and we're a purposefully small program — around thirty to thirty-five students at any one time with six faculty. I take on two to three students myself. But no one ever has more than five students, so it's a good faculty to student ratio. Due to our size the writing community is the tightest and most bonded and most friendly I've ever seen. All our visiting writers comment on that. We are also highly focused on fiction and non-fiction — narrative prose — and have an environmental writing track. Finishing our degree, the student has a full book manuscript in hand.

UNIVERSITY OF SOUTHERN MAINE

Stonecoast
Poetry, Creative Non-Fiction, Fiction, Popular Fiction, Cross-Genre
Portland, ME
2 years, 5 residencies
www.usm.maine.edu/stonecoastmfa

The interviewees

Annie Finch, director, is the author of four books of poetry, including *Calendars* and *Eve*. Her books on poetics include *The Ghost of Meter* and a collaboration of essays, *The Body of Poetry: Essays on Women, Form, and the Poetic Self.*

Patricia Smith is the author of five books of poetry, including *Blood Dazzler*, chronicling the tragedy of Hurricane Katrina, and *Teahouse of the Almighty*, a National Poetry Series selection. Her work has appeared in *Poetry*, *The Paris Review*, *TriQuarterly*, and many other journals, and has been performed around the world. Patricia is an instructor — and graduate — of the Stonecoast program.

Carol Berg, alumnus, has poems forthcoming or in *Fifth Wednesday Journal*, *Pebble Lake Review*, *Rhino*, *Sweet*, *Tattoo Highway*, and elsewhere. She works as a writing tutor at Pine Manor College in Massachusetts.

The program

Annie Finch, director: Many things make Stonecoast special. To name just a few: our popular Stonecoast in Ireland program; our philosophy of academic flexibility and rigor, evident in student-initiated elective workshops on topics from Writing About Race to the Graphic Novel, a wide range of third-semester project options, and a thoughtfully organized mentor selection process; our Rhythms of Poetry foundational course for entering poets; our Writing Nature focus; our openness to cross-genre work; our concentration options in scriptwriting, translation, and performance; our Popular Fiction track, with the fascinating conversations across genres that that engenders; our attention to building a truly diverse community characterized by risk-taking and shared respect; and what must be one of the coolest graduation dances in any creative writing program, DJ'ed each residency by a multiple-time National Poetry Slam winner Patricia Smith.

Faculty/teaching philosophy

Annie Finch, director: In the Stonecoast MFA faculty, I look for a diverse gathering of truly rare individuals: talented, skillful, productive, and well-recognized writers who are also generous, patient, imaginative, erudite, challenging, and non-egocentric teachers and stimulating, open-minded, energetic, inspiring members of the Stonecoast creative community. Yes, that's a lot of adjectives — and every one of them is true.

Patricia Smith, faculty/alumnus: I choose to be a Stonecoast instructor for entirely selfish reasons — I wanted to keep learning. While I admit that I bring certain strengths to the table, the environment at Stonecoast is one that satisfied a continuing curiosity about my passion. The revelations never stop. Also, I love working closely with students who are on the verge of becoming spectacular; it's a thrill to see that light come on behind their eyes, to know that they're falling in love with what they do.

Carol Berg, alumnus: The thesis portion of my program was intense. My mentor at that time liked to communicate via the phone and we would go over my poems in depth. Most often my mentor would suggest writing more and where I might write more, which was eye-opening to me and taught me a great deal about the element of revising. My mentor was never prescriptive, but rather listened to my poems carefully and seriously, which in turn taught me how to open up a poem and explore it further. The phone conversations could last an hour at least. But I was always buzzing after them. I felt on fire.

Residency/community

Annie Finch, director: Stonecoast residencies are a lively yet meditative experience in a stunning natural environment, designed to provide valuable and substantial new ideas to absorb into your writing during the following semester. Think of the most creatively stimulating literary conference you've ever attended, combined with a festive reunion of dear friends old and new. Workshops in the morning, classes in the afternoon, readings from faculty, visitors, and students at night. Then there's a wonderful talent show called Stonecoast Follies, plenty of student open mics, and that rocking graduation dance.

Patricia Smith, faculty/alumnus: The words I've often used when describing the Stonecoast residences are "amusement park." Not that there's unleashed revelry, daring rides and corn dogs, but because it's a sensory explosion, so much going on, so many choices, and almost all of them are good. For someone like me, who got introduced to poetry by getting up on stage and doing it, the residencies offer an unparalleled opportunity to catch up on what I missed: seminars on Robert Creeley, a celebration of the villanelle, deciding once and for all why I am definitely not enamored of Emily Dickinson. I couldn't indulge myself so much in any other place. And it's definitely broadened my social circle, especially since I've found friends and creative colleagues among both students and faculty.

Once the residency is over, I relish the intense one-on-one time with my mentorees over the semester. It's this close, challenging work that makes being a faculty member rewarding.

Carol Berg, alumnus: The residencies were incredibly special. Driving the twisty back roads of Maine, it felt like I was driving into another world, another nation, where I would be able to talk in my favorite language to the people of my favorite country about what we were most passionate about. And I knew that everyone else felt that way.

Format/study

Annie Finch, director: One of the most gratifying parts of directing Stonecoast is to see how often the program really does change people's lives. Every one of our students seems to me to be a success story, from the one who sold two novels in her last semester at Stonecoast, to the one teaching memoir writing to women recently emigrated from Somalia, to the one who collaborated on a multimedia show involving poetry, film, and music, to the one accepted into a prestigious PhD program to apply feminist theory to medieval literature. Among the particular success stories we're most proud of are those of two alums who are now teaching for us, National Book Award finalist Patricia Smith, and novelist and non-fiction writer Jaed Muncharoen Coffin.

Patricia Smith, faculty/alumnus: Since I was already mid-career and had published several books, I hoped that the schools would want a working writer aligned with their program . . . Stonecoast was the only program that felt flexible enough for an established author who still had a lot to learn.

Carol Berg, alumnus: The fourth semester was fine-tuning the poems for my thesis . . . and perhaps this is one of the hidden jewels of a low-residency program. I had to take a major role in my studies. This was surely practice for after I graduated. I chose which poets to read — although my mentor would make suggestions, it was I who decided. This was determined at the beginning and throughout the semester. I chose what poems I would revise and which I would discard, another key element for a writer to learn.

SPALDING UNIVERSITY

Fiction, Poetry, Creative Non-Fiction, Playwriting, Screenwriting, Writing for Children and Young Adults
Louisville, KY
2 years, 5 residencies
www.spalding.edu/academics/mfa

The interviewees

Sena Jeter Naslund, director, is the author of *Ahab's Wife*, *Four Spirits*, *Abundance: A Novel of Marie Antoinette*, and *Adam & Eve*.

She has taught more than thirty years in traditional and low-residency graduate programs.

Kathleen Driskell, associate program director, is the associate editor of *The Louisville Review*. Her books include *Seed Across Snow* and *Laughing Sickness*. Kathleen served as the first Chair of the Low-Residency MFA Directors' Caucus, which now meets annually at the AWP conference.

Richard Goodman is the author of *French Dirt: The Story of a Garden in the South of France* and *The Soul of Creative Writing*. He has written for many national publications, including the *New York Times*, *Harvard Review*, and *Vanity Fair*. He teaches creative non-fiction at Spalding.

Molly Peacock, faculty, has authored six poetry books, including *The Second Blush*, and several prose titles including the memoir, *Paradise: Piece by Piece*. Her latest is a biography, *The Paper Garden: Mrs. Delany Begins Her Life's Work at 72*. Molly is one of the creators of Poetry in Motion on the nation's subways and buses; she is also the general editor of *The Best Canadian Poetry in English* series.

Diana M. Raab, alumnus, is the author of several poetry and non-fiction books, including *The Guilt Gene*, *My Muse Undresses Me*, and *Healing With Words*.

Brian Russell graduated from the Spalding MFA program in May 2010, where he served as a student editor of *The Louisville Review*. His book, *Meeting Dad*, was published in 2010.

Katerina Stoykova-Klemer, alumnus, is the author of a bilingual poetry book, *The Air around the Butterfly*, and an English language chapbook, *The Most*. She is the founding editor of Accents Publishing.

Christopher Klim is the author of six books, including the novel *The Winners Circle*. He serves as the chairman of the Eric Hoffer Award for Books and Prose, is the Executive Editor of the annual anthology, *Best New Writing*, and is a journalism professor at the College of New Jersey. He was a student at the time of interview.

The program

Sena Jeter Naslund, director: We encourage our students to live their lives as writers and the Spalding MFA program provides an ideal model for the writing life. This is a non-competitive atmosphere; we all know we have to work hard to get ideas. Our low-residency program provides greater quantity and quality of feedback with established, published authors. We have a large faculty with a low student to faculty ratio.

Christopher Klim, student: The Spalding program is a special place that both nurtures and disciplines writers — not in an inhibiting way, but in a way that prepares you for the writing life while elevating your prose and craft ... The editorial feedback that I received from my semester mentors has been phenomenal; it has changed my writing.

Cross-genre study is important for the program director. Each semester residency concentrates in part on one of the disciplines. You can spend an entire semester in a different discipline. There are workshops open in other genres. Last semester I turned one of my short stories into a script, which was filmed and shown to the students. I participated in every aspect of the project from acting to filming and editing and production.

Faculty/teaching philosophy

Sena Jeter Naslund, director: We ask two things of our faculty: to be emotionally supportive and offer intellectual stimulation. The faculty members choose the method of communication with their students. Some make phone calls, while many provide digital recordings of their feedback; this is beneficial for conveying the tone of voice in each response to the student.

Kathleen Driskell, associate director: We encourage our students to become comfortable with public readings. Each student has to do a graduate reading and our faculty enjoys attending this event. In each residency, too, we host several readings. Students sign up for a scheduled time and we usually have between forty to fifty readings at each residency.

Also, our faculty are very happy to work with students on novels, rather than just short stories. Our fiction instructors provide suggestions for ways to improve both the manuscript overall and the finer details, and this is of great value to our students. We have had students from other programs transfer to Spalding for this very reason.

Molly Peacock, faculty: What attracted me to Spalding is the atmosphere established by Sena Jeter Nasland and Karen Mann, and now supported by Kathleen Driskell, Katy Yocum, and Gayle Hanratty. The creative life and the imagination are paramount at Spalding. It is a program with high standards and no competition. "The competition is in the library," Sena is fond of saying. It values cross-genre work, and as a poet and non-fiction writer I, too, value writing in more than one genre. Most of all, I cherish the fact that I am treated so well as a faculty member. I'm listened to, and my own creative life is recognized. The program lets me play to my strengths as a writer and a mentor, just as it lets students play to their strengths.

Richard Goodman, faculty: I work generally with five students. They send me a series of packets with their work, five in total, throughout the semester. I'll email them if I have questions and vice versa. We talk on the phone once, sometimes twice.

Diana M. Raab, alumnus: There was a poignant moment [for me]. It was my third semester and I was struggling with my memoir's structure. I had been back and forth on various ideas, but none felt right. The mentor who I was working with at the time suggested we go to lunch. We brainstormed for another structure and suddenly we both had an epiphany which not only brought tears to both of our eyes, but lead to the book's final published structure. The solution was just so logical and that was a moment I will never forget.

Brian Russell, alumnus: A student at Spalding has a good deal to do with designing the study plan in cooperation with one's assigned mentor. We create a semester study plan for the mentor to review and approve. In terms of selecting mentors, we have an opportunity to meet available mentors, to ask them pertinent questions, and then we submit a "Mentor Preference Form" to the MFA office and the office assigns us a mentor . . . I've been very pleased with the level of communication with my mentors.

Residency/community

Sena Jeter Naslund, director: The main goal during residency is to improve their own personal writing and to develop an awareness of others' writing. As such, we offer craft lectures and plenary lectures applicable to all genres. We also bring in editors and publishers during the residencies and place an emphasis on publishing. Our students have had well over one hundred books published, including a few *New York Times* bestsellers. Our students do very well. We're trying to improve literary standards through publishing education.

Kathleen Driskell, associate director: Our residencies include workshops, lectures, panel discussions, readings, and a number of featured guests. Everyone socializes with one another and we eat very well! We offer an orientation for our first year students and we usually reunite alumni and faculty during a dinner.

We have students who work together to organize readings and we have incredibly active alumni. Now, every spring residency there is an alumni homecoming and we feature recently published works by our graduates during a public reading.

Brian Russell, alumnus: Residencies are very busy, chock-full of lectures and workshops and other extra-curricular events. Residency is both exhilarating and exhausting. One of the greatest aspects of residency is interacting with a large community of writers. Writing is such a solitary endeavor that to spend time with a number of other writers for ten straight days is a wonderful gift. Many of us at Spalding stay in touch with each other regularly during the at-home time to provide each other with support and an empathetic ear.

Richard Goodman, faculty: They're exciting, intense, and very inspiring. I once told Karen Mann, one of the founders of the program, that it was like being in a foreign country where everyone speaks the same language. It's the only situation I know of where you can walk up to absolutely anyone for those two weeks and say, for example, "What do you think of semicolons?" We have a two-and-a-half hour workshop every morning. It's normally led by two writers in the fall and just one in the spring when the workshops are smaller. That's the heart of the residency.

During the residency, every teacher has to give a reading and a lecture. I love to hear the other teachers read and lecture, especially outside of my genre. There are some wonderful poets and novelists, for example, that I can't wait to hear. But I also love to hear the students read. The graduation readings are very moving. Their families are there, babies and parents and grandparents. It's more than just a piece of paper.

Format/study

Sena Jeter Naslund, director: We offer a nine-month semester for students who need to pace their course load. It is equal to the six-month semester, but provides 50 percent more time to complete the same work. This has been especially beneficial for working adults, like teachers. Students have the choice to attend the spring Louisville residency or the summer international residency and, in addition, can take up to ten years to complete the MFA.

Kathleen Driskell, associate director: Students have several options for the residencies, one of which may include the summer international residencies. We polled our students and found there was general appeal for including this option. We are pleased to be moving toward more global awareness in writing. The international residencies provide for the student an introduction to a city and oftentimes many students go back to visit on their own.

Molly Peacock, faculty: Four semesters of a brief-residency program can prepare a student for the exigencies of creative life. If a student can internalize the deadlines and use them, and if a student can internalize the positive voices of reinforcement from mentors, then the inner structure that a writer must maintain — I'd call it the writer's poise — can be achieved. If the student relies on the program to structure the writing life without internalizing it, then the student suffers a terrible bump after it stops. How to go on? Everyone needs writing friends.

I have a friend from graduate school, the poet Phillis Levin, with whom I have shared nearly every poem I have written in the past thirty years. Phillis has done the same with me. I know this is an unusual friendship, but it began by our professor, Cynthia Macdonald, saying that no one produces art as exciting as those one considers one's peers. The Spalding postgraduate community is a very strong one, and staying in touch, simply reporting in, enlivens those inner deadlines and keeps the exchange about what matters, the imagination, going. Careers matter, of course, but the imagination means the world and, for artists, *is* the world.

Diana M. Raab, alumnus: We were each responsible for making our study plans which were then approved by our chosen mentor. Many people enrolled in the program with manuscripts which they had been working on for years. It was the perfect milieu to cultivate them into publishable work.

Katerina Stoykova-Klemer, alumnus: The Spalding program has improved my writing, and since I started there, I began having works published in journals. By the time I graduated, I had a full-length bilingual poetry book published by an international publisher, and an English-only chapbook scheduled for publication the following year.

Also, I have established a network of friends — writers, with whom I intend to keep in touch in the future. It is always important for writers to be plugged into the community. I have developed about ten very close friendships with authors for whom I feel confident that we will be significant in each other's lives. I feel that I have a professional relationship with virtually all of the other students that I have met throughout the program.

UNIVERSITY OF TEXAS AT EL PASO
Poetry, Fiction, Playwriting, Screenwriting, Essay, Translation
El Paso, TX
3 years, 0 residencies
www.academics.utep.edu/Default.aspx?tabid=42392

The interviewee
Lex Williford, director, holds an MFA from the University of Arkansas. His book, *Macauley's Thumb*, was co-winner of the 1993 Iowa School of Letters Award for Short Fiction.

The program

Lex Williford, director: [UTEP is] the first bilingual [English and Spanish] program in the US. We've taken tremendous risks over the last few years moving toward a more bilingual international program, but those risks have paid off in the sense that our mission has drawn students who might not have otherwise had a chance to workshop their creative work, students with remarkable talent and drive.

Faculty/teaching philosophy

Lex Williford, director: I've been surprised how much I enjoy teaching online. I'm a teacher who loves the face-to-face spontaneity of live workshops, and I was afraid I would lose all that when I began teaching online. Ultimately, I didn't. In fact, sometimes my online workshops can be more fun, more productive, and professional than face-to-face workshops. Everyone has a bit more time to think about their responses, so those responses are often more articulate and clear.

Our instruction runs both wide and deep, and our students leave this program with a real-world equivalent of the knowledge they might have from the best on-campus MFA programs in the US. That will continue to be our goal.

Residency/community

Lex Williford, director: We now have many students from all over the US and the world, one in China, for example. Ours is becoming a truly international program, and our goal of transcending boundaries both geographical and otherwise has largely succeeded.

Format/study

Lex Williford, director: Technically, students do not have to be bilingual, but we do encourage some effort towards bilingualism. Our online MFA seems to be a bit less "bilingual" than our on-campus program, but that may change over time. For students who aren't bilingual, we have monolingual courses, but most of our courses fall under the beginning and intermediate bilingual designations. Students have a choice of different levels of monolingual or bilingualism.

VERMONT COLLEGE OF FINE ARTS
Poetry, Fiction, Creative Non-Fiction, Literary Translation
Writing for Children & Young Adults
Montpelier, VT
2 years, 5 residencies
www.vermontcollege.edu

The interviewees

Louise Crowley, director, has worked with the VCFA low-residency MFA in Writing for twenty-eight years.

Melissa Fisher is the director of the MFA in Writing for Children & Young Adults program at Vermont College of Fine Arts.

Sue William Silverman has been on the prose faculty at Vermont College of Fine Arts since 2003. Her book on craft is *Fearless Confessions: A Writer's Guide to Memoir*.

Audrey Friedman, alumnus, has been published in journals such as *Comstock Review*, *Newport Review*, *California Quarterly*, and *The Griffin*. She is the author of *Gallery of the Surreal*, a chapbook.

Malcolm Campbell graduated in 2008. He is the author of two travel guidebooks and is at work on his first novel.

Jeanie Chung's stories have appeared in *Timber Creek Review*, *Madison Review*, and others. Prior to writing fiction, she was a journalist for twelve years; she graduated in 2005.

Claire Guyton, alumnus, is a freelance writer and editor. She's working on three short story collections and interns for *Hunger Mountain*.

Michael Hemery, alumnus, has published essays with *Lumina*, *New Plains Review*, *Passages North*, *The Portland Review*, *Post Road Magazine*, and the book *Fearless Confessions: A Writer's Guide to Memoir*.

Carolyn Walker entered the program at age fifty-two, after twenty-five years working in journalism. She graduated from the creative non-fiction program in 2004. Her work has appeared in *Crazyhorse* and *The Southern Review*.

Rich Farrell, student, expects to graduate in 2011. Prior to starting at VCFA, he taught high school for eight years in San Diego, California.

The program

Louise Crowley, director: We believe in a program that is both highly rigorous and focused as well as one that is consistently friendly and supportive; those two viewpoints don't necessarily blend together well in a lot of places but it's what we have always fostered here at VCFA. And, what, perhaps, also makes us unique is such a long-standing history that brings a quality and stability to our students that is recognized by them at once. We were one of the very first low-residency programs in the country, established in 1981. We were the first program in the country to offer a fully developed program focused entirely on an MFA in Writing for Children & Young Adults (in 1997). And, we believe in offering our students a wide variety of experiences — such as dual-genre study, translation, postgraduate semesters — but without diluting the rigor and focus that should accompany a top-tier MFA in Writing program.

Melissa Fisher, WC&YA director: The Writing for Children & Young Adults program provides a rare forum for intensive and serious discussions on the craft of children's literature, and yet at the same time fosters the creative aspects as well in a highly supportive environment. We continually explore the needs and interests of the students, and provide new initiatives such as the Picture Book Certificate semester and the Cross-Discipline semester for writers who wish to student in poetry, fiction, or non-fiction for adults. Students are encouraged to take risks in their writing but also do this in a rigorous context. Since the faculty work with an average of five students per term, the one-on-one attention from each advisor offers direct and personal response and insight to the student's writing, and the independent study demands work habits that set the groundwork for successful and disciplined writing habits after graduation.

Michael Hemery, alumnus: Since graduating from the MFA program, I have published nine short stories in various books and literary magazines. I've also been chosen as the non-fiction editor of *Hunger Mountain*. Success is typical of a VCFA graduate ... The MFA not only made me a better writer, but opened up networking opportunities that otherwise would not have been available. I am currently submitting my collection of stories to agents and publishers and working on my second body of work.

Faculty/teaching philosophy

Sue William Silverman, faculty: I hope to offer students a nurturing learning environment — but one that is also rigorous, that fully respects a student's craft and her or his decision to be a writer. In other words, I think it's possible to be both encouraging and rigorous. I take their work very seriously, take their commitment to art seriously, while, at the same time, offering them a safe place to share their words. I think students learn from what they do well, as well as by better understanding the areas of craft that still need more of a focus. So as much as I praise and encourage, I also challenge and push until any given piece reaches its full potential *and* until any given student reaches his or her own full potential as well.

What I don't expect is for a student to write like me! Rather, it's important for me, as a teacher, to listen ... to listen to each student and help her or him "hear" their own voice.

Melissa Fisher, WC&YA director: We strive to bring a variety of voices from the field of children's literature and look for published authors with teaching experience who want to become part of a community of writers. The faculty work collaboratively with the students in a non-hierarchical manner, so we look for faculty who wish to fully participate in the writing process. Our faculty uphold a balance of continual encouragement and tall expectations; they know that it's important to both nurture the students as well as set high goals and demands in order for the students to get the most out of their time here.

Rich Farrell, student: I worked with Jess Row first semester. He helped me turn the focus of my writing inward, and really forced me to understand the intentionality of what I was doing. Second semester, I worked with Ellen Lesser. She meticulously worked with my stories and really forced me to go deeper and work harder, but also helped me believe in what I was doing.

Audrey Friedman, alumnus: Each semester our advisors worked with us to develop goals, to create a reading plan, to discuss student interests. They also read some of our recent work to customize the semester's work to our own strengths, weaknesses, and preferences. The student always had input.

Claire Guyton, alumnus: Each of my mentors was very different from the others and not always what I anticipated, but exactly what I needed at each stage of my development.

Jeanie Chung, alumnus: My four advisors were all very different, but I got a lot from each one of them: Doug Glover, my first-semester advisor, once wrote me a twenty-eight page packet letter . . . That shows how committed he is to his students — and, perhaps, how much I had to learn. He is all about structure in fiction; Xu Xi is probably more willing to be flexible in terms of letting the student have more input. She also has read everything — not just contemporary American litfic — and is wonderful for reading suggestions. As a writer of color, I'd say working with her was helpful from a lot of standpoints; I worked with Ellen Lesser primarily because I did an author interview for my critical thesis and I knew she had done one too. That said, I found her to be a very intuitive reader and often better able to know what I was trying to do than I did; Abby Frucht is similarly intense as Doug, but on a more micro level. She will look at every word you write and make you think about whether it's the right one.

Malcolm Campbell, alumnus: Each mentor gave important insight into my work. Without attempting to mold my voice, my mentors individualized their guidance to point me to further influences from which I could learn. On a practical level, my last advisor, Sue William Silverman, convinced me to begin my novel versus spend another semester working on short stories. That's what I'm doing now, with a great deal of joy and also confidence for its future in the publishing world.

Carolyn Walker, alumnus: I had wonderful faculty from the beginning to the end of my studies. Erin McGraw, my first instructor, opened my writing up in ways I couldn't have imagined before going to Vermont. I went from a newspaper columnist confined to a box size, to a writer of books! She showed me how to expand and deepen my writing. Laurie Alberts nominated me to represent VC in a student writing competition sponsored by *The Writer's Chronicle*, and she gave me a referral to her agent.

Residency/community

Rich Farrell, student: The residencies are a very open, very relaxed time but packed full of readings, lectures, and workshops. They become a time to build social connections with other students and to engage more deeply with the faculty. Most of the lectures are top-notch. Students are able to attend CNF, Fiction and Poetry lectures without regard for a particular area of study. My three workshop experiences have been outstanding. Not only is the level of student participation supportive and worthwhile, but the faculty uses the time to talk about broader issues of craft.

The community is very supportive, nurturing, and extensive. Many grads I met at residency stay in touch. It seems like each month another story or novel is being published by a VCFA graduate, and now some of those people are my friends.

Michael Hemery, alumnus: The atmosphere of the residencies is a perfect balance of arduous work and opportunities for connecting with fellow writers. The students in the program are some of the most intelligent and kindest people I've ever encountered. Conversations could fluctuate from intense debates on Sartre to boisterous laughter about the nonsensical. I've met some of my best friends through this program — people who are still reading my work, and people I respect beyond words.

Audrey Friedman, alumnus: I loved that you shared the campus with your advisors, which meant getting to know them outside of a formal classroom setting. This is so beneficial, for in sharing writing we open ourselves to others, and trust in this relationship is a big factor. There was time for this to happen . . . The relationships built with other students were as important to me as building relationships with my teachers. I was exposed to people of many cultures, people with different esthetics.

Malcolm Campbell, alumnus: After the initial nervousness of meeting your classmates, the faculty, and learning your way around campus, the schedule picked up quickly into a non-stop carnival of dozens of intellectual rides from which to choose. I was unprepared for how thought-provoking and varied the lectures would be: everything ranging from close examinations of specific craft elements of the masters to practical how-to advice regarding finding agents, handling the long periods of solitude, and the necessity of building a community of writer friends to carry you beyond the short, two-year experience.

Carolyn Walker, alumnus: The residencies were the highlights of my life for two years. They were hosted on the grounds of Vermont College, along with an international residency held in Slovenia. During that time, I had my writing critiqued in workshop settings, gave readings, listened to lectures, guests, and panels regarding the art of writing, and made fabulous new friends. I wouldn't trade the exhilaration of the residency for anything. I felt stimulated and renewed each time.

Format/study

Audrey Friedman, alumnus: I worked with Clare Rossini during my thesis semester. She allowed me to follow my own interests, but was there to suggest how to fine-tune my project. I could not have asked for a better reader of my work, both the thesis and the poetry. This was one of my best semesters in the program. I learned much from the process of writing the thesis that transferred into my own creative processes and improved my work.

Melissa Fisher, WC&YA director: Alumni return to campus each summer as part of the Alumni Mini-Residency, which overlaps with the second weekend of the MFA program's event, giving them an opportunity to meet with students and faculty and some MFA events as well as participate in master classes and meet with editors and agents. We've recently added YA [young adult] literature to the offerings for the Postgraduate Writers' Conference. And we're facilitating more regional events around the country for those who aren't able to make it back to Vermont. I think that especially in this field of writing, this program invites a deep level of discussion about writing for young readers that continues to draw students and alumni back to the campus and to each other.

Claire Guyton, alumnus: VCFA's MFA program is a studio program that promises intensive help with writing, not with publishing. Having said that, every semester there was a panel discussion or an informal talk devoted to some aspect of publishing, and I found each of these helpful given that I am new to writing and knew absolutely nothing about publishing when I started the program. In my final residency a former editor of a prestigious literary magazine gave an excellent talk on how to handle submissions. His advice has been extremely helpful.

Carolyn Walker, alumnus: I participated in the Slovenia residency as a postgraduate. This was a fabulous experience. A different, special kind of camaraderie was formed among students and faculty in this smaller setting — something intimate and wonderful. We sampled everything new: food, friendship, study experiences, writers and writing, the sites. These kinds of experiences can only "grow" you as a person and writer.

WARREN WILSON COLLEGE
Fiction, Poetry
Asheville, NC
2 years, 5 residencies
www.warren-wilson.edu/~mfa/newwebsite/homepage.php

The interviewees
Debra Allbery, director, is the author of *Walking Distance*. Her poems have appeared in *Yale Review, Kenyon Review, Poetry, Iowa Review, TriQuarterly, Ploughshares, Prairie Schooner*, and others.

Heather McHugh, faculty, is the author of thirteen books, including *Upgraded to Serious*. She served as a chancellor of the Academy of American Poets, and in 2000 was elected a member of the American Academy of Arts and Sciences.

Laura Cherry, alumnus, received the Philbrick Poetry Award for her chapbook, *What We Planted*. Her poems have appeared in journals including *Los Angeles Review*, *Borderlands: Texas Poetry Review*, *Newport Review*, and anthologies such as *Letters to the World*.

Kathleen Jesme, alumnus, is the author of three volumes of poetry: *The Plum-Stone Game*, *Motherhouse*, and *Fire Eater*.

K. Alma Peterson, alumnus, is the author of *Befallen*, a poetry chapbook. Her poems have appeared in *Hayden's Ferry Review*, *The New Orphic Review*, *Perihelion Review*, and others.

Ian Randall Wilson, alumnus, teaches in the fiction program at the UCLA Extension. He is the author of *Great Things Are Coming*. His fiction and poetry have appeared in many journals including *The Gettysburg Review*, *North American Review*, and *Puerto del Sol*.

Scott Nadelson, student, is the author of two story collections, *The Cantor's Daughter* and *Saving Stanley: The Brickman Stories*. He teaches creative writing at Willamette University in Salem, Oregon.

The program
Debra Allbery, director: We'll celebrate our thirty-fifth year at Warren Wilson in 2011. Any program that has endured that long has had both the right core values from the start and has had the flexibility to learn and adapt as it grows. Our Academic Board continues to fine-tune our policies as needed, and we solicit suggestions from students at the conclusion of every residency.

I first taught here in 1995; I was drawn to the program through the effusive recommendations of friends already on the faculty. I found it exhilarating — the quality of the students, the commitment of the faculty, the pure focus on craft. This program is so thoughtfully designed, so thorough in its tending of a writer's apprenticeship, and so attentive to student feedback; my only "vision for the future" is to continue the good work of our founder, Ellen Bryant Voigt, and the directors who have preceded me: encouraging and sustaining the program's formidable strengths and being open to any needs for change that might arise.

Faculty/teaching philosophy

Debra Allbery, director: We seek excellence in teaching, excellence in writing, and a shared sense of commitment to our community and to our art. Our faculty bring a wide range of teaching experiences and esthetic preferences to the program. We have a dedicated and quite accomplished core of veteran faculty members — in any given semester, usually about half of the faculty have a long history with the program — but we continue to add new voices to the mix.

Our low student–faculty ratio — usually three to one, but never more than five to one — allows for each student to experience at least four extensive and sustained mentorships during his or her tenure in the program. The residency — through team-taught workshops and a wide range of craft classes and lectures — provides interaction with at least twenty to thirty experienced writer-teachers over the course of a student's enrollment. This access to such a range of approaches and esthetics is essential in helping each student to discover and develop an individual voice — our graduates don't sound like each other, and don't sound like our faculty, either — and to hone his or her own critical abilities.

K. Alma Peterson, alumnus: All of the faculty I worked with were really skilled at homing in on the strengths and weaknesses of my writing. I felt that the program, the collective wisdom of its faculty, was able to guide my progress, by assigning me the mentors each semester who were best suited to my progress as a poet.

Kathleen Jesme, alumnus: I had many wonderful experiences. I don't want to name names, because that would leave out other names. All of my faculty mentors were outstanding. The day I would receive my packet back from my mentor was always revelatory. Mentors would often write ten- to twenty-page letters in response to the work. That was amazing.

Laura Cherry, alumnus: My faculty experiences at Warren Wilson were excellent across the board. Steve Orlen was my first supervisor, and he was incredibly generous and gentle and elicited from me many semi-narrative poems that were unlike anything I'd done before. Dan Tobin and Brooks Haxton were more scholarly and academic, and encouraged me to do reading that I'd have been unlikely to do otherwise, but which was very helpful. Stuart Dischell was my final-semester supervisor, and he midwifed my thesis collection as well as the class we were required to teach. I'm still amazed by the time and the quality of attention all four supervisors brought to their teaching.

Residency/community

Heather McHugh, faculty: Though by nature I'm something of a recluse or hermit, anybody can sense that the residencies foster an uncommonly devoted and uncommonly generous community, both inside and outside the curricular events — not least and perhaps paradoxically because the program is so selective, and because it is so dedicated to the highest pedagogical standards.

Ellen Bryant Voigt, who designed the low-residency MFA writing program, continues to attend every residency; she confers on proceedings, and elicits from them, gifts of scrupulous attention and breathtaking pedagogical integrity. Not only students, but distinguished faculty as well, recognize this quality of attention and integrity. They come because of it; and the students continue to nurture it, in an ongoing way, after graduation.

Kathleen Jesme, alumnus: The Warren Wilson alumni conference is held yearly. I have gone to a couple. I also maintain personal and professional relationships with many, many people I met through Warren Wilson.

Ian Randall Wilson, alumnus: I went on to start a literary journal, *88: A Journal of Contemporary American Poetry*, and published a number of WWC alumni. I also started a chapbook series through Hollyridge Press and published alumni and faculty members. There's a group of five men around my age who all went to the program and we try to get together in the summer and attend a writers conference. The alumni put on a summer conference and I've gone to that with good result.

Laura Cherry, alumnus: I made fast friends whom I love to this day. I found the classes to be at exactly the right level for me, to match and stretch my interest and curiosity in many, many topics. The atmosphere was friendly and challenging, personally and intellectually.

The interactions with other students felt like relationship building, not like networking. There were late-night dances in a gym. There were fresh peach pies baked in dorms. There were softball games. It was like a heavenly college for writers, and also deeply exhausting. I couldn't wait to go home and I couldn't wait to get back.

Scott Nadelson, student: The highlights for me are always the classes given by graduating students; to see where people have come after two or three years in the program, what they've learned and how passionate they are, is thrilling. The real testament to how well the residencies are put together is that no matter how exhausted I am when they are over, I can't wait to start writing the moment I get home.

Format/study

Debra Allbery, director: More than half of our students choose to expand upon their MFA experience by taking an "Extra," fifth, semester; fiction students also have the option of taking a Novel Semester. An Extra carries with it the same requirements of our first and second semesters: a minimum of five exchanges with a supervisor, a substantial amount of creative work, twelve to fifteen annotations, and fifteen to twenty books read. During the Novel Semester, available for students who already have 100 pages of a novel underway, the student will turn in novel chapters and maintain an analytical journal in response to his critical reading.

Ian Randall Wilson, alumnus: I looked at my supervisor as a writer whom I respected and from whom I could learn something. They did not disappoint. Because each supervisor is assigned three students each term, there was very close contact with them and close examination of your work during the time when you're away from the residency. I appreciated that attention. I appreciated the exposure to poets I'd never read before.

Scott Nadelson, student: The program has challenged me to see my work with fresh eyes, to take risks, and to deepen my under-standing of craft. It has also sharpened my critical abilities and given me new skills to take into the classroom as a teacher. I have come away with a body of work I am proud of and a community that I am thrilled to be connected with.

WEST VIRGINIA WESLEYAN COLLEGE
Poetry, Fiction, Creative Non-Fiction
Scheduled to launch 2011
Buckhannon, WV
2 years, 5 residencies
www.wvwc.edu

The interviewee
Irene McKinney is the director of the new low-residency MFA program offered by West Virginian Wesleyan College. She is also the West Virginia State Poet Laureate.

The program
Irene McKinney, director: This is a two-year program culminating in a Master of Fine Arts in Creative Writing degree, requiring four residencies on Wesleyan's campus or in field studies abroad, and a final residency in which the student presents the creative thesis, gives a public reading, and teaches a class.

We are in the heart of the Appalachian Mountains, and our program is grounded in the region. An important part of the program is our emphasis on writing out of a sense of place, this place and other travel destinations. The geography, history, literature, and myth of the region can be a powerful creative stimulant. As an option for one residency, students may choose to spend it in Ireland or other locations. Many of our teachers are accomplished writers who are committed to writing about place and environment.

Faculty/teaching philosophy
Irene McKinney, director: Extensive, directed reading is essential in developing strong, accomplished writing. Teachers work with students during residencies to plan their course of study, and may assign relevant readings from the past, as well as current work. In addition to their own writing, students concentrate for one semester on a substantial critical essay, which explores issues and techniques they find useful in their own creative projects.

Residency/community

Irene McKinney, director: The program has a strong place-based emphasis, and many of the writers taking part will be deeply interested in the Appalachian region, and by extension, other regions and environments. The program is not exclusively Appalachian, but is committed to a passionate interest in the natural environment, and allows one travel residency as an option, in Ireland, Belize, or other Wesleyan-sponsored destinations.

Format/study

Irene McKinney, director: Format of course work emphasizes one-on-one dialogue. The semester's work is not an online course, but an ongoing communication by phone, regular mail, and occasional email between the apprentice writer and the mentor. The student–teacher ratio never exceeds four to one, and usually the teachers will be responsible for two or three students. During the residencies, students attend lectures, workshops, and short craft courses in fiction, poetry, and creative non-fiction. We believe that the connection between student and mentor should be candid, professional, and intimate.

WESTERN CONNECTICUT STATE UNIVERSITY
Creative and Professional Writing
Danbury, CT
2 years, 4 residencies
www.wcsu.edu/writing/mfa/low-residency.asp

The interviewee

Brian Clements, coordinator, is the author of over half a dozen books of and about poetry, including *Disappointed Psalms*. He is the editor of *Sentence: A Journal of Prose Poetics* and of the small press Firewheel Editions.

The program

Brian Clements, coordinator: This program was specifically designed to give writers professional career options other than teaching, and most of our students begin working as professional writers while they're still in the program.

Faculty/teaching philosophy

Brian Clements, coordinator: Because every student in our program specializes in one creative genre and one practical genre, we have great need for professional writers who have done both — who are great novelists but have also worked as reporters and editors, like Don Snyder; great writers of non-fiction who have long, established careers as magazine journalists, like Daniel Asa Rose, Elizabeth Cohen, and Mark Sundeen; poets who are also playwrights and grant writers, like Paola Corso, and so on. Versatility is the greatest asset for a professional writer, and that quality is demonstrated in our faculty.

We are truly unique because we are the only MFA program that trains students in both the creative and the practical sides. In fact, our program assumes that the creative and the practical are not mutually exclusive — they are false discriminators. Everyone who writes professionally knows that one can't succeed without creativity, and all good writers of fiction, poetry, drama know that problem solving is just as important as imagination. Our program takes those facts as basic premises and helps them to build careers around those skills.

Residency/community

Brian Clements, coordinator: We make a conscious effort to keep our graduates involved in the program as mentors, as workshop leaders, and as panel participants at residencies. Our graduates frequently are the best advisors to our new students, because they have been through the program and are able to provide a perspective that faculty are not able to provide. The community we create at our residencies is intense and tight-knit; our graduates tend not only to stay in touch with the program, but with each other, even though they're scattered around the country.

Format/study

Brian Clements, coordinator: Our program also provides our students with very practical training on the business side of writing, experience in dealing with agents and editors, and hands-on learning experiences in required internships and enrichment projects. The classroom alone is not enough to train professional writers; they need experience doing what professional writers do — writing for deadlines, writing for specific audiences, learning to adapt.

WESTERN STATE COLLEGE OF COLORADO
Fiction, Poetry, Screenwriting
Launched in summer 2010
Gunnison, CO
2 years, 3 residencies
www.western.edu/academics/creativewriting

The interviewees
Mark Todd has served on the faculty at Western for over twenty years. He serves as program director for the MFA in Creative Writing and also teaches in the college's undergraduate Creative Writing Emphasis. His publications include three novels and two collections of poetry, including *Wire Song*.

Barbara Chepaitis, faculty, is author of seven published novels, including *Feeding Christine* and *These Dreams*, and a non-fiction book, *Birds of Paradise*.

Jack Lucido teaches film and filmography, including screenwriting, and he directs both the undergraduate Film Studies program and the MFA concentration in screenwriting. His work has won a CINE Golden Eagle Award, a Broadcast Educator's Association Festival of Media Arts Award of Excellence, and an Emmy nomination. His professional experience includes work on such films as *June Bug* and National Lampoon's *Pucked*, as well as the PBS series *Simple Living*.

The program
Mark Todd, director: The philosophy of the program is to offer a curriculum that encourages writers who want to reach mainstream audiences. There's a sea change on the horizon, mostly seen through isolated courses here and there, comments in the key trade publications by authors and critics admitting they like genre and popular literature, and the proliferating conferences that focus on mainstream writing. Sniffing those breezes — and having passions for this kind of writing ourselves — we've designed a curriculum that embraces and applauds aspiring writers who want to make a living outside the Academy with their writing as well as poets who want to reinvigorate poetry and reclaim lost, larger audiences.

We wanted to develop niche programming that wasn't already "done to death" in current MFA offerings, but it also needed to be a curriculum that we felt passionate about. We found both niche and passion by focusing on a program that addresses the world of writing and writers that target audiences beyond traditional academic literary circles. The program offers three concentrations: Mainstream and Genre Fiction; Poetry with an Emphasis in Formal Verse; and Screenwriting for Hollywood, Independent Film, and Television. Starting the summer of 2011, the program will also offer a Certificate in Publishing.

Faculty/teaching philosophy

Mark Todd, director: Our program takes advantage of the low-residency approach to attract not only students but also faculty, and we're tapping a pool of successful mainstream authors, poets, and screenwriters from across the country. Our school may be small but our faculty spans the continent. We've also developed a rotating advisory council of authors, screenwriters, and poets with national and international reputations, on hand during summer residencies to share and interact with our students.

Barbara Chepaitis, faculty: All the faculty are professional writers who have gone through the process of finding editors, agents, directors, producers, etc. We'll be teaching from experience, and we'll all include specific coursework that's about fundamentals such as writing good queries, where and how to network, how to target specific markets and publicize your work, and more.

Residency/community

Mark Todd, director: Students will attend three summer residencies in late July of two weeks each on our campus in Gunnison, Colorado, high in the Rocky Mountains. That's an unfair but natural advantage that we'll exploit to the fullest, and our summer curriculum includes blocks of time to take advantage of the recreational destination playground at our feet. Nevertheless, our summer residency experience is primarily a time to build a sense of literary community at multiple reading recitals, panel discussions, as well as agent and editor pitches, plus face-time classes with the same faculty that students will work with during non-residency tutorials.

Format/study

Mark Todd, director: The [optional] Certificate in Publishing will take one year to complete, including residency involvement for two consecutive summers and online participation during the academic year between those summers. The certificate is geared to help writers become savvier about the publishing process, and participants will prepare a book for actual publication — going through the acquisitions process, dialoguing with authors and poets, proofing, designing the final product, planning the marketing, and initiating contacts with distributors. The certificate will, in alternating years, produce an anthology and a single-author book, and each year the project book will be published by our new college press.

Jack Lucido, faculty: The screenwriting program is based in independent feature film. With the recent success of lower budget films we will be centered there. Also, [with] a good strong study of classic and canon film, their associated screenplays, film genre and specific constructs, and the form of the peculiar screenplay itself — like no other writing form — we will equip students to earn a living writing scripts. Television drama and situation comedy will be included as well. Students will be able to aim for major Hollywood studio projects if they so choose . . . The connections of our faculty will be at the disposal of students.

Barbara Chepaitis, faculty: [The Mainstream and Genre Fiction concentration] is an area that's not often included in either graduate or undergraduate study, so it fills an unmet need. I know that when I was in graduate school, working on books like *The Fear Principle*, which is cyberpunk suspense, I was writing outside the norm for such programs. I was fortunate to have two professors who accepted what I did, and were able to help me with it, but I think it's important to have curriculum that actually is designed to work with these forms.

From talking with young writers and students at conferences and workshops I've found that they're clamoring for this. They want support and structure to learn the skills involved in writing science fiction or the mystery, and they can't find it easily. I also believe that popular fiction can and should be done well, with a sense of poetics as well as engaging narrative. Like good Shaker furniture, such works can contain an elegant clarity of style, if the writer knows how to get the job done.

WILKES UNIVERSITY
Fiction, Poetry, Creative Non-Fiction, Playwriting
Wilkes-Barre, PA
1½ years, 4 residencies (MA)
2½ years, 5 residencies (MFA)
http://wilkes.edu/creativewriting

The interviewees
Bonnie Culver, co-founder and director, has had more than twenty of her plays produced from New York to Los Angeles by colleges, regional theatres, and equity companies. Her professionally produced plays include *Lifelines*, *Accident*, and *Sniper*. She is currently at work on a novel/screenplay called *Harmony Lake*.

Jim Warner is currently the assistant director of Graduate Creative Writing Programs at Wilkes University and the associate editor and business manager of Etruscan Press. He is the author of two poetry collections, including *Too Bad It's Poetry*. His poetry has also appeared in *Word Riot, The HazMat Review, Drunken Boat, Cause and Effect*, and various other journals.

J. Michael Lennon, co-founder, is the late Norman Mailer's authorized biographer and has written/edited several books about him, including *Normal Mailer: Works and Days*. He is past president of the Norman Mailer Society, past president of the James Jones Society, and a member of the executive board of the Norman Mailer Writers Colony. His work has appeared in publications such as *The New Yorker* and *Paris Review*.

Philip Brady, faculty, has published three collections of poems. His latest book is a collection of essays, *By Heart: Reflections of a Rust-Belt Bard*. His poetry and fiction have appeared in over fifty journals, including *The American Literary Review* and *The Belfast Literary Supplement*.

Kaylie Jones, faculty, is the author of several novels and a memoir, *Lies My Mother Never Told Me*. Her novels have been translated into many languages including French, Dutch, German, Japanese, Italian, Polish, Turkish, and Spanish.

Brian Fanelli completed his MFA from Wilkes University in 2010. His poetry has been published in journals such as *Chiron Review*, *Word Riot*, *Blood Lotus*, and *My Favorite Bullet*.

Amye Barrese Archer, student, is a full-time graduate assistant in Wilkes University's Creative Writing Low-Residency Program. She is in her second year, and while she is hard at work on a memoir, she is a poet at heart. She is the author of a chapbook, *No One Ever Looks Up*. Her work has appeared, or is forthcoming, in *PANK Magazine*, *Twins Magazine*, *The Ampersand Review*, and others.

The program
Bonnie Culver, director: In the years we spent developing this program, the faculty and board members were clear we must find a way to vet not only the final manuscripts, but also the program as a whole. We included agents, editors, publishers, and producers because we wanted the practical, marketing response such inclusion would bring to us. Therefore, all theses are read by an outside reader who does not know the student. These readers respond to the work and cite its strengths, weaknesses and offer suggestions as to how best to move, revise the thesis towards publication. Students revise these drafts in the MFA based upon the critiques received by market professionals, moving them towards publication or production. Again, this is the real writing world that incorporates the tougher business piece of writing directly into the program requirements. Lastly, it has forced all of us — students, faculty, board members — to ramp up our own work, hold a higher bar for excellence than we may have if the projects were read only internally, rather than by these industry pros.

Philip Brady, faculty: I've been involved in the Wilkes Low-Residency MA and MFA program since its inception. I've seen the program grow from a small group of enthusiastic and dedicated faculty and students to a thriving MA and MFA program that includes faculty with an extremely broad array of interests and credentials, and a student community that is accomplished, vibrant and voracious to learn. As a former director of a traditional MFA program, I've had the chance to compare the Wilkes low-residency program with traditional academic programs, and I'm very impressed with the unique features the Wilkes program offers.

The strengths of the Wilkes program, it seems to me, lie in its breadth, its heart, and its practicality. Many non-traditional kinds of writing are taught here. In addition to the poetry, fiction, creative non-fiction, and playwriting, Wilkes offers mentorships in screenwriting, young adult fiction, fabulist writing, mystery writing, and other forms often unfairly excluded from academic programs.

Faculty/Teaching Philosophy

Bonnie Culver, director: We look for serious working writers who are gifted teachers. We only hire faculty who can hear, see a novel, poem, script, or non-fiction piece as the student wishes to write it. Such faculty mentor in terms of craft and technique. However, they guide students and help them uncover what it is that they are saying rather than tell them. Meanwhile, our faculty are all writing.

Amye Archer, student: There are online classes used throughout the program, but the first semester foundation courses are the most intensive. In those courses you share writing ideas and clippings with five or six other students who are studying the same genre. It's a wonderful icebreaker. I think the anonymity of the online courses is helpful at first because you can write freely without being self-conscious.

The mentorship that I experienced was wonderful. Because you are long distance, you get to have these intimate phone chats with your mentor. My mentor is big on social media, so we chat online all of the time. It's really like she became my friend through the process.

Brian Fanelli, alumnus: I personally liked my interactions with the faculty members during non-residency terms. They always responded to my questions and emails within a day or two, and their feedback was solid. They looked at my poems line by line and really worked hard with me through multiple drafts of my work.

They also expanded my knowledge of contemporary American poetry and frequently introduced me to new poets. I also enjoyed the low-residency aspect of the program because it allowed me to work thirty or forty hours a week and still complete my MA and MFA.

Residency/community

Bonnie Culver, director: We include several modules during the residency courses that walk students through [the publishing] process. We also have meetings, pitch sessions, and information sessions with agents, editors, etc., as part of the residency course to assist students in preparing their manuscripts. Faculty have been wonderfully generous in continuing to follow and to assist alums in making needed contacts to seek publication.

Amye Archer, student: The first residency I ever went to changed my life. And I'm not exaggerating. For the first time in my life I was surrounded by writers and was being treated as a writer.

Brian Fanelli, alumnus: My experiences at the residencies were invaluable, especially the courses on publishing/networking. I learned how to write a proper cover letter, research journals, and how to approach editors, as well as how to use social media to promote other writers and my own projects. Furthermore, the residencies provided the opportunity to meet other students also studying poetry. Since then, we've shared full manuscripts and poems with each other before sending the work out to journals and contests. I'm sure I'll have these friends for a long time, and I'm happy to have a solid writing group now.

Format/study

Bonnie Culver, director: In just a few short years, we have become one of the largest programs — low and residency included — in the country. Through careful faculty selection and their commit-ment, we have built a supportive, but tough, producing writing community. As its director, I have the best job in the world.

Kaylie Jones, faculty: Most of our students end up writing pretty good novels or non-fiction books. But every once in a while one of us will mentor a student who has a real talent, a driving force and an understanding of humanity that sets him or her above the rest. That is when this is no longer a job, but a passion.

Jim Warner, assistant director: As someone who has been a part of the program since its start, I am very proud of what our writing community has become . . . From the very first residency where the student population was almost outnumbered by our faculty, to now having over a hundred students from twenty-five plus states, it's amazing to see the same degree of intimacy and passion from everyone involved. I feel like I've grown right along with the program.

When I started here half a decade ago, I was just a graduate assistant. Today, I am the assistant director of this program and know that my development within the program mirrors my maturation as a poet and a member of our writing community. It's been community first from day one, and it's what allows us to be successful.

Brian Fanelli, alumnus: I am now far more serious about writing than I was prior to joining the Wilkes program. Because I had to complete a full-length collection of poems within a few semesters, I got into the habit of writing daily, and I see myself sticking to that habit long into the future. Since joining the program, I've also had my poems published in a few journals, I feel more confident about my work, and I now have a group of friends that are fellow writers and are willing to share feedback on my work and share their work with me.

Mike Lennon, co-founder: There is a strong emphasis on providing information and analysis on the way the worlds of professional publishing and producing function. We all provide tips and insights about our own professional contacts and the mores of the publishing world. We bring experts from every part of the New York publishing scene to residencies: agents, editors at big publishing houses and small magazines, copyright lawyers, the VP for publicity at Random House, copy and style editors, book reviewers, theater directors, movie producers — anyone who can open a door and provide more than a glimpse of the world after the MFA. And faculty stay with their students, providing a permanent lifeline, an ear, a shoulder, guidance. Students are exposed to the spectrum of literary activity from journaling and initial conception to book tours and media interviews. Proximity to New York is a real asset, as are the extensive connections faculty members have with literary, theatrical, and film professionals.

Philip Brady, faculty: Wilkes has affiliated itself with a national literary press, Etruscan Press; a national book contest, the James Jones Contest; an arts magazine, *Provincetown Arts*; a conference, the Norman Mailer Conference; and a screenwriting incubator run by Robert May. The program offers students the chance to meet and talk with agents, publishers, producers, and editors as well as writers and teachers. Wilkes focuses on writing as a way of life, not merely an academic discipline. Many alumni from Wilkes will attest to the life changes brought about during their time in the program. What's more unusual is that such changes aren't limited to students. Dr. Culver's program has created a synergy that provides enormous potential for growth in all facets of its community: writers, teachers, and professionals, as well as students.

CHAPTER 7

The Residency Experience

THROUGHOUT CHAPTER 6, YOU have read a wide variety of residency experiences. These additional comments offer a few more detailed descriptions, personal experiences, and tips for incoming students.

A closer look

Anne Caston, faculty, University of Alaska, Anchorage: UAA's residency sessions happen on the campus in mid-summer, with students and faculty housed in the dorms and taking meals together at the Creekside Eatery on campus. During this twelve-day residency session, the program offers a robust schedule of readings, workshops, seminar classes, and distinguished guest speakers, artists, and scientists. Near the halfway point, the students get a "day off" for a little R&R while the academic board and director meet to assign the mentorships, pairing the student writer with a faculty writer/mentor for the year's work away from campus. There are also field trips during the residency sessions, which allow students to experience the Alaskan landscape.

On the final evening of the session, there is a social in the Wolf's Den where everyone gathers for a final time of music and dancing and saying farewell until the next summer's residency. There is a strong sense of cohort among our graduates: many of them become friends and remain so long past graduation. The camaraderie among faculty and students balances the long months of solitary reading and writing between residency sessions.

Patsy Sims, director, Goucher College: During the summer residencies, students participate each morning in a three-hour workshop with their fall-semester mentor and the other students assigned that mentor, with no more than six per mentor. In the afternoon, we have a lecture given by a faculty member or guest writer, editor, or agent; in the evenings we have faculty and student readings, followed by an informal social hour called Study Hall. In the time slot between the lecture and dinner, we have a variety of activities: one-on-one student–faculty conferences, a library database session to familiarize students with the various databases available to them from home (including LexisNexis), and a variety of individual breakout sessions on various topics by the faculty members.

The spring semester begins with a weekend mini-residency in late January when each faculty member and his or her assigned students meet for three days of intense writing workshops in the mentor's home community or at a location deemed convenient to the group. Students arrive on Friday for a late-afternoon writing workshop. Saturday is devoted to writing workshops and one-on-one conferences, with a final workshop on Sunday. The intimate nature of these mini-residencies enables groups to establish a rapport that greatly enhances their online discussions throughout the semester.

International appeal
Carol Berg, alumnus, University of Southern Maine: One benefit of the USM Stonecoast program was the opportunity to spend a residency in Ireland, with the wonderful poets Annie and Ted Deppe. The focus was on Irish literature and so the readings and visiting writers were in various genres as well. The small group allowed for a more intimate experience in discussing and exploring the alternate genres.

Tips for the newcomer
Dawn Paul, alumnus, Goddard College: Rest up, get your work organized in advance, read the work of the advisors that interest you. Let go of your expectations. Think about what you want and be prepared to make it happen. Expect to work very hard and play hard. It's not a time for quiet contemplation and getting a lot of writing done. You can do that at home. That said, try to block out

a little time for yourself so you don't go crazy. I used to go for a run every morning.

Mandy Farrington, student, Antioch University LA: I worked during one of my residencies and only took three days off. It was doable, but not as engaging as it was to do nothing but attend seminars and readings during the ten-day period.

Meg Kearney, director, Pine Manor College: Our own students have advised each other: Don't be shy. Step into the circle. As writers, we tend to be loners, or at least we tend to be people who feel quite comfortable sitting in a room alone for hours at a time. It's difficult for some of us to be part of a group. But it's the friends one makes while in a program — those friends being fellow students as well as faculty members and staff — who not only provide much-needed support during those four semesters, but serve as invaluable readers, guides, and cheerleaders well beyond graduation.

CHAPTER 8

Non-Residency Semesters

You HAVE READ NUMEROUS accounts regarding the time management skills and self-discipline required to find success with the non-residency workload. The following comments offer a few additional details and experiences worth contemplating in preparation for low-residency MFA studies.

Online interaction

Wayne Ude, director, Northwest Institute of Literary Arts: Our online courses are asynchronous, a bit of jargon that means students and faculty may post material any time. With asynchronous online classes, those who are still up and at their best at two in the morning may converse with those who rise at six and are at their best then. Those who aren't as quick on their feet as others can take their time to develop their ideas before posting them without worrying that the discussion may have moved on to some other point — the earlier discussion will still be posted and the new contribution welcomed.

In addition to online classes, our online campus includes several discussion areas which faculty, students, and alumni may participate in, as well as student-only, student–faculty, and individual one-on-one faculty sites for each student in each course, which replace standard office hours.

Stephen Haven, director, Ashland University: Students benefit from the one-on-one attention of their faculty mentors and from online discussion with other students and faculty during non-residential semesters. Each faculty mentor serves as a catalyst for an online discussion forum during fall and spring semesters and responds individually in writing to packets of student creative work.

Clifford Garstang, alumnus, Queens University of Charlotte: Each month we'd swap submissions by email. The week of the swap would be busy doing critiques and writing up summaries, and then we'd circulate our comments. It was always interesting to see what others said about the same submissions. Then the group instructor would provide his or her comments, often also commenting on the comments that we all made.

It was very helpful to have all that commentary in writing, for revision purposes. In the face-to-face workshop, you may be depending on your notes when it comes time to revise, so in some ways the distance learning component is superior.

Jessie Carty, alumnus, Queens University of Charlotte: Online workshopping was great for me. I was really able to spend time with the poems I was critiquing. I felt less inhibited by critiquing online. I am glad that my program had in-person critiquing during the residencies and online workshopping during the term because it gave the whole experience more balance.

Mentor feedback
Abby Frucht, faculty, Vermont College of Fine Arts: First, I mark the fiction and creative non-fiction manuscripts liberally as I read. These jottings and suggestions indicate my immediate ongoing response to the material and manifest themselves as a kind of dialogue between the prose and me, a model for the kind of dialogue that my students, I hope, will come to have with their works-in-progress. Some of what I write is meant to demonstrate the range of alternatives available to writers every step of the way and to drive home the fact that when we write, we are making choices often without naming them as such to ourselves. I want my students to make the smallest choices — as to word choice, punctuation, and syntax — deliberately.

Other of my immediate comments represent my attempts to encourage an abundantly playful, vital energy to be brought to the text. Much of this I call riffing, which is when we plug into a scene and free associate for a while on the page, to see where it goes.

None of my suggestions, riffs, or editorial comments are meant to be prescriptive. I can't emphasize this strongly enough. Rather than edit my students so that it will be in closer accordance with my own tastes or style, I like to introduce a method by which they might discover, identify, and refine their own literary instincts and impulses. That's my biggest hope for every semester, that my students come away from it able and eager to engage with their manuscripts in playful, analytical, experimental, surprising, and purposeful ways.

In addition to marking the manuscripts as above, I write comments on the back page or two of each one, shaping questions and concerns that invite our close attention. These notes, along with the notes, comments, and questions that my students sent along when they mailed in their packets, provide the template for my letters in return. And while I'm always happy to answer emails, I want to be sure, as well, that the program encourages us all to experience the rigorous spells of solitude that writing requires and that, in turn, nurture writing. So, ask away by email if you like, I always say to my students, but if I feel that you are compromising those important spells of solitude, or if I feel that you might be better off struggling over the questions on your own for a while in order that you might have the pleasure of discovering the answers for yourself, believe me, you'll be the first to know.

Time management: writing habits for life
Peter Oresick, director, Chatham University: Students should be comfortable with online technologies and the daily time commitment required in order to perform successfully in virtual classrooms. Students should also remember that a low-residency program is the same amount of work as a traditional program.

Often we hear prospects talk about the flexibility of low-res programs — they don't have to move or to quit their jobs. In short, they don't have to change their lives. We argue that they do. Even though low-res students do not drive to campus, park, sit in a three-hour class, go out to a bar afterwards with their classmates, then drive home, they do need to carve out twenty hours or more a week for classes, reading, and writing.

Jim Warner, assistant director, Wilkes University: I think working online with a mentor forces you to develop better writer habits and practices. You are on your own — you don't have the artifice of going to a classroom Monday-Wednesday-Friday for fifty minutes to workshop with a class. Online, it's you and your work, and it becomes your responsibility to figure out how to reconcile your writing life with your day-to-day life. In a lot of ways, that first drafting semester is probably the most difficult in the program. All of a sudden, you have two weeks to deliver contracted content — no daily check-in, no class assignments, nothing but you and your writing.

Knowing how to plot out your day and organize your writing time is probably as important as anything you generate in the program. In eighteen months, you start and complete a full manuscript — knowing it's possible gives you the permission to write.

Robert Peake, alumnus, Pacific University: Completing the suggested twenty to twenty-five hours of coursework per week on top of holding down a full-time job was tough. But it was like boot camp. Two years of getting up early before work to write, reading after work, and spending time in the evenings and on weekends revising work and sending out poems, seems to have been long enough to groove new habits. Ten months after my final residency, I continue to sustain a life well engaged with writing.

Low-residency taught me what longevity takes — the patience and persistence, the commitment that poets like Wallace Stevens or William Carlos Williams had, maintaining a demanding career while still structuring one's life to be able to write often, and fiercely.

CHAPTER 9

Pedagogical Preparation

THE MFA IS A terminal degree — the required qualification to teach creative writing at the college level. However, competition is tight and there are no guarantees for future employment. If you are interested in teaching, the comments included in this chapter will clarify the realities of the job market, and provide a few of the pedagogical learning experiences provided through low-residency MFA programs. There are others, of course, and if you are interested in pedagogical training, you should ask what opportunities are available in the programs you intend to apply for.

First, however, it may interest you to note that while the MFA and the PhD are terminal degrees, the MA may limit your options. Clark E. Knowles, a Bennington College graduate, learned this the hard way. He pursued an MFA after obtaining an MA and now teaches writing at the University of New Hampshire.

Clark E. Knowles, alumnus, Bennington College: I came to writing a bit late — starting a serious practice when I was thirty. I went to the University of New Hampshire and earned an MA in Writing and lucked into a lectureship there, directly after my graduation. I didn't know enough at the time to ask how much difference the "F" in between the "M" and the "A" made in the world. I had no idea that the MA was not a terminal degree, and since I had no ambitions of becoming a PhD candidate, I settled into teaching composition and tried to write. Although I was fairly prolific immediately after getting the MA, getting a few stories published and getting the attention of an agent, I also discovered the unfinished business of the degree. I realized that if

I wanted to teach in a tenure track position anywhere, I'd have to get that terminal degree.

After attending a few writing conferences, I started looking at low-residency programs. For me, low-residency was the only way to go. I'd already put much energy into the MA, so I felt that I'd already had the on-campus experience. Plus, I had a two-year-old daughter, a home, friends, and family. I was rooted in my community . . . In the fall of 2002, the time seemed right, my job was secure, my wife and daughter were supportive, and I applied to Bennington College, was accepted, and started the journey.

Putting things in perspective

David Stevenson, director, University of Alaska Anchorage: It's difficult to get teaching experience in a low-residency program. On the other hand, I have known many MFA students in traditional programs who spent an inordinate amount of their time in graduate school teaching and not enough time writing. My belief is that if students put their writing first, and succeed with it, future teaching opportunities will open up for them. We also have a literary practicum in our curriculum, which is, in effect, a kind of internship. This is where our students can build some teaching experience into their degree program.

Rick Mulkey, director, Converse College: First, I would never suggest students work toward an MFA degree because they want a teaching degree. I think the only real reason to complete an MFA program is because a student wants to improve as a writer, has a passion for writing and reading, and because that person can't imagine living a life without writing and reading. When that's the case, and they can put all their energy and enthusiasm into doing it and write regularly, then an MFA is a worthwhile pursuit.

Having said that, if a writer also wants to teach, I think the writer should broaden his or her definition of teaching. Don't limit the options to only teaching at a college or university. There are community and regional arts centers and literary arts programs that need teachers. Writers can develop their own writing workshops to lead, and there are writing-in-schools programs, and prison writing programs, among others. When the definition is broadened, one can see the possibilities for teaching are numerous.

Tod Goldberg, director, University of California Riverside: It is exceptionally difficult to get a job as a professor of creative writing without significant publications, so focusing on that foremost should be your goal. Beyond that, I'd say invest yourself in the literature you're reading, take your critical work as seriously as your creative and spend time learning from your own professors.

Ann E. Michael, alumnus, Goddard College: Many MFAs contain no teaching component at all. I am really glad that Goddard did; it helped me very much, but it was my responsibility and that was helpful, too. Really, no one is going to job hunt for you — you have to learn how to do it yourself someday! Those students who had trouble motivating themselves to set up teaching experiences may also have had some trouble finding teaching jobs later, I don't know. My teaching component led to a series of jobs, ultimately full-time, in academia.

Meg Kearney, director, Pine Manor College: Most undergraduate and graduate programs that are looking for creative writing teachers require an MFA degree. The most competitive positions are also looking for writers with books, but if you're willing to start out teaching composition, it is possible to land a job without significant publication.

One of the main things gained by being part of an MFA community are the contacts made during the course of those two years. Faculty members, program guests, and even fellow students can become, in the future, sources of recommendations and jobs.

My main piece of advice, then, is to keep in touch with the contacts you make while in graduate school, and be realistic about the kind of teaching you might have to do — meaning comp classes — as you work your way up the proverbial ladder.

Program-specific opportunities
Luanne Armstrong, faculty, University of British Columbia: [In UBC's Teaching Creative Writing course] we spend quite a bit of time discussing the differences and similarities between teaching creative writing, teaching English, teaching composition, and also teaching writing across all the academic disciplines, and the role of writing in other programs, such as PhD programs. So

they get a very broad-based idea of what kinds of opportunities are available to teach writing and how they can be, and will need to be, flexible and adaptable enough to make a good living as writers and teachers.

Most people who graduate with an MFA in Creative Writing are likely going to end up applying for some kind of teaching position, or perhaps teaching in a community based program or a continuing education program. In any case, they are always going to need a good CV, a teaching philosophy and a number of course outlines or syllabi that they can use. I want my students to be prepared and feel confident when they go to apply for a teaching position; they have experience, they have solid theory and they have the tools to do a good interview.

Frank Montesonti, faculty, National University: National offers two important classes for prospective teachers — composition pedagogy and the pedagogy of creative writing. Composition pedagogy is a particularly useful class where we create the teaching portfolio students will need to apply for jobs teaching at the college level.

In our most recent alumni survey, we were happy to see that 35 percent of students reported they had been hired to teach at a two or four year college after graduation. This very high number, considering not all students seek employment in higher education, is most likely due to the fact that we offer courses on both the pedagogy of creative writing and composition.

Steve Heller, director, Antioch University LA: For those who are interested in supporting their writing by teaching, I recommend two things: (1) Keep writing and submit your work for publication; (2) Consider AULA's Post-MFA Certificate in the Teaching of Creative Writing. This one-semester program is open to anyone who holds an MFA in Creative Writing from an accredited institution. The Post-MFA program begins with a residency workshop on writing pedagogy and a number of pedagogy-related orientations, seminars, and lectures. During the five-month project period, the student completes a pedagogy reading list and writes a critical paper on writing pedagogy.

Most important, the student completes a supervised teaching placement that MFA faculty help arrange in the student's home community. The student completes the program as an informed, experienced writing instructor — someone who has seriously studied writing pedagogy and put theory to practice in the classroom. Students who complete this program are ready for the job market.

Wayne Ude, director, Northwest Institute of Literary Arts: Alumni of ours and other MFA programs may take classes on a postgraduate basis. Among those is our only class which focuses on teaching, English 600: Methods of Teaching Creative Writing. Though this course discusses teaching both traditional and online for-credit classes, it also explores other kinds of teaching: at writers' conferences and literary centers, in local non-credit workshops, and during school visits.

Annie Finch, director, University of Southern Maine: Our pedagogy focus provides a structure for students to make teaching an integral part of their MFA program. Students can begin as early as the first semester to plan a third semester pedagogy project based in a teaching internship in their home community. Students have done wonderful projects involving teaching everywhere from colleges and high schools to elementary schools, prisons, and shelters, and have gotten excellent teaching jobs after graduation in schools from leading prep schools to nationally recognized graduate creative writing programs.

Paul Selig, director, Goddard College: Students develop a creative writing course, which they will offer in their own community under the auspices of a sponsoring institution. Where a practicum takes place depends on a student's teaching interests. We've had practica take place in schools, colleges, community centers, libraries, prisons, and hospitals. At the completion of the practicum, the student submits a reflective essay on the teaching experience, along with supporting materials — course outlines, evaluations, outside observer reports — to his/her faculty mentor for review. Students are mentored by their advisors throughout the practicum and all students take a preparatory workshop prior to the semester in which they teach.

The MFA is the preferred degree for teaching creative writing at the college level, and we feel we would be remiss if we did not require our students to have an experience of this. At Goddard, we believe that students need to give their learning back to their community and the practicum is one of the ways in which students demonstrate this. New students who are already teaching writing may use their existing teaching work for their Goddard practicum.

Kathleen Driskell, associate director, Spalding University: We offer a Teaching Practicum, as one of our enrichment courses, which includes a workshop at residency that provides a wonderfully rich "teaching laboratory" for five or six students. During the workshop, we discuss practical teaching matters, current pedagogy for creative writing, and each student has the opportunity to lead a workshop and to present a creative writing exercise or two to their peers.

We also talk about practical teaching matters. For example, we discuss how to set up a syllabus and what to expect when first working as an adjunct. At residency, we also present lectures specific to teaching. In the past, those lectures have focused on teaching the Introduction to Creative Writing Workshop to undergraduates. It's important for our students interested in teaching to know that providing instruction to undergraduates calls for a very different set of teaching tools than needed in a workshop of graduate students. A new teacher has to remember that in an intro course, the instructor normally is going to present curriculum in three or more genres, so we also discuss how to prepare for those cross-genre lessons. One of the great things about Spalding is that our students are already exposed to other genres.

When students return home to teach in their practicum, they might choose to conduct class online, in continuing education, or at universities. We provide consultations to help them figure out how to convene and plan for a course, whether that class meets for six weeks or a fifteen-week semester. We work closely with our students to help them develop syllabi, lesson plans, and select readings for their courses.

I remember how wonderful it was as a new teacher to be able to bounce ideas off someone else or how helpful it was to have someone to ask about what seemed to be small teaching concerns; Spalding's mentoring provides the opportunity for our students to have that kind of dialogue. Our students who enter the classroom do very well. They feel confident and prepared to begin their teaching careers.

CHAPTER 10

Learning from Experience

As you consider whether a low-residency MFA program is right for you and your lifestyle, you will want to take into consideration the many experiences and tips shared throughout this handbook. A few interviewees had additional tips for both prospective applicants and newly accepted incoming students. The following experiences and observations offer additional perspectives on preparing for the realities of low-residency MFA studies.

Before you apply

Clark E. Knowles, alumnus, Bennington College: Low-residency programs are wonderful for people who want to experience living the writing life. They are writer-centric in that you have to do the work. No daily classes to keep you on your toes. But — and I think this is important — they will not make you a writer. That is a lesson taught too little in all MFA programs across the board, not only low-residency programs. It will make you write stories, or poems, or whatever, but it will not make you a writer. That is something that needs to come from another place.

The MFA helped me clarify my writing life and to find out what needed work and what I was doing correctly, but it did not make me a writer. I talked to many, many people who were looking forward to leaving the program and becoming writers, or who thought that doing the work of the program would transform them somehow and when they graduated, they'd get to the real work of their creative selves — and I suppose even I thought that to some extent — but the reality is that once the thrill of being in a program is over, there is still the long lonely blank page and filling it is as dreadful and exhilarating as it was the first time I sat down to write.

So my advice is to wait before you spend the money and the time. Do the work without a classroom. Then, if you feel as if a key ingredient is missing, jump into a program.

Laraine Herring, alumnus, Antioch University LA: It's not a cheap experience, so make sure you are really able to commit to it. Most low-res programs don't have teaching assistantships or fellowships or other kinds of scholarships. Make sure your family recognizes that this is something you are doing, and that, short of the house catching on fire, this is your first priority. I would hate to think of people spending the money and time to do an MFA program and not really immersing themselves in the experience.

With a low-residency program, you have to be the one to make the time. You're not living on campus or hanging out in a student union. You make your own writing community, and the first place that relationship is forged is with yourself. You should be a good self-motivator, and a very strong time manager. And, oh yeah, you should love to write and read more than anything else in the world. An MFA won't make you rich, but it can enrich your soul.

Jessie Carty, alumnus, Queens University of Charlotte: If you are considering a low-residency program really do your research. Try to think of what you want from the experience to see if you are a good match for a given program. There are lots of blogs and message boards that can give you valuable information from current students and alumni of programs.

You also have to weigh the costs that are not covered by loans: books, travel expenses. Once you are in a program, participate as much as you can especially since most low-residency programs do hold a pretty decent price tag, which is rarely covered by financial aid. Remember that you will be meeting the kinds of people who are your potential readers for life. But, most of all, enjoy every minute of it. It goes by way too fast!

Diana M. Raab, alumnus, Spalding University: I have been a writer my entire life, so the MFA program did not really teach me *how* to write. What it did teach me is how to be more critical of my work and the work of others. It taught me how to offer constructive criticism to my colleagues and how to be a precise editor and to appropriate questions. In reality, we learn a lot by reading the work of others and we did plenty of this in workshop. More often than not, we learn more from reading bad writing than we learn from reading good writing.

Tips for incoming students
Anne Caston, faculty, University of Alaska Anchorage: First and foremost, a student must be a self-disciplined writer in order to succeed in this kind of program. And a student must be willing to establish a relationship to his/her art that endures over a lifetime, beyond the three years of graduate study we offer. There's really no workshop, no class, no "how-to" manual that offers a short cut to success in the writing life — and literature is filled with examples of poets who were not published in their lifetimes or who were unappreciated for their work. This program is as close as a student writer can get to the rigors of a writing life: long periods of solitude and work with companionable interludes with like-minded others.

Stephen Haven, director, Ashland University: To understand the sensibilities of their mentors, students should always thoroughly read the books of their faculty. They should also work with as many faculty mentors as possible and only then choose a thesis advisor. Students benefit from being exposed to a range of esthetics in a range of faculty mentors. After working with multiple faculty mentors, students will be better informed in choosing thesis advisors who might provide the most useful critical feedback during the thesis semester.

Alice Mattison, faculty, Bennington College: If students choose a low-residency program, they must learn to write in the place where they live, surrounded by the people who will continue to surround them. If they need to learn how to get writing done in the press of family life and work life, they'll learn that while they are students. They won't graduate after two years in an artificial environment in which they do little but write, only to find themselves unable to find writing time because their boss is pushy, their mother is sick, their child is needy, or it's more fun to do something else.

Melanie Faith, alumnus, Queens University of Charlotte: One of the most exciting and also tiring experiences about the MFA is that students need to be open-minded about having their work critiqued. A writer learns that it is impossible to take all suggestions into the editing process, but that *several* of the suggestions might actually be feasible or strengthen the piece. Part of the learning curve as an MFA student is learning to sift through fellow writers' suggestions.

Stefon Mears, student, Northwest Institute of Literary Arts: An incoming student needs to realize that low-residency does not mean low impact: these are full, graduate-level classes and will require a lot of time and effort. It would be useful during the weeks leading up to the first residency to examine one's daily routines and start determining what is expendable.

Keeping up with classes will probably require about twenty hours each week, and one may find that spreading those hours out becomes less stressful than trying to accomplish everything on weekends. That said, everyone has activities that are personally important, and these should not be sacrificed in the name of study time. The cost in stress outweighs the savings in time.

CHAPTER 11

Life After the MFA

WHEN YOU COMPLETE YOUR program, your writing life is only just beginning. Now comes the hard part. Without the faculty mentorships, residencies, and assignment deadlines, you are left to your own time-management and motivational devices to continue to produce work that makes you proud to be a writer.

I asked Diane Lefer, who taught at Vermont College of Fine Arts for twenty-three years and has authored several book-length works of fiction including *California Transit*, if she had any suggestions for students preparing for life after the MFA.

> If you go straight through without a leave of absence, you've been on a relentless treadmill of producing and revising work. Some students have a period of creative collapse right after graduation. Not to worry. Your brain needs to recover and assimilate everything that was thrown at you and you need to reconnect with the family and friends you neglected while working on the MFA. You will write again — beautifully and very soon.
>
> *Diane Lefer, former faculty, Vermont College of Fine Arts*

In addition to a selection of tips from directors, faculty, and alumni, I have included a brief Q&A with Loreen Niewenhuis, editor of Spalding University's MFA alumni association newsletter. As you prepare for life after graduation, remember that writing is a process and a commitment, and many of the skills you learned in your program are meant to keep you writing, long after the MFA.

Building a life as a writer

R. T. Smith, faculty, Converse College: It's important that graduates not become addicted to the pinball machine of the workshop/conference/festival circuit. There comes a time when reading a Flannery O'Connor story before the fire, taking a walk and then staring at the page is what you should be doing, instead of clustering with other writers and networking, socially or "professionally." It's mostly a solitary activity, writing, and one has to learn to love a room with no sound but the soft sniper fire of the keyboard.

Sue William Silverman, faculty, Vermont College of Fine Arts: Since, throughout the program, students work every month to meet their packet deadlines, I suggest to graduating students that they *pretend* they still have packet deadlines. In other words, I encourage students to continue to set goals and meet deadlines. This seems to work with many alums. I also encourage my former students to check in with me from time to time and let me know how the writing is going. That helps them to still feel connected to the program.

Teaching perspectives

Laraine Herring, alumnus, Antioch University LA: My MFA program gave me the discipline to write and complete a novel while working a fifty-plus hour job. I learned to manage my time and to create a permanent place of prominence for my writing. Without the MFA, I wouldn't have been able to teach full-time at the college level. I honestly think that teaching writing has helped make me a better writer.

Martin Donoff, director, Fairleigh Dickinson University: My advice is to publish and keep publishing. While the MFA is the requisite degree for teaching at the university level, the degree alone is not a ticket to a tenure-track or even a full-time job teaching creative writing. Most creative writing programs — graduate and undergraduate — look for a record of publication before even considering a candidate.

Publishing

Laura Nathan-Garner, alumnus, Bennington College: When I first applied to MFA programs, I had grand visions of publishing the Great American Essay Collection. But after I graduated from Bennington, I ended up writing largely for commercial audiences because this paid the bills. I wrote two travel guides, wrote copy for websites, worked for book developers and publishers on a variety of topics, and wrote and blogged about health and lifestyle topics. This might seem like a poor use of my MFA, but it surprises me how many of these opportunities I can trace back to the MFA, both directly and indirectly . . . All of these projects have opened the door to other opportunities.

Susan Tekulve, faculty, Converse College: Book publications and prizes are great, but those things don't always happen right away, and you really can't rely on outside forces to be consistently affirming or even nice. A lot of times, being a writer is about going to the writing even when you haven't heard a positive word from an editor for months, or possibly years. So it's really destructive to focus only on the publishing aspect of writing. The students I see benefiting the most from the MFA are those who are more concerned about writing the best poem or story or essay that they can write at a certain moment in time.

The alumni connection

Jenn Scheck-Kahn, alumnus, Bennington College: I participate in the Bennington Collective, which is an alumni group. Participants are divided into pods of four people who share and evaluate ten pages of work once a month. I'm still in touch with a few of my instructors and see the students in my city who have become friends.

Meg Kearney, director, Pine Manor College: We keep alum involved in a number of ways: through our graduate assistant-ships, our graduate guides (an advisee program that links alum with current students), our monthly e-newsletter, and our annual gathering at AWP. Alumni also receive discounts to our audit-ing program, which enables writers from the outside community to attend select classes at our summer and winter residencies. Our alumni point person also hosts a biannual "life after the

MFA" lunch at our residencies, which graduates are invited to attend.

Debra Allbery, director, Warren Wilson College: The alumni community is a remarkably vital and supportive one. Our graduates meet for annual alumni conferences, and keep connected through the alumni listserv. The Friends of Writers website posts alumni notes, news, and publications. We also offer an Alumni Residency Fellowship; graduates can apply to attend an MFA residency as part of our staff, recording lectures and readings; a small stipend is offered to offset travel costs.

Q&A with Loreen Niewenhuis, alumni tips

Loreen Niewenhuis holds an MFA in Fiction Writing from Spalding University. Her short fiction has appeared in many journals including *The Antioch Review* and *The Bellevue Literary Review*. She edits the MFA alumni association newsletter.

Can you tell us how the alumni association developed?

There was a core of probably four alumni who came together to start the association, but Terry Price really did the majority of the planning and early meeting with the MFA staff before the rest of us got involved. Terry felt it was essential that we work with the program to develop the association. It has worked out well, I think, for both returning alumni and for students still in the program. We are constantly welcoming new grads into the association and both the excitement level and involvement level are on the upswing.

What happens during homecoming and how are such activities organized?

Homecoming always happens the last few days of the spring residency, and alumni are encouraged to come back at that time. Since the MFA program focuses almost exclusively on the craft of writing, the association works with the program to offer lectures or panel discussions more geared toward professional development and networking. And we try to have some fun time scheduled, too, time to hang out or do something as a group. We also try to do a brunch with faculty and the grads from that semester. We also celebrate the success of our alumni by featuring those who have been published/produced in the past year. We feature them during a special reading followed by book-signing/sale.

The association is constantly brainstorming and watching for interesting topics at conferences or seminars we attend and we bring these ideas to a meeting with someone from the MFA staff when we plan homecoming with them.

What advice might you have for starting an alumni association or networking group for post-grad fellowship?

Try to work with the program. Start small with a few dedicated people doing specific things, and then build from there. You'll probably need a website for general information, and a newsletter is a great idea, too. Remember, you need to communicate with all alumni.

How did the alumni newsletter begin, what does it include, and how is it beneficial to graduates?

We knew we would need some way to communicate with scattered alumni. A PDF newsletter seemed like the way to go. The program's newsletter is called "On Extended Wings," so we named ours "SOARING." Once we got someone who knew iPages onboard, we recruited several alumni to be editors and it kind of came together. We do articles on published/produced alumni, reports from conferences, and pieces about teaching after getting your MFA, pieces on alumni who start a new literary magazine or chapbook press, and many other topics.

We also communicate details about homecoming and then report on it afterward. Any alumni can write for the newsletter. The newsletter is the voice of the association. In addition to great content for alumni, we hope that it also pulls us together so that we can support each other. SOARING is archived on our website and people are welcome to check it out for ideas: http://spaldingmfaalum.com.

CHAPTER 12

AWP Membership and Services

YOU LEARNED A LITTLE about the Association of Writers and Writing Programs (AWP) in Chapter 3, when we covered the "AWP Hallmarks of an Effective Low-Residency MFA Program in Creative Writing." AWP is a national, non-profit organization that offers a number of services for writers and writing instructors that you might want to take advantage of; these include a guide for writing programs, the Annual Conference & Bookfair, grants and awards, online community discussions, and job listings for both academic and non-academic writing positions.

While many AWP services are open to non-members, some online services — such as the AWP Job List — are available to members only. Membership is open to writers of all levels and experiences, and students are provided with a discount on annual dues. All members receive a subscription to *The Writer's Chronicle*. The AWP Annual Conference & Bookfair is beneficial for all writers — in or outside of academia, published or unpublished — and you do not need a membership to attend. More information about AWP services is available online at www.awpwriter.org.

Prospective students, and writers working independently outside of a program, can — in some ways — benefit the most from AWP services. One member, who is both a low-residency MFA graduate and current faculty member, has this perspective to offer:

Patricia Smith, faculty/alumnus, University of Southern Maine: AWP is woefully underutilized. I think it's seen as an outlet for people who are at a "certain level" of the MFA experience — but it's most valuable for those *seeking* that level.

National Conference & Bookfair

Arguably one of the most anticipated writing events in any given year is the AWP Annual Conference & Bookfair. Hosted in a different North American region each year, writers from all walks of life converge at the Conference and participate in hundreds of writing-related panel discussions, lectures, open forums, and on- and off-site literary readings. But that's a fairly formal overview.

What you really need to know is that the Conference draws in more than 8,000 attendees and more than 500 publishers — publishers that want to meet you. The Bookfair, which runs concurrently with the Conference, is the primary networking hub where writers are invited to interact and have informal conversations with editors, publishers, and writing program representatives.

If you are a prospective student, or even just considering the graduate degree for "someday" in the future, the Bookfair is the best way to meet an entire spectrum of program reps all under one roof. Each program has a designated booth or table where directors, faculty, alumni, and current students make themselves available to answer questions, provide information, and share their personal experiences. There really is nothing like having a one-on-one conversation with people who know, *really know*, the programs you might be applying to, so this is one of my top recommendations for prospective students.

In addition to the writing programs, the Bookfair is also a great way to introduce yourself to hundreds of literary magazines, publishers big and small, and other writing-related organizations and service providers. As you walk through aisle after aisle, in a maze of booths and tables, your back will start to hurt for all of the swag you have stashed away in your AWP-provided shoulder bag. But it's so worth it. Through your Bookfair journey, you will find incredible discounts on books and pick up complimentary back issues of lit journals, writing magazines, and other promotional items, not to mention so many business cards and contact names you will need to take a break to organize and recoup — but just for a bit, because there is so much more waiting for your discovery.

The events last a few short days, but provide a year's worth of motivation and inspiration. Through personal conversations with editors, publishers, and program reps, you will be on fire with the desire — the need — to get back home and write until your pen is dry. But don't dare leave the conference until you have soaked up every last piece of information, and met every last editor and director.

You will walk — or crawl — away from the conference feeling exhausted, but more creatively refreshed than when you were on day one. That's not only because of the official Conference offerings, but also because of the fantastic discussions about writing you had with writing friends old and new. All of those "friends" you have online? They'll see you at the conference. All of the editors you work with via email and over the phone? You'll catch up over a lunch. If you can only attend one such event in your lifetime, go to the AWP Conference & Bookfair. It will provide you with enough oomph to last well beyond the few days when writers from various geographic regions invade a (slightly unsuspecting) city to create *the* literary nucleus of North America for one short week.

You needn't be a member to attend the conference, but there are registration fees and travel costs to consider. However, the Bookfair is open to the general public at no cost on the closing Saturday. Thus, if you are working with a strict budget, you can still absorb and benefit from the aforementioned perks. This really is an event that needs to be experienced at least once in your life as a writer.

But don't just take my word for it. I asked a few current members to share their thoughts on some of the AWP services that are beneficial to low-residency applicants. In addition, Kathleen Driskell shares a brief overview of the Low-Residency MFA Directors' Caucus. I have also included a brief Q&A with Matt Burriesci, AWP Acting Executive Director, wherein he provides a few more details about AWP services and membership.

Stan Rubin, director of the Rainier Writing Workshops at Pacific Lutheran University, is the current Chair of the Low-Residency MFA Directors' Caucus that meets annually at the AWP Conference.

> Go to at least one national Conference. Select a few panels in advance and try to attend them. You'll learn something and meet peers. Spend a lot of time at the Bookfair. Scope it out, and then return to specific

tables that interest you. It's the greatest concentration of publishers, editors, and literary organizations you'll ever see in one place. Meet people. Your mind will open with possibilities.

Stan Rubin, director, Pacific Lutheran University

Kelly Davio serves as managing and poetry editor at *The Los Angeles Review* and reads poetry for *Fifth Wednesday Journal*. She holds an MFA in poetry from Northwest Institute of Literary Arts, and teaches English as a Second Language in Seattle, Washington.

The AWP Bookfair is a wild and wonderful place. Writers, editors, and publishers teem about a convention hall, waiting, making awkward small talk, and selling their wares. Somewhere in all that madness and sensory overload, there's the potential to make a real human connection between writer and editor. It's those moments of artistic understanding and enthusiasm about the work that make the AWP Conference worth it; if every writer can come back with a few good leads on homes for her new work, the Bookfair has been a success.

It's invaluable for writers to meet the magazine editors who've published their work in the past. Editors don't want to publish your work and then never speak to you again; if an editor published you, it's because something about their tastes and your writing clicked. At AWP, you can cultivate relationships by making a personal connection.

Kelly Davio, alumnus, Northwest Institute of Literary Arts

The Low-Residency MFA Directors' Caucus

The Low-Residency MFA Directors' Caucus is held annually at the AWP Conference, and it's important to know the significance behind its development and what the group is doing for low-residency students and programs. In addition to her role at Spalding University, Kathleen Driskell is the Founding Chair of the Low-Residency MFA Directors' Caucus and offered this brief overview of its development:

In 2000, only a handful of low-residency MFA programs existed; by 2006, more than thirty had been founded and low-residency directors were looking for ways to have meaningful conversations about curriculum and administrative development specific to our programs. With the help of AWP, we convened the first Low-Residency MFA Directors' Caucus in 2006 at the Atlanta Conference. Three dozen directors showed up to help develop our Hallmarks and explore programmatic concerns. The Caucus continues to discuss ways to offer our graduate students the very best educations in creative writing. We're grateful to AWP for its support and are pleased not only to be in the larger conversation of our professional organization, but also to find that all programs, traditional as well as low-residency, benefit from conversation about our many innovations.

Kathleen Driskell, associate director, Spalding University

Q&A with Matt Burriesci, AWP Acting Executive Director

Can you comment on the developments in low-residency programs you have witnessed throughout your career?

I suppose the largest development has been the growth. The low-residency model is probably the fastest-growing segment of the MFA degree. The model is appealing to people who can't leave their careers or families for extended periods, but it's also appealing to those who are looking for the kind of educational experience one can get from a low-residency program. In a way, the low-residency model embraces a timeworn tradition of writer–student mentorship. I am not endorsing the low-residency model over the traditional residency model, which has other advantages; I'm just stating that it's a different experience.

How can prospective students use the "AWP Hallmarks" to their advantage?

Students should use the Hallmarks to evaluate the programs they apply to. The Hallmarks were developed over several years with the input of the country's most experienced and dedicated low-residency program directors. These directors care deeply about providing great education for their students, and maintaining high standards in the low-residency curriculum. The Hallmarks are there to help students evaluate a program's curriculum, philosophy, and faculty.

Why should prospective students consider a membership with AWP before deciding on a program?

Membership in AWP is a great way to learn about MFA programs, but it's also an incredible resource for the individual writer. AWP's membership includes a comprehensive listing of jobs available for writers, both in the academic and non-academic markets. It also comes with a subscription to *The Writer's Chronicle*, where writers can get the inside scoop on what's happening in the field of literature, and in the programs themselves. Of course the *Chronicle* also features great essays on the writer's craft, interviews with today's most important literary voices, and discussions of important issues in the field of literature. It also has a current list of publication opportunities, and grants and awards available to writers. Members [of] AWP also gain access to an online archive of more than 1,000 articles from the *Chronicle*, dating back several decades. Membership is a way to support literature in the country, as AWP advocates on behalf of writers. It's also a community where people meet to share ideas and work. Once writers join AWP, they often stay as members for years or decades.

Can you tell us about AWP career services?

AWP's career services center is a dossier service for writers seeking jobs. Writers can have transcripts and letters of recommendation sent to us, and we'll keep them forever. We'll also send them out to jobs for you.

Why should prospective students attend the Conference?

AWP's Annual Conference & Bookfair is one of the most important literary gatherings in North America, with more than 400 readings, lectures, and panels on contemporary literature. The Bookfair features more than 500 small presses, publishers, and literary magazines, and often you can walk right up and talk to the editors. It's a great chance to network with other writers, to see your favorite writers, and basically to have a great time and celebrate our country's diverse and impressive literary culture.

How can student members get involved with AWP events and programs?

Students should always propose events for AWP's Conference. The proposal process is open to all, members and non-members alike. Although the process is quite competitive, we're always looking for excellent discussions, panels, and readings. They can also friend us on Facebook and, of course, every writer should be a member of AWP!

Extended Interviews

THROUGHOUT THE HANDBOOK, YOU have become acquainted with a number of directors, faculty, alumni, and current students. While there simply isn't space to share every complete interview, this section provides a few extended interviews to share even more personalized experiences and perspectives. The interviewees herein are shared in alphabetical order, by program name.

Converse College: Leslie Pietrzyk, faculty

Leslie Pietrzyk is the author of two novels, *Pears on a Willow Tree* and *A Year and a Day*. Her short fiction has appeared in many journals and magazines, including *The Iowa Review*, *New England Review*, *The Sun*, and *TriQuarterly*.

How long have you been an instructor with Converse College?

The program began in June 2009, with its first residency and first class of students. I started teaching fiction in the program at that time and have continued since.

In your opinion, what makes the Converse program unique?

The Converse program maintains a very low mentor–student ratio, which ensures lots of personal attention for each student.

What advice would you offer to students considering a low-residency program?

While all graduate writing programs call for students who are disciplined and self-motivated, I think this is only more so in a low-residency program. Though the work submission deadlines are clearly delineated, there's no voice reminding you what to do when, no regular class meetings to keep you on track. A student needs to be organized, and needs to be willing to do the hard work to become a better writer. The mentor wants to help, but it's always up to you. The more you put into this type of program — coming up with ideas for your reading list, researching other writers, thinking about projects to work on — the more you will get out of it.

What does the low-residency model provide for students?

What I like about the low-residency model is that it offers the best of both worlds. There is the workshop, and the opportunity to share work and get a broad perspective on it; it seems to me that sharing work that has been revised with the mentor is an especially effective use of the workshop time . . . The newer material, then, is ideal to share with the mentor, who can offer undivided attention and very specific comments that will help move the work forward. The combination of both approaches is not to be underestimated, in my opinion.

I would also remind students in a low-residency program to take advantage of the social aspects of the residency period. You may be tired — actually, I know you will be utterly exhausted — but try to find time to hang out with the faculty and other students after readings and at meals. There's much to be learned from these more casual, off-the-cuff conversations. Don't hole yourself away.

What are the residencies like at Converse College?

I very much enjoy the residencies. It's great to spend ten days immersed in conversations about writing, with all these writers, to feel as though we're all in this enterprise together learning how to improve our work. I try to attend most craft lectures and readings myself, which aids in the teaching as I'm able to reference in our workshop various talks from throughout the week. Also, when a workshop meets every day instead of weekly, the bond forms quickly and tightly: I think our discussions tend to get to the heart of the matter more rapidly than the more traditional once-a-week workshops that I also teach. And I love the student readings at the end of the period: it's inspiring to see people read after only a semester in the program and to hear how their work has progressed in such a short time.

You've participated in a variety of AWP activities. How can prospective and current students make the most of a membership with AWP?

Attend the conference! That's a great way to keep the bonds with your former teachers and former fellow students. I like to say that eventually you'll run into every single writer you've ever met at AWP and, surprisingly, they will remember you!

Northwest Institute of Literary Arts: Kobbie Alamo, alumnus

Kobbie Alamo was a student at the time of this interview. She has since graduated from the fiction program and teaches expositional and creative writing at both the college and high school levels. Literary agent Andrea Hurst is representing her most recent novel.

Why did you choose this program?

There were so many factors that went into my decision to attend NILA. However, at the end of the day, NILA won out because of three main reasons: (1) Who the players are. The instructors are incredible! (2) What they're doing. Take a look at the impressive publishing record for both faculty and students. (3) How they make students feel. There is an intimacy with this program that I believe is unique to *this* program in *this* place.

How has the program benefited your writing life?

I have learned so much about writing! That probably seems like a "no duh" response, but I have attended many, many writers' conferences, seminars, and events. Goodness, I've even taught writing. So I wasn't expecting to learn much about the actual craft of writing. What an egotistical mistake! My very first semester, when I took Craft of Writing: Form and Technique in Fiction with professor Wayne Ude, I realized there was significantly more to learn. As far as my career? I'm pleased to say I met my agent at one of the residencies.

Tell us about your experience with the thesis project.

Since the fiction thesis for NILA is an entire novel, intimidation plays a role. My advisor actually suggested my thesis — there was a short story I had written that she enjoyed and thought it could be expanded and made into a novel.

The process is fairly simple: create an outline, create a schedule, and then follow both. The way my advisor worked with me was, for the first half of the novel, I would upload each chapter as it was completed and she would make critiques and comments. After the first half, I just plowed ahead and then submitted the entire novel, having incorporated the critiques from the first half. The most important piece to the thesis portion is communication. I feel blessed that communication worked very well with my advisor.

What are the NILA residencies like?

The residencies are the most unique aspect of the entire program. The schedule is created for classes to be conducted in the mornings, and they're great. But it's the afternoons that keep me tethered. The afternoons are a required segment for students, under the heading of the Profession of Writing, and they're filled with guest speakers and facilitators, ranging from authors to editors to agents to publishers to book binders to screenwriters to PR folk to, well, I think you get the idea. We students are exposed to every aspect of the profession of writing, with a treasure trove of material.

And as wonderful as the presentations are, and they are, it's also a wonderful opportunity to meet these experts in a warm and inviting setting. To have lunch or dinner at a table with a mix of students, presenters, and faculty is an unsurpassed experience. Sure it's good for networking, but it's more than that. It's making relationships that have the potential to last a lifetime. I forget about the networking and just enjoy the atmosphere and the new friendships.

Another part of what makes the residencies special is the location. Whidbey Island is a quiet, peaceful environment rich with natural beauty. At my January residency I watched seals frolicking in the water outside my bedroom and had bald eagles nesting in a tree near the kitchen. With the cove surrounded by trees and lapping water, well, there just isn't anywhere on earth more conducive to igniting the muse. This peaceful setting helps the entire atmosphere at the residencies. People are more tranquil, more open to each other.

How should incoming students prepare for the MFA?

In my opinion, the number one requirement for an incoming student is good organizational skills. Good time management and self-motivation is crucial to success. Some students plan to work a few hours every day, which is what I did and found it easier to manage the workload this way, but others give all of their required hours in large chunks over a day or two. If you have good organizational skills, the study direction falls into place.

I do recommend finding a way to have access to an academic library. For me, as a part-time teacher at a community college, I was able to utilize the library and, also important, have access to scholarly journals. However, this is not required and many of my friends have made it successfully through the program without such access.

Queens University of Charlotte: Georgia Banks-Martin, alumnus

Georgia Banks-Martin is the author of *Rhapsody for lessons learned or Remembered*, a collection of ekphrastic poems. Her poetry has appeared in *African-American Review*, *Pearl Magazine*, *Prick of the Spindle*, *Thanal Online*, and other journals.

Why did you choose to do an MFA?

When I began my MFA at Queens University of Charlotte, I was employed as a seven-to-twelfth grade Language Arts teacher. I had taught in public schools for eight years and was generally unhappy. I had become overtaken by a need to improve my own writing skills and to be involved with something that required and respected my creativity.

Can you share your experience with the thesis portion of your program?

The term in which the thesis is completed is the most stressful at Queens. The graduating student is enrolled in classes, so she must keep up with submissions and critique, while writing her thesis and craft seminar. I did my major writing over the summer and focused on rewriting and filling in of ideas during the fall. Some of the stress was relieved through some rather detailed discussions with my mentor.

What were the residencies like?

The residencies are hard work. We begin on Sunday evening right after dinner when we meet our instructors and group members and exchange manuscripts. These manuscripts must be critiqued for group discussions, which begin with a large group on Monday morning. At the end of the week, instructors meet for an hour one-on-one with their students. In these meetings, students can speak with the instructor about concerns they may have about their work. The instructor also gives a full evaluation of the student's work submitted for the week and gives suggestions of areas that the student might wish to explore or improve. This is also the time where individual goals and expectations can be expressed.

Each person has her own way of relieving stress, but students do have a tradition of hanging out at a local restaurant, Providence Café, after classes. There you can eat and have a nice drink; most just go to drink and talk to friends and instructors in a less formal setting.

During the program, what assistance did you receive in learning how to approach publishers and editors?

During each residency students are required to attend a program-wide panel. The topic changes each term but some of them did address elements of the publication and submission process; for example, one was on book proposal writing. After graduation, alumni can attend the Alumni Program. This is a writing conference offered bi-yearly and allows students to take advanced workshops with renowned writers in their fields, as well as speak one-on-one with professional editors who will review and critique their manuscripts.

Do you continue to communicate with the Queens community?

After graduation, we are encouraged to take part in small writing groups. Each month, the group members submit new work or problematic work for critique. Some of us still email and Facebook each other on a regular basis. A few of us are in involved in more professional relationships, which involve promotion and publication.

Seton Hill University: Cynthia Ravinski, alumnus

Cynthia Ravinski is a graduate of the Writing Popular Fiction program at Seton Hill University. While at SHU she wrote a Fantasy novel, *Dreams of Stone*. When she's not writing fantasy, her interests include lapidary and jewelry making, fiber arts, and exploring the great outdoors.

Why did you choose to enter a graduate writing program?

I had decided to continue my education in writing after I received my BFA. However, I wanted to wait a couple years to gain more life experience, save up some money, and try my hand at getting published before venturing into another degree. I was very lucky as I found a job, part-time albeit, in publishing. This was another great form of writing education. I did not succeed in getting published before attending SHU.

Can you share any experiences from working with your faculty mentors?

I went into the program assigned to David Bischoff as my mentor, who I worked with for my first year. Instead of nitpicking all my grammar errors as I built the first draft of my novel, he looked for my weaknesses and worked with me on little side assignments to improve my craft. What he helped me with the most was motivation. He knew exactly what to say to help me writing and slogging through the draft.

At SHU, third-semester students pick their next mentor. We switch to ensure our projects get more than one set of eyes on it. I was incredibly lucky that I got my first choice mentor, Timons Esaias, for the last half of the program. As a mentor he was brutal, honest and exacting, but still entirely constructive and funny all at the same time. As he read my manuscript, he clearly classified all my mistakes into groups and offered suggestions, or resources on how to fix the problem and never telling me what I should have written instead.

Can you describe the non-residency semester work?

After residency, I returned home with a head full of motivation and inspiration for the writing term. The first thing on my mind was always the daunting page count I'd have to complete by the end of the semester. As I was writing a full-length fantasy novel I had to complete at least one hundred pages to graduate on time. Every month a section of new pages were due to the mentor and the members of our critique group — one to two other people. After two weeks we were responsible for having read and critiqued our partner's work. After two weeks, we also should have received feedback from our mentor and partners to apply to the pages. At the end of the semester, all our rough pages would be revised and turned in to the mentor.

I kept a reading journal, which I turned in to my mentor at the end of every semester. I read a mix of fantasy and classic literate, non-fiction how-to writing books, and scholarly criticism books adding up to four or five per semester. I kept a journal detailing my reactions to the books, what I learned about writing or my genre, how I didn't like the way an author executed a craft element, or when I discovered a new foundation element of the genre. Three semesters of this work prepared me for the fourth semester requirement of writing my "genre paper," an eight to ten page essay describing how my thesis novel fit into the genre. The genre paper took the place of the reading journal for the fourth semester.

Then there was the online portion. The program ran a discussion board of threads and a chat foyer. In the threads, we had to post a comment, or add to a discussion at least once a week. Three times a semester, a required one-hour chat occurred in which mentors, alumni, or professors would lead an hour-long discussion.

What were the SHU residencies like?

The SHU residency is seven days of intense learning. We arrived the night before classes started for a required welcome session. I always looked forward to this. For the first time in half a year, I would be able to see my old friends and meet all the new students . . . Learning days were very long, sometimes up to twelve hours. Classes started at 9 a.m. and ended at 4 p.m. These were workshops and modules, each lasting three hours. Although these were very laid back, every student works very hard during these hours.

Mentors and professors taught modules focusing on basic craft elements as well as various aspects of writing and publishing. Almost every module I remember attending consisted of lecture, writing exercises, sharing and discussion. These modules were so much better than simply reading a book about how to improve your craft. You had someone up there who knew what they were doing sharing with you the little gems of information they had learned the hard way.

One evening per residency is set aside for mentor meetings. Every student has one hour scheduled with his or her mentor. Nerve wracking or enjoyable, this was when I could make eye contact with the reader of my manuscript, get feedback on my work habits, talk about the next steps for me on developing my work. Also, this was when students and mentors agree on the upcoming writing term's contract, detailing the page counts and books to read for the upcoming three months.

What assistance did you receive in learning how to approach publishers and editors?

Just as SHU is enthusiastic about teaching good craft to its students, it is just as eager to teach the business of writing. After all, the point of writing is to get it out there. There is a required module dedicated to the business of writing, which highlights the importance of agents and details the process of publishing novels. As this is one of the most common subjects brought up by students, mentors frequently shared their personal experiences, good and bad, and offered suggestions to students about pitching their work and querying publishers.

One final way the program assisted me in learning how to approach agents and publishers was, in fact, requiring me to do it. At least every four semesters the program brings in a group of agents and editors to cover every genre. Students with completed or nearly complete novels must pitch. For this, we are forced to use all the pitching skills we've picked up going through the program to be as successful as we can here. Although I didn't sell my book while pitching to Betsy Mitchell of Del Rey books, another of my peers did.

Have you benefited from your experience in the program?

SHU gave me innumerable tools to promote myself in a writing career. I know what to expect from agents and editors as a new writer. I won't be shocked at every step of the way and will know how to make good business decisions.

In two years, I've gone through almost every stage of writing a book at least once, with the guidance of professionals. Next time I do it, I will know what to expect and how to handle it myself. The active alumni network will always provide me support and confidence in my work to keep me going.

Other than student loans, how accessible is financial aid at Seton Hill?

There are three scholarships offered by the alumni association; the school offers a 25 percent scholars discount off tuition. The application is an essay.

Any other thoughts you wish to share?

A writing program is kind of like a way to force you to write and parade networking opportunities in front of you. You don't need a program to learn how to do these things. A program just puts them all into one place; that's what you are paying for, as well as the attention your work will receive from professionals.

Being aware of standard publishing and networking opportunities while going through programs, or before going through a program, will be more helpful than just taking what they give you in the package. Be aware of the writing world and its opportunities because when the two years end, you will have the support of your community, but you will have to stand on your own feet.

Spalding University: Kathleen Driskell, associate director

Kathleen Driskell is the associate editor of *The Louisville Review*. Her books include *Seed Across Snow* and *Laughing Sickness*.

Tell us about the screenwriting option at Spalding

We're very proud of Spalding's screenwriting option and have put a good deal of energy and resources toward building a great MFA program. Screenwriting students are in workshop during residency, and attend lectures with the practicing screenwriters on our faculty and visiting industry guest speakers. When our students leave the residency, they mentor with a working screenwriter throughout the at-home portion of the semester.

In addition to this instruction, our screenwriting students have the opportunity to move script to the screen in our Film Production Seminar. This film is very short, of course, and features only a small portion of the screenplay, but it is enormously helpful for our students to see their own work filmed and edited. Also, our students receive professional readings of their scripts-in-progress presented by actors before the students begin their fourth semester in which they polish and complete a screenplay to be presented in the creative thesis.

How does the screenwriting option contribute to the overall MFA program?

We believe in the power and future of film at Spalding and know that all students are enriched by our having a screenwriting program. It's wonderful to see our students and faculty members present their scripts in our residency reading series. It gives all of us, whether poets or picture book writers, new ways to think about our own writing processes.

We also have many students studying in other genres who wish to cross over and study screenwriting for a semester. Recently, because we have a screenwriting program, we were able to offer a semester in Film Adaptation for our prose writers. Fiction and creative non-fiction students interested in adapting prose for the movies were able to study screenwriting for an entire semester. They were assigned a screenwriting mentor to help them move their prose writing to screenplays. We continue to look for ways to "blur" the genres in order that our students have the best opportunities for their own writing.

What can you tell us about the Writing for Children program?

Our Writing for Children and Young Adults program includes graduate instruction in picture books, middle-grade readers, young adult fiction and creative non-fiction, plays, and screenplays for children and young adults. In the first semester, our students are in workshop with other writing for children and young adult authors. In the second and third semester, they have the opportunity to focus on the craft of writing and study in particular genres. A student who wants to write screenplays for young adults will work with a screenwriting mentor. A student who would like to write a novel in verse for middle-aged readers will study with a poetry mentor. In their last two residencies, students return to the writing for children and young adults workshop to study.

We place a great deal of emphasis on craft within this program. Often students who study writing for children and young adults are isolated from the other writing students. We recognize that our Writing for Children and Young Adults student writers have unique emphasis on their audience, but they participate alongside the others at each residency.

What can you tell us about the international summer residencies?
Unlike other programs that offer study abroad experiences we go to a different world city for each residency. Recent students have studied in Paris, London and Bath, Barcelona, Buenos Aires, and Tuscany. This is a sort of grand tour that we provide our students and faculty. In addition to studying hard in workshop and during lectures and other curriculum sessions, we also take in that part of the world as part of our "texts." How can a trip to the Louvre or to Stonehenge not be valuable to a writer?

Our tuition for the summer semester is the same as for fall and spring semesters in Louisville on Spalding's campus, though obviously there is extra travel expense involved. Studying in the summer also allows our students to take a nine-month semester instead of a six-month semester. The students do the same amount of work, but the work is spread out over a longer period of time. This is especially wonderful for teachers or those who have difficulty schedules at home.

Spalding University: Cathy Shap Nickola, alumnus
Cathy Shap Nickola teaches at Mott Community College in Flint, MI. Her poems have appeared or are forthcoming in publications such as *Florida Review* and *Public Republic*. She graduated from Spalding's poetry program in May 2009.

Why did you choose to pursue an MFA when you did?
I went to a writer's conference, Bear River, in northern Michigan and one of my mentors there, Laura Kasischke, introduced me to the concept of and suggested I apply to a low-residency program. At the time I had four smallish children at home and my writing wasn't taken all that seriously by those around me; worse, I found myself always putting my family's needs before my creative work because I didn't really have the necessary discipline. I hoped that being in a writing program would give some legitimacy to my work — an idea I now find fairly ridiculous — and would force my family and me to simply make time every day for my creative work.

Once I started the program I realized that the degree would help me get back to my teaching career, which I had given up when I became a mom. Having completed the program I can say that the experience did indeed help me establish a consistent routine. I learned how to be disciplined and how to juggle my responsibilities as a mom with my responsibility to be a good steward of my work.

Why low-residency? How did that work for your lifestyle?

Low-residency ended up working really well for me as a stay-at-home mom with four kids, because it allowed me to create my own writing and studying schedule and to do most of my work from home. The residencies were exactly the sort of vacation I had always dreamed of: time away from the kids doing something that challenged me while mingling with other terrific writers, who were equally excited about being away from their routines, all of us thrown together into this insane vortex of creativity. It was exhausting.

Can you share your experience in working with the faculty at Spalding?

The fabulous thing about these residencies at Spalding is that you're assigned one mentor and you work one-on-one the entire semester. I was lucky to be assigned to Molly Peacock my first semester; she was so encouraging and would spend hours on the phone with me giving me private lectures on the history of poetry. Debra Kang Dean was also amazing. Working with her often felt as if I had been apprenticed to a Jedi master of the line.

In some ways, studying under these writers can seem so intimidating, so it takes a certain willingness on the part of the student to just let go of her own limiting beliefs and to engage with each mentor as if each is an equal. That's when the energy shifts, and the writing grows.

I studied under Greg Pape the year he became Poet Laureate of Montana; he guided me through the writing of my thesis. The highlight for me, honestly, was when he sent me some of the new poems he was still working on for a new collection, asking me for my thoughts. Greg works with his students via snail mail and cassette tape. We would write letters and I would record myself reading my poems onto tape and then he would send the tape back and read my work back to me with comments and suggestions thrown in.

It took a lot of courage for me, at one point, to send him my honest thoughts about one of his poems. I questioned a couple of lines. I remember stammering on tape, "Oh, please forgive me for saying this . . ." but he was very gracious about it, and his willingness to share his work with me and to both accept and challenge my comments taught me so much about the importance of both vulnerability and stewardship.

What were the Spalding residencies like?

The residencies at Spalding are heavenly, frankly. We were housed in the Brown Hotel, a luxurious historical hotel in downtown Louisville. The days are filled with readings and lectures by the faculty and graduating students, as well as visiting faculty and writers such as W. S. Merwin. Does it get any better than that?

The nights are filled with just the very best sort of "party": poets, screenwriters, playwrights, actors, musicians with guitars handy, novelists, essayists all gathered together either on the overstuffed-let-me-just-sleep-here-couches or at one of the local pubs drinking, singing, talking, arguing, laughing until three or four in the morning, though not every night, of course!

By the end of it all, by day ten, there are no words left in the atmosphere. Everyone looks deflated and exhausted, but also stricken, because no one really wants to leave that lively and engaging atmosphere.

Do you keep in touch with the Spalding community? How so?

I've gone back to see peers give readings and graduate. I keep in touch via email with six or seven other writers from the program somewhat regularly. If someone drops off for a while, we all know they're being productive. I have two or three other writers from the program with whom I share work. Right now my daughters and I are reading aloud the novel written by one of my talented peers. We record our readings and then we send her the tapes with the hope that it will help her as she edits the work before sending it out to publishers. I care very much about my friends' creative work and life.

In your experience, how can writers benefit from a low-residency MFA? What would you say to prospective students?

If you're a writer like me, for example, who lives in a small town with limited access to a vibrant and thriving artistic community — and I imagine this is a good number of us — then what any MFA program will do is provide you with such a community for a limited time. Once you complete your degree, of course, it will be up to you to maintain and continue to create a smaller version of that community, and it's often challenging even with the degree under your belt.

The degree can help you to get a teaching position at the college level, or maybe some good connections with various journals to improve your chances of publication, but it won't guarantee you great writing, or even a better job in today's economy. It will improve your writing certainly. It will expose you to many different styles of writing. And the residency experiences themselves I often felt were like any really intense retreat — you meet fascinating people with whom you quickly develop close bonds because you're sharing such an intimate part of yourself, your creativity, day and night far away from your daily reality. It's fun. And it should be fun. And then you return to reality full of inspiration and ideas and you have six months to write your heart out before the next residency.

I have friends who graduated from traditional MFA programs and the biggest difference I could see between their experience and mine was that I learned to be a lot more comfortable with long stretches of writing time during which I received no formal feedback unless I really sought it out. I figured out how to make my writing life fit into the rest of my life in a consistent daily way. I didn't have to leave family or work to go off for a couple of years to pursue this degree; the program sort of came into my life, home, and family as they were and we all adjusted. After completing the program I really just carried on with what I had already been doing the last two years.

I write in the mornings certain days, and evenings others, and on the weekends when time and family commitments allow. The lack of formal deadlines makes it a lot easier for me to skip days and even weeks, so that's where I think the friendships that were formed during residency can come in handy. It's nice to get the occasional email asking, "So what are you working on now?"

But it's also probably not a good idea to be overly dependent on that.

You're a writer if you're writing, and the more you write, and more importantly read, the better you'll eventually get. An MFA program speeds that up a bit and introduces you to some great people, but it's not inexpensive. It's fun. It's interesting. It's another experience. But Kay Ryan isn't writing the way she's writing because she went to any kind of MFA program. Pattiann Roger's poetry isn't what it is because of a residency experience. Keep it all in perspective.

Vermont College of Fine Arts: Phyllis Barber, faculty

Phyllis Barber is the author of seven books, including *Raw Edges: A Memoir*. She has taught in the Vermont College of Fine Arts MFA in Writing Program since 1991 and lives in Denver, Colorado.

What do you hope to offer your students?

What I've hoped to offer my students is encouragement based on my own particular experience with the life of writing. I hadn't come through academic channels . . . so when I decided to write, I realized I had a lot to learn. But I was determined as well as intense about this determination. Over the years I had met many VC students who were equally determined to call themselves a writer so when I became a teacher, I hoped to assist them through the maze . . . One of my main efforts over the years has been to help students not only see the micro- and macro scope of their work and to develop their technique as writers, but to help them believe in their own voice and their own worth.

Do you face any challenges teaching in a low-residency format?

As an instructor in a low-residency format, I've faced the challenge of being able to be familiar enough with my students' work so that they feel they are fully supported in their effort to write. We only have eleven days at the residencies, but when we all go home, I've tried to stay in good touch with each student so that they don't feel alone in their efforts. It has been very important to me to become thoroughly acquainted with each student's work in order to help him or her become the writer he or she wants to be. I try not to have an agenda about what I want for them, except for their success, and try to be in tune with what they want to do and say with their writing.

Tell us about the VCFA residencies

A Vermont residency is very busy and stimulating. We have workshops — an hour for each student's twenty pages of writing in fiction and creative non-fiction; lectures — the graduating students and members of the faculty give lectures regarding all manner of concerns about the writing craft, the writing life, those who populate the writing scene, and the philosophy of the venture; readings given by faculty, visiting writers, graduating students, and shorter versions given by the other students at the nightly student reading; and all manner of discussions about writing in the halls, in the lunchroom, and while walking across campus.

The atmosphere is exceptionally supportive, and an unspoken effort is made to make students feel like writers rather than to set up a competitive atmosphere about who is best or better. Every effort is made to acclimate new students to the residency and to help everyone feel that they have a listening ear should they need one. There is usually a talent show of some sort — some residencies have more "talent" than others — where all one needs to do is drop a handkerchief to get applause. Participants are totally supported as they demonstrate their skills, or not-so-skillful skills, and laughter and good will is rampant.

How might students maintain a sense of community after graduation?

After the MFA graduation, a student needs to keep writing, to set up a definite schedule, and to not spend most of their time thinking about writing — an easy thing to do. I also recommend that graduating students become involved with writing groups so that they have a deadline to keep and have someone who both needs and is willing to give a response to the writing in the group. It's also nice to be involved with community writing organizations such as The Loft in Minneapolis, Minnesota, and Lighthouse Writers in Denver, Colorado, or help establish such a thing in their own communities.

What advice do you have for students considering a low-res program?

Having experienced a traditional university situation as well as the low-residency program, I believe strongly that the low-residency program can support students in ways that a traditional university can't. The one-on-one component with four different advisors is something that can't be found at most universities. Granted, there is the communal life at traditional schools, but it's amazing how strongly supportive each class at Vermont College becomes through the four semesters and how close ties remain after they leave the program. I would advise prospective students to do their homework about the kind of program they want and to know exactly what it is that they do want from their advisors and their chosen school. That kind of clarity makes for a good experience with a low-residency program.

Vermont College of Fine Arts: Jeanne Lyet Gassman, alumnus

Jeanne Lyet Gassman is the recipient of a creative writing fellowship from the Arizona Commission on the Arts. Her work has been published in literary magazines and she teaches writing workshops and classes in the Phoenix, Arizona metropolitan area. She is currently working on an historical novel set in the first century AD. Jeanne was a student at the time of this interview, but she graduated in 2010.

You have more than twenty-five years of experience as a writer and instructor. Why did you choose to pursue an MFA at this point in your career?

When I first started writing seriously, there weren't many MFA programs available. The demands of raising a family and financial constraints made it difficult to consider pursuing an advanced degree for many years. To compensate, I was mostly self-taught during those twenty-five years, attending writer's conferences, taking the random workshop or class, or participating regularly in critique groups. I benefited from this self-directed study and managed to write and publish on a fairly regular basis, but it wasn't enough.

I was also acutely aware of my limitations and knew that I needed either a good mentor or a good advanced writing program to help me bring my craft to the next level. As soon as time and finances allowed, I decided to pursue my MFA so that I could further develop my writing craft.

Why did you choose Vermont's program?

When I decided to pursue an MFA in writing, I researched the low-residency programs thoroughly, seeking a program that would best fit my needs. Vermont's excellent reputation and stellar faculty put it at the top of my list.

Can you tell us about the structure of your program of study?

The low-residency MFA in Writing program at Vermont consists of four semesters and five residencies. You begin each semester with attendance at a residency where you meet with your faculty advisor and work out a semester plan of study. The additional fifth residency is your graduating residency, in which you present a lecture on an approved topic and a reading of your work. During each residency, you are required to attend a minimum of eight lectures. You are also required to attend your writing workshop. In addition, you must complete evaluations of lectures, the workshop, the readings, panel discussions, etc. You and your advisor also create a semester reading list and study plan. Workshop materials are submitted in advance of the residency.

Once you return home, you begin your semester work. Every semester is divided up into five reporting periods, called packets, that are due to your advisor approximately every four weeks. The first two semesters are devoted to concentrated reading, writing, and analysis of the craft. The reading list consists of a minimum of ten books. For each packet, you are required to submit two critical essays based on your reading/analysis of the craft and approximately twenty-five to thirty pages of creative work. The advisor responds to your work within a few days of receipt with a detailed letter of suggestions and comments as well as written comments on the packet material itself.

During the third semester, you are required to write a critical thesis, with a minimum of 5,000 of your own words for prose that is a detailed study of some element of craft. You also continue to submit creative work in your packets. The fourth semester, you write your creative thesis — a minimum of seventy-five pages for prose — and prepare a lecture for your fifth residency. This material is still submitted on the packet deadline schedule, and your advisor works with you to polish your creative thesis and help you refine your lecture.

What were the VCFA residencies like?

Residencies last ten days and are jam-packed with lectures, readings, panel discussions, workshop, and social activities. It's easy to burn out if you don't pace yourself or take some time to rest. Workshop discussions can be very intense, especially for those who aren't accustomed to the workshop environment, but the faculty work hard to make it a nurturing experience.

There are usually two to three lectures every day as well as workshop, and readings. Often a visiting author will conduct small group discussions. There may be one or two panel discussions during the residency on such topics as teaching or publishing with small presses. Social activities include informal gatherings, dances, talent shows, ball games in the summer, receptions, and parties. Students and faculty dine together in the cafeteria, so there are numerous opportunities to visit with both students and faculty members. About one-third of students choose off-campus housing but still eat in the cafeteria.

Tell us about the Vermont community

Since this is a low-residency program, almost no one in the program lives near me. However, I communicate regularly with several of them via email. We support each other by providing tips on publishing opportunities and reading each other's work.

I've made lifelong friends and discovered wonderful new writers. One of my greatest joys is reading about a fellow student's success. It's an inspiration to all of us. The faculty and students maintain contact beyond the formal constraints of the program via email and correspondence.

What advice would you offer to a student considering a low-residency program?

First of all, understand that this is not a part-time degree. Unlike a residency program, which has vacations such as spring, summer, and winter break, the two-year, low-residency MFA is non-stop for two years. Beginning with the ten-day residency, each semester is almost six months long, ending less than three weeks before the next residency. Vermont recommends that students plan on committing a minimum of twenty-five hours per week to program requirements. After the first semester, my weekly time commitment has been closer to thirty hours per week. Effective time management is essential. If you are a procrastinator or someone who needs reminders to finish work, a low-residency program may not be the best choice.

Warren Wilson College: K. Alma Peterson, alumnus

K. Alma Peterson is a graduate of the MFA Program for Writers at Warren Wilson College. Her poems have appeared in *Hayden's Ferry Review*, *The New Orphic Review*, *Perihelion Review*, and others. She is the author of *Befallen*, a poetry chapbook.

Why did you pursue an MFA? And why low-residency?

My career was unrelated to writing at the time I thought about an MFA. I own a real estate appraisal company, and it's a job that doesn't sap my creativity, which affords me time to write. I considered myself a serious poet, and applying to an MFA program seemed the next step.

Low-residency was the only option that suited my work situation: full-time job, self-employed. Low-residency allowed me to plan for the times I would be away from home and work, and to generate new material on my own schedule, which was essential for me. Attending regularly scheduled classes, even near my home, would have been much less conducive to sustained productivity.

Why Warren Wilson?

I met the founder, and some of the faculty, of Warren Wilson at the Ropewalk workshops, and was extremely impressed with the rigor of their teaching, and their literary and educational success. I had also become acquainted with several graduates of Warren Wilson in my area, Minneapolis/St. Paul, MN, who held the program in high regard; these were poets whose writing and teaching styles I admired, and who were eager to talk about Warren Wilson. I liked what I heard, and became convinced that Warren Wilson was the best program. I very much wanted to be accepted there.

What was your experience with the residencies?

The residencies are very intense: the brainpower of the assembled students and faculty is mind-blowing! I always felt privileged to be

a part of it, and always a little intimidated. Because I'm an intro-
vert, the social stimulation, even with "my tribe" was exhilarating,
but exhausting. Returning from the residencies, there was always
a period of re-entry: it was difficult to quiet the constant stream
of chatter coming from my mouth — settling back into a work
and home routine took time, especially since I was fired up to do
nothing but write.

The residencies are chock full of lectures, readings, meetings,
new friendships, and subsequent reunions. From morning to
night, everyone is consumed and consuming ideas and presentations about the craft they love and are committed to improving. I
will never forget the marvelous cast of characters I met, the enduring friendships I made. There was burnout, there was anticipation,
and there was anxiety — the gamut of emotions. I remember
wondering how we could be so hungry all the time when the only
thing running was our brains.

We stayed in dormitories during the residencies and ate in the
cafeteria. The undergraduate program at Warren Wilson College
has programs in sustainable agriculture and other green concerns,
and the food in the cafeteria was very good! Off campus, the
nearby towns of Swannanoa and Asheville, NC, had good restau-
rants and fun shopping. We had one day off in the middle of each
residency; some people caught up on sleep, and others explored
the area: Blue Ridge Mountains, and Parkway, Biltmore, etc.

The lectures started at 9 a.m. every day, and continued through
the day. We were required to summarize the lectures, and turn in
those summaries. Fiction and poetry lectures were always open
to students in both genres, and even though I had — and have
— no ambition to write fiction, the fiction lectures were valuable
and interesting, since many craft elements overlap genres. The
daily workshop sessions held us to a high standard, analyzing
student work in strict terms of craft. We used a methodology that
allowed us to get beyond personal taste and pushed us to focus
on the success of each poem, rather than subjective reactions
to it.

What was your experience with the non-residency semesters?
The one-on-one work with a different faculty member each
semester was terrific; this aspect of low-residency programs means
that each faculty gets to know the writer's work in depth. Packets

of significant amounts of work are exchanged, on an agreed upon frequency, and I always found that there was flexibility if need be. At the same time there is an in-depth familiarity, the distance factor — not being in class, or even seeing the mentor writer at all after the residency — minimized the effects of personality. By that I mean, that it was all about the writing, not how well two people got along, or clicked in person.

During the semester, a great deal of work was required; I was highly motivated, yet I often wondered if I would be able to generate enough, much less enough good, material. The faculty I worked with always seemed to strike the right balance of encouragement and criticism, were always appreciative of my sensibilities. Warren Wilson has an essay semester, which is devoted to writing a scholarly paper. I was not looking forward to that semester, but it turned out that having to choose a topic, and find works of poetry to support it, really broadened my understanding of poetry. I also gained confidence, having never written a scholarly paper before.

What can you tell us about working with your faculty mentors?
At each residency, we prepared a summary, characterizing our writing, our ambitions, our processes, etc. There was an opportunity to indicate which faculty we wanted to work with. The faculty convened, and pairings of faculty with students were posted. We then met with our faculty person to discuss and make a semester plan. This was a collaborative process, and required several meetings.

During each semester, the faculty mentor determined, packet by packet, whether sufficient work was being generated, and that the annotations were in-depth and useful to my writing. During the essay semester, each draft was approved, as the essay was developed. I was able to send poems to my essay faculty mentor, and I received a very valuable letter, addressing the future of my writing, that I still refer to often.

As I recall, there were five or six packets of work exchanged during the semester, either by snail mail or email. Each packet had several annotations, which addressed various aspects of the craft of poetry, as well as new poems, or revisions of poems. The teacher's response to each packet included a lengthy letter, accompanied by notated poems, and suggested revisions. Sometimes rewrites of annotations were required, if they did not adequately explore their subject.

What is the Warren Wilson community like? Have you stayed in touch with anyone?

I made close friends in the program, and stay in touch with several. The intensity of the residencies is conducive to stimulating discussions, in which affinities are discovered quickly and enduringly. Even in a community of writers, who are all to some extent kindred spirits, it was important, and wonderful, to have best pals. The workshop sessions and craft classes were also situations where we could get to know the faculty, as well as other students, from the Q&A during and after the lectures.

There is a listserv for alumni of the program, which I am part of, and I have met and become good friends with alums in my area. The listserv is an incredible resource, sounding board, and network. There is also an annual alumni conference, which I have not yet attended, but it's in my plans.

How do you retain that sense of community post-graduation?

I am very motivated and disciplined about my writing, and I think developing a habit — writing at a certain time of day, or in certain places — is very important to keeping the creative juices flowing. Being part of a writing group, or exchanging work with writers who both appreciate and are able to offer helpful criticism, are invaluable for the writing life. In the Twin Cities, The Loft is a fantastic resource for all things writerly. Getting out there and doing readings, and participating in open mic sessions are also important to emerging and establishing oneself as a serious writer.

Do you have any final thoughts to share?

I felt that all of the writers who were accepted at Warren Wilson were emerging writers, assuming the term means writers with talent who hadn't yet honed their craft. The residencies were mostly about absorbing all one could, and working with the mentors was about generating new work based on what was absorbed. The program gave me in four semesters what would have taken me decades to learn on my own.

Quick Reference

ALL OF THE FOLLOWING programs are included, alphabetically, within Chapter 6. Within this quick reference, the chapter references listed below some program websites indicate where additional comments may be located.

University of Alaska Anchorage
Poetry, Fiction, Non-Fiction
Anchorage, AK
3 years, 4 residencies
www.uaa.alaska.edu/cwla
Chapters 4, 7, 9, 10

Albertus Magnus College
Poetry, Fiction, Non-Fiction
New Haven, CT
2 years, 3 Saturday residencies each semester
www.albertus.edu/masters-degrees/mfa/index.html

Antioch University Los Angeles
Poetry, Fiction, Non-Fiction
Culver City, CA
2 years, 5 residencies
www.antiochla.edu/academics/mfa-creative-writing
Chapters 2, 3, 7, 9, 10, 11

Antioch University Midwest
Individualized Liberal and Professional Studies

Fiction, Poetry, Playwriting, Screenwriting
Yellow Springs, OH
2 years, 2 residencies
http://midwest.antioch.edu/ilps/cw/index.html

Ashland University
Poetry, Creative Non-Fiction
Ashland, OH
2 years, 3 residencies
www.ashland.edu/graduate/mfa
Chapters 8, 10

Bennington College
The Bennington Writing Seminars
Fiction, Poetry, Non-Fiction
Bennington, VT
2 years, 5 residencies
www.bennington.edu/go/graduate/mfa-in-writing
Chapters 2, 9, 10, 11

University of British Columbia
Fiction, Poetry, Non-Fiction, Children's, Translation, Screenwriting, Playwriting
Vancouver, BC
2 years, optional residencies
www.creativewriting.ubc.ca
Chapter 9

University of California Riverside
Palm Desert Graduate Center
Fiction, Poetry, Memoir, Screenwriting, Playwriting
Riverside, CA
2 years, 4 residencies
http://palmdesertmfa.ucr.edu
Chapter 9

Carlow University
Fiction, Poetry, Non-Fiction
Pittsburgh, PA
2½ years, 4 residencies
http://gradstudies.carlow.edu/creative/index.html

Chatham University
Focus on Nature, Environment, and Travel
Pittsburgh, PA
2 years, 2 residencies
www.chatham.edu/ccps/mfa
Chapters 4, 8

Converse College
Fiction, Creative Non-Fiction, Poetry
Spartanburg, SC
2 years, 5 residencies
http://old.converse.edu/mfa
Chapters 1, 9, 11; Appendix A

Drew University
Poetry, Poetry in Translation
Madison, NJ
2 years, 5 residencies
www.drew.edu/grad-content.aspx?id=39651

Eastern Kentucky University
Fiction, Poetry, Creative Non-Fiction
Richmond, KY
2 years, 2–4 residencies
www.english.eku.edu/mfa

Fairfield University
Poetry, Fiction, Creative Non-Fiction, Screenwriting
Fairfield, CT
2 years, 5 residencies
www.fairfield.edu/mfaonline
Chapter 5

Fairleigh Dickinson University
Poetry, Fiction, Creative Non-Fiction
Madison, NJ
2 years, 3 residencies
http://mfa.fdu.edu
Chapter 11

Goddard College

Fiction, Poetry, Creative Non-Fiction, Playwriting, Screen-writing
Plainfield, VT or Port Townsend, WA
2 years, 5 residencies
www.goddard.edu/masterfinearts_writing
Chapters 7, 9

Goucher College

Creative Non-Fiction
Baltimore, MD
2 years, 5 residencies
www.goucher.edu/x1166.xml
Chapters 4, 7

Hamline University

Writing for Children & Young Adults
Saint Paul, MN
2 years, 5 residencies
www.hamline.edu/gls/academics/degree_programs/mfa_cl/index.html

City University of Hong Kong

Fiction, Poetry, Creative Non-Fiction
Kowloon, Hong Kong
2 years, 5 residencies
www.english.cityu.edu.hk/mfa

Institute of American Indian Arts

Fiction, Poetry, Non-Fiction, Playwriting, Screenwriting
Santa Fe, NM
2 years, 5 residencies
www.iaia.edu

University of King's College, Halifax

Narrative Non-Fiction
Halifax, NS
2 years, 5 residencies
www.ukings.ns.ca

Lancaster University
Master of Arts (MA) in Creative Writing
Lancaster, UK
2 years, 1 residency
www.lancs.ac.uk/fass/english/postgrad/creativewriting

Lesley University
Fiction, Poetry, Non-Fiction, Writing for Stage & Screen, Writing
for Young People
Cambridge, MA
2 years, 5 residencies
www.lesley.edu/gsass/creative_writing/index.html

Murray State University
Fiction, Poetry, Creative Non-Fiction, Writing for Children &
Young Adults
Murray, KY
2 years, 4 residencies
www.murraystate.edu/chfa/english/mfa/index.htm

Naropa University
Jack Kerouac School of Disembodied Poetics
Fiction, Poetry, Non-Fiction, Translation
Boulder, CO
3 years, 2 residencies
www.naropa.edu/academics/graduate/writingpoetics/mfalowres

National University
Fiction, Poetry, Non-Fiction, Screenwriting
La Jolla, CA
2 years, 0 residencies
www.nu.edu
Chapter 9

University of Nebraska
Fiction, Poetry, Creative Non-Fiction, Playwriting
Omaha, NE
2 years, 5 residencies
www.unomaha.edu/unmfaw
Chapter 4

New England College
Poetry
Henniker, NH
2 years, 5 residencies
www.nec.edu/graduate-and-professional-studies/mfa-in-poetry
Chapter 4

University of New Orleans
Poetry, Fiction, Non-Fiction, Playwriting, Screenwriting
New Orleans, LA
2 years, 3 residencies abroad
http://lowres.uno.edu

Northwest Institute of Literary Arts
Whidbey Writers Workshop
Fiction, Poetry, Creative Non-Fiction, Writing for Children &
Young Adults
Freeland, WA
2 years, 5 residencies
www.writeonwhidbey.org/mfa
Chapters 2, 5, 8, 9, 10, 12; Appendix A

Oklahoma City University
The Red Earth MFA
Fiction, Poetry, Non-Fiction
Oklahoma City, OK
2 years, 5 residencies
www.okcu.edu/english

Oxford University
Master of Studies (MSt) in Creative Writing
Oxford, UK
2 years, 3 residencies
http://awardbearing.conted.ox.ac.uk/creative_writing/mstcw.
php

Pacific Lutheran University
Rainer Writing Workshops
Fiction, Poetry, Creative Non-Fiction
Tacoma, WA

3 years, 4 residencies
www.plu.edu/mfa
Chapters 4, 5, 12

Pacific University
Fiction, Poetry, Creative Non-Fiction
Forest Grove, OR
2 years, 5 residencies
www.pacificu.edu/as/mfa
Chapter 8

Pine Manor College
Solstice Creative Writing Programs
Fiction, Poetry, Creative Non-Fiction, Writing for Children &
Young Adults
Chestnut Hill, MA
2 years, 5 residencies
www.pmc.edu/mfa-program-overview
Chapters 4, 5, 7, 9, 11

Queens University of Charlotte
Fiction, Poetry, Creative Non-Fiction, Writing for Stage &
Screen
Charlotte, NC
2 years, 5 residencies
www.queens.edu/graduate/programs/creative_writing.asp
Chapters 4, 5, 8, 10; Appendix A

Seattle Pacific University
Fiction, Poetry, Creative Non-Fiction
Seattle, WA
2 years, 5 residencies
www.spu.edu/prospects/grad/academics/mfa

Seton Hill University
Popular Fiction
Greensburg, PA
2 years, 4 residencies
www.setonhill.edu/academics/fiction
Chapter 2; Appendix A

Sewanee: The University of the South
Sewanee School of Letters
Fiction, Poetry, Creative Non-Fiction
Sewanee, TN
5 years, 4 residencies
www.sewanee.edu/SL/SLHome.htm

Southern New Hampshire University
Fiction, Non-Fiction
Manchester, NH
2 years, 4 residencies
www.snhu.edu/5749.asp

University of Southern Maine
Stonecoast
Poetry, Creative Non-Fiction, Fiction, Popular Fiction, Cross-Genre
Portland, ME
2 years, 5 residencies
www.usm.maine.edu/stonecoastmfa
Chapters 1, 5, 7, 9, 12

Spalding University
Fiction, Poetry, Creative Non-Fiction, Playwriting, Screenwriting, Writing for Children and Young Adults
Louisville, KY
2 years, 5 residencies
www.spalding.edu/academics/mfa
Chapters 2, 4, 9, 10, 11, 12; Appendix A

University of Texas El Paso
Poetry, Fiction, Playwriting, Screenwriting, Essay, Translation
El Paso, TX
3 years, 0 residencies
www.academics.utep.edu/Default.aspx?tabid=42392

Vermont College of Fine Arts
Poetry, Fiction, Creative Non-Fiction, Literary Translation
Writing for Children & Young Adults
Montpelier, VT

2 years, 5 residencies
www.vermontcollege.edu
Chapters 2, 4, 8, 11; Appendix A

Warren Wilson College

Fiction, Poetry
Asheville, NC
2 years, 5 residencies
www.warren-wilson.edu/~mfa/newwebsite/homepage.php
Chapters 1, 4, 11: Appendix A

West Virginia Wesleyan College

Poetry, Fiction, Creative Non-Fiction
Buckhannon, WV
2 years, 5 residencies
www.wvwc.edu

Western Connecticut State University

Creative and Professional Writing
Danbury, CT
2 years, 4 residencies
www.wcsu.edu/writing/mfa/low-residency.asp

Western State College of Colorado

Fiction, Poetry, Screenwriting
Gunnison, CO
2 years, 3 residencies
www.western.edu/academics/creativewriting

Wilkes University

Fiction, Poetry, Creative Non-Fiction, Playwriting
Wilkes-Barre, PA
1½ years, 4 residencies (MA)
2½ years, 5 residencies (MFA)
http://wilkes.edu/creativewriting
Chapters 5, 8

Additional Resources

IT WOULD TAKE AN additional handbook to list all of the resource-ful websites for writers and prospective graduate students. The following is a mere sampling of those particularly useful for prospective low-residency applicants.

Organizational Resources

The Association of Writers and Writing Programs (AWP) main website: www.awpwriter.org

"The AWP Official Guide to Writing Programs" includes a searchable database of residency and low-residency MFAs, MAs, PhDs: http://guide.awpwriter.org

"AWP Hallmarks of an Effective Low-Residency MFA Program in Creative Writing," available for free PDF download: www.awpwriter.org/pdf/loreshallmarks.pdf

FAFSA, Free Application for Federal Student Aid: www.fafsa.ed.gov

IRS Publication 970, Tax Benefits for Education: www.irs.gov/publications/p970

Magazines for Writers

Poets & Writers: www.pw.org

Quill & Quire: www.quillandquire.com

The Writer: www.writermag.com

The Writer's Chronicle: www.awpwriter.org/magazine/index.htm

Writer's Digest: www.writersdigest.com

Writers' Journal: www.writersjournal.com

Blogs

Erika Dreifus wrote the section on "Choosing a Low-Residency MFA Program in Creative Writing" for the second edition of Tom Kealey's *Creative Writing MFA Handbook* (Continuum, 2008): http://practicing-writing.blogspot.com/2005/11/on-subject-of-funding-for-low.html

Tom Kealey, author of *The Creative Writing MFA Handbook*, hosts this blog, which occasionally includes questions and comments about low-residency programs: http://creative-writing-mfa-handbook.blogspot.com

Acknowledgments

THANK YOU TO MY editor David Barker, and the team at Continuum Books, for seeing the life in this project when it was a mere seed of an idea. On that note, I must also acknowledge Continuum Books author Tom Kealey, for setting high standards with *The Creative Writing MFA Handbook*. Tom, thanks for pioneering the guide. I hope to offer prospective low-residency students what you have provided for full-residency applicants.

I also owe a great deal of thanks to Christopher Shier, for his attention to detail as a second-reader, and for cleaning and refilling the coffee pot — about ten times a day. Chris, if I had known you were this helpful under deadline, I would have married you that much sooner.

There were a number of students, alumni, and faculty not interviewed for this book that randomly offered words of appreciation and enthusiasm for this project. Thank you for your encouragement and for contributing to my general understanding of the various programs.

Most important, I wish to thank all of the interviewees from each of the programs for offering up far more feedback than I could have possibly included, but which is valued for the overall contribution to the development of this project. Thank you to the following institutions and people for your generosity of time and words, and for sharing your experiences with prospective students.

University of Alaska Anchorage: David Stevenson, Judith Barrington, Anne Caston, Jeff Oliver, Sandy Kleven

Albertus Magnus College: Sarah Wallman

Antioch University Los Angeles: Steven Heller, Larraine Herring, Mandy Ferrington

Antioch University Midwest: Rebecca Kuder

Ashland University: Stephen Haven, Ruth Schwartz, Joy Gaines-Friedler, Grace Curtis, Joan Hanna

Bennington College: Sven Birkerts, Alice Mattison, Clark Knowles, Laura Nathan, Jenn Schek-Kahn, Winona Winkler Wendth

University of British Columbia: Andrew Gray, Luanne Armstrong, Elaine Beale

University of California Riverside: Tod Goldberg, Mark Haskell Smith

Carlow University: Ellie Wymard, Celeste Gainey, Michelle Stoner

Chatham University: Peter Oresick

Converse College: Rick Mulkey, Leslie Pietrzyk, Susan Tekulve, R. T. Smith, Jeffrey R. Schrecongost

Drew University: Anne Marie Macari, Alicia Ostriker

Eastern Kentucky University: Tasha Cotter

Fairfield University: Michael C. White

Fairleigh Dickinson University: Martin Donoff, Anne Woodworth

Goddard College: Paul Selig, Ann E. Michael, Bridgette Mongeon, Dawn Paul, Tina Broderick

Goucher College: Patsy Sims

Hamline University: Mary François Rockcastle

City University of Hong Kong: Xu Xi

Institute of American Indian Arts: Jon Davis

University of King's College, Halifax: Stephen Kimber

Lancaster University: Lee Horsley, Graham Mort

Lesley University: Steven Cramer

Murray State University: Squire Babcock, Ann Neelon, Leah Stewart

Naropa University: Junior Burke

National University: Frank Montesonti

University of Nebraska: Richard Duggin, Kate Gale, Timothy Black, Stephanie Austin

New England College: James Harms, Mariela Griffor

University of New Orleans: Bill Lavender

Northwest Institute of Literary Arts: Wayne Ude, George Shannon, Stefanie Freele, Kelly Davio, Kobbie Alamo, FeLicia A. Elam, Stefon Mears

Oklahoma City University: Danita Berg

Oxford University: Rebecca Rue

Pacific Lutheran University: Stan Rubin, David Biespiel, Natalie Haney Tilghman

Pacific University: Shelley Washburn, Marvin Bell, Peter Sears, Robert Peake, Jennifer Miller, Nomi Morris

Pine Manor College: Meg Kearney

Queens University of Charlotte: Michael Kobre, Daniel Mueller, Georgia Banks-Martin, Jessie Carty, Melanie Faith, Clifford Garstang

Seattle Pacific University: Gregory Wolfe

Seton Hill University: Albert Wendland, Shelley Bates, Heidi Ruby Miller, Jason Jack Miller, Cynthia Ravinski, Nicole Taft, Matthew Duvall, Natalie Duvall

Sewanee: The University of the South: John Grammer

Southern New Hampshire University: Robert Begiebing

University of Southern Maine: Annie Finch, Patricia Smith, Carol Berg

Spalding University: Sena Jeter Naslund, Kathleen Driskell, Katy Yocum, Karen J. Mann, Gayle Hanratty, Richard Goodman, Molly Peacock, Cathy Nickola, Loreen Niewenhuis, Diana M. Raab, Christopher Klim, Brian Russell, Katerina Stoykova-Klemer

University of Texas El Paso: Lex Williford

Vermont College of Fine Arts: Louise Crowley, Melissa Fisher, Phyllis Barber, Abby Frucht, Diana Lefer, Sue William Silverman, Jeanie Chung, Malcolm W. Campbell, Audrey Friedman, Claire Guyton, Michael Hemery, Eve Rifka, Carolyn Walker, Rich Farrell, Jeanne Gassman

Warren Wilson College: Debra Allbery, Heather McHugh, Laura Cherry, Kathleen Jesme, K. Alma Peterson, Alison Powell, Ian Randall Wilson, Scott Nadelson

West Virginia Wesleyan College: Irene McKinney, Doug Van Gundy

Western Connecticut State University: Brian Clements

Western State College of Colorado: Mark Todd, Barbara Chepaitis, Jack Lucido

Wilkes University: Bonnie Culver, J. Michael Lennon, Jim Warner, Philip Brady, Kaylie Jones, Brian Fanelli, Amye Archer

And, while he is not affiliated with any one program, I would also like to thank Matt Burriesci, AWP Acting Executive Director/Director of Development & Advancement, for generously responding to my questions.